"If you make any noise, I'll kill you."

Shea wanted to scream but couldn't. The man's hand was so big that it covered almost her entire face, pressed so tightly against her mouth and nose that she could not breathe. Shea began to panic.

She was a swimmer and had very strong legs, and when she kicked them out, it caused the headboard to knock against the wall between the two bedrooms . . .

---

I've always been a heavy sleeper, but this woke me up. I could hear soft whimpering and a strange sound of movement coming from the guest room where Shea was sleeping. In my mind, the combined noises could only have been our fifteen-year-old daughter in the throes of some bad dream. Something told me to go check on her anyway, having no idea what real nightmare was awaiting.

# Caught in the Act

A Courageous Family's Fight to Save
Their Daughter from a Serial Killer

JEANNIE MCDONOUGH
WITH PAUL LONARDO

BERKLEY BOOKS, NEW YORK

**THE BERKLEY PUBLISHING GROUP**
Published by the Penguin Group
Penguin Group (USA) Inc.
**375 Hudson Street, New York, New York 10014, USA**
Penguin Group (Canada), 90 Eglinton Avenue East, Suite 700, Toronto, Ontario M4P 2Y3, Canada
(a division of Pearson Penguin Canada Inc.)
Penguin Books Ltd., 80 Strand, London WC2R 0RL, England
Penguin Group Ireland, 25 St. Stephen's Green, Dublin 2, Ireland (a division of Penguin Books Ltd.)
Penguin Group (Australia), 250 Camberwell Road, Camberwell, Victoria 3124, Australia
(a division of Pearson Australia Group Pty. Ltd.)
Penguin Books India Pvt. Ltd., 11 Community Centre, Panchsheel Park, New Delhi—110 017, India
Penguin Group (NZ), 67 Apollo Drive, Rosedale, North Shore 0632, New Zealand
(a division of Pearson New Zealand Ltd.)
Penguin Books (South Africa) (Pty.) Ltd., 24 Sturdee Avenue, Rosebank, Johannesburg 2196,
South Africa

Penguin Books Ltd., Registered Offices: 80 Strand, London WC2R 0RL, England

The publisher does not have any control over and does not assume any responsibility for authors or
third-party websites or their content.

CAUGHT IN THE ACT

A Berkley Book / published by arrangement with the authors

PRINTING HISTORY
Berkley mass-market edition / March 2011

Copyright © 2011 by Jeannie McDonough and Paul Lonardo.
Cover photos: Shutterstock.
Cover design by Pyrographx.
Interior text design by Laura K. Corless.

ISBN: 978-0-425-23543-0

BERKLEY®
Berkley Books are published by The Berkley Publishing Group,
a division of Penguin Group (USA) Inc.,
375 Hudson Street, New York, New York 10014.
BERKLEY® is a registered trademark of Penguin Group (USA) Inc.
The "B" design is a trademark of Penguin Group (USA) Inc.

PRINTED IN THE UNITED STATES OF AMERICA

10  9  8  7  6  5  4  3  2  1

Most Berkley Books are available at special quantity discounts for bulk purchases for sales,
promotions, premiums, fund-raising, or educational use. Special books, or book excerpts, can also
be created to fit specific needs.

For details, write: Special Markets, The Berkley Publishing Group, 375 Hudson Street, New York,
New York 10014.

*This book is dedicated to my daughter, Shea McDonough, who by the grace of God is still with us. Her beauty lies not only in the resiliency of her spirit, but also in the strength of her character. Throughout this tumultuous journey, she has remained true to herself and has not allowed the negativity of the past events to alter her perspective toward life. Wherever her path may lead, may angels continue to watch over her.*

# Acknowledgments

This book is an account of the facts of what happened when my family came face-to-face with a serial killer intent on hurting our daughter. I began writing about my family's encounter with Adam Leroy Lane as a way to express my thoughts, fears and concerns throughout this continuing journey—an outlet for my frustrations, not only relating to the initial experience, but also to our attacker's lengthy progression through our system of justice. This unexpected test of inner strength and character has provided me clarity of spirit, which has proven to be as equally life-altering as the attack itself, and I hope that this account might benefit others.

Life can change in an instant, for better or for worse, and when that instant comes, there's nothing you can do about it. You don't need to be religious to appreciate life as the gift that it is, but when you've had a brush with death, you no longer take anything for granted. If I could go back in time and alter the events of July 30, 2007, I would do anything to spare Shea and my family from that life-changing experience. However, I also would not have wished it on any other family, and ultimately, all things considered, things turned out as best as anyone could hope. In that sense, I have learned to embrace what happened and the wonderful people I have come to know as a consequence. It has solidified my belief that Adam Leroy

Lane was sent to our house by a higher power with the knowledge that we would somehow have the fortitude to stop him. Whether that fortitude was aided in some way by help from above or dumb luck is of secondary concern.

There are many people I would like to recognize as having a major impact on my decision to write this book. First of all, I want to acknowledge the two beautiful women whose lives were taken from them by the hands of an angry, thoughtless and brutal killer. Darlene Ewalt and Monica Massaro were sadistically struck down in the prime of their lives. They will always be remembered by our family, and their spirit will live on in all of us. Our thoughts and prayers go out to their family members and friends, who have suffered such tragic and senseless losses.

It is equally important for me to thank the various law enforcement agencies and personnel who have influenced the investigation, prosecution and imprisonment of Adam Leroy Lane. I want to acknowledge the following individuals: Chelmsford Police Chief James Murphy, Deputy Chief Scott Ubele, Officer Robert Murphy, Sergeant Frank Goode, Officer Bruce Darwin, Detective George Tyros and his wife, Detective Rebecca Tyros, Detective-Sergeant Todd Ahern and Detective Jeff Blodgett. To be commended as well are the members of the Middlesex District Attorney's Office: Assistant District Attorney Kerry Ahern, Assistant District Attorney Tom O'Reilly, District Attorney Gerry Leone and our victim advocate, Dora Quiroz. A special thanks goes to our close friend Mike Champagne for providing tremendous support to our family during the trial proceedings.

Vitally important as well were all of the detectives within the New Jersey State Police Department who played an instrumental role in the Massaro investigation. Their support and commitment will always be appreciated. In particular,

Detective-Sergeants Geoffrey Noble, Jeff Kronenfeld and James Kiernan, as well as Detectives Justin Blackwell, Timothy Coyle, Nicholas Oriolo and Tom McEnroe. Also, Sergeant Kevin Burd and Lieutenant Jeff Farneski, of the Hunterdon County Prosecutor's Office, and Margaret Paul, the forensic scientist from the New Jersey State Police Lab who went above and beyond in her efforts to link Adam Lane to the case forensically. There are numerous other professionals in various law enforcement agencies who have worked on the Massaro and Ewalt cases, as well as other potential cases that Adam Leroy Lane may yet be linked to. Our thanks go out to all of them as well.

Special recognition should also be given to Jennifer Storm, the Ewalt family's victim advocate. Her assistance and support leading up to and throughout Adam Leroy Lane's hearing was an enormous help to me. Her expertise and guidance enabled me to report on aspects of the proceedings that I would not have otherwise been able to recount.

I would like to further express a heartfelt appreciation to our family, friends and the entire Chelmsford community. There were countless calls, cards, flowers and food that renewed our belief in the goodness of the human spirit. We never could have anticipated the friendships that would be strengthened and formed in the wake of such turmoil. In the days following this ordeal, we received an overwhelming show of support and compassion, and our family will always remember the kindness shown by so many people. I also want to recognize Principal Allen Thomas, who reached out to us on behalf of Chelmsford High School with an expression of concern and commitment to our daughter's adjustment following the trauma of the attack. Without the support of Dan Rosa, the school psychologist, and Christine Lima, Shea's guidance counselor, I am certain that Shea's future prospects would not be as bright. The level of personal concern they demonstrated and their professional input have been invaluable.

I would also like to thank my friend Piotr Chadzynski for providing support and encouragement to me in the final writing stages of this book. A special thank-you to my coauthor, Paul Lonardo, for taking on this project. Paul's expertise, guidance and craftsmanship have spun my ramblings into a cohesive piece of writing. To our agent, Linda Konner, thank you for believing in our ability to bring this story to script and helping us every step of the way. Above all, I would like to express my gratitude to our editor at Berkley Publishing, Shannon Jamieson Vazquez. She stuck with us through this emotional roller-coaster ride with her unwavering patience and continual interest. She had a magical way of taking what was written and polishing it with such precision that the significance of the words became clearer even to me.

Of paramount significance as well is the acknowledgment of our son, Ryan. I know that he has questioned himself many times about what role his absence that night may have played, but it will always be my conviction that his absence very likely may be the reason we all survived. Ryan will never fully comprehend how thankful I am that everything happened exactly the way it did.

Most important, I must pay tribute to my husband, Kevin. Without a doubt, I wouldn't have been able to write this if it weren't for him. His encouragement, support and enthusiasm with regard to my writing have been incredible. Certainly, none of this would have been possible if he hadn't done what he did that night. A local news reporter once described my husband as being a "silent hero." I couldn't have put it more aptly, and I thank God every day for the many blessings he has brought to my life.

—*Jeannie McDonough*

There are only two ways to live your life. One is as though nothing is a miracle. The other is as if everything is a miracle.

—ALBERT EINSTEIN

# Prologue

With the kids getting older, it was more difficult to spend time together as a family. Besides the holidays, July was the one time of the year that everyone put aside his or her individual plans and shared one another's company. That year, 2007, it began on the Fourth of July, which we celebrated in Rockport, Massachusetts, a quaint seaside community on the North Shore. With Independence Day falling in the middle of the week, on a Wednesday, it was only a brief diversion from our workaday worlds. There was nothing particularly remarkable about the trip, but it was a pleasurable break from the ordinary, even if the kids never seemed to stop texting their friends and Kevin talked about the work he had to do the next day. The best part was we were all in the same place with close family, and that place was on the beach on a beautiful summer day, capped off by an evening fireworks display. What was not to love about that?

So everyone was busy making other plans, including

myself, but isn't that when the true experiences of life are supposed to occur, at least according to John Lennon? We were all assuming, anyway, that we would be getting back to our daily routines and the imagined futures we had planned. But something very unexpected was out there, and it was coming our way. All the suntan lotion and fruity umbrella drinks could not keep it away . . .

# Chapter 1

"WHO ARE YOU?"

Friday, July 13, 2007

Darlene Ewalt was sitting on the back porch of her home at 2:00 a.m., talking on the phone with her friend Chet Gerhart about the cruise that she was going on with Chet and his wife, Pat, scheduled to set sail in October. The Gerharts had purchased four tickets to paradise, a Caribbean family vacation they had originally expected to take with their two teenage sons. However, the boys had misbehaved, so as punishment, their parents decided to leave them behind, making two tickets available. Over dinner just a night earlier, the Gerharts offered the tickets to their best friends, Todd and Darlene Ewalt. Darlene jumped at the opportunity.

Darlene had married young and raised two children, and for many years there had not been a lot of time for her. But now, at only forty-two, there was still plenty of life remaining and experiences that awaited. For far too long her travel destinations had been limited to the supermarkets and football fields around the small Pennsylvania town where she lived. She could only dream of far-off adventure and exotic places, and this was her opportunity to make her fantasy a reality. The cruise could mark the beginning of a new chapter in her life, and bring her closer to the man she married and still loved.

Todd Ewalt was a carpenter by trade, but he was also a dedicated youth football coach. That was how the Ewalts came to know the Gerharts, when Todd had coached their kids. But the upcoming cruise was in the fall, and so was the football season; Todd couldn't do both. He had a difficult choice to make.

Darlene knew how much her husband enjoyed working with the kids, but she was shocked when he politely declined the Gerharts' offer, opting to stay behind. Todd wasn't comfortable missing a week of football in the middle of the season. They both knew he wasn't going to change his mind, so there was no point in arguing about it. But Darlene was just as determined to go on the cruise, with or without her husband. Todd knew how much the trip meant to his wife, so he gave her his blessing to set sail without him. Despite making plans to spend time apart, neither Todd nor Darlene harbored any bitterness or animosity toward one another for their independent decisions. So it was decided that Darlene would join the Gerharts on the Caribbean getaway in October while Todd stayed home and coached football.

The cruise was all that Darlene could think or talk about the next day. There were several girlfriends who were considering coming with her in Todd's place. Which one of them could get the time off of work, temporarily disengage themselves from family and other obligations, and come up with the money in time to reimburse the

Gerharts for the all-inclusive ticket were all factors in this Caribbean lottery.

As day turned to night, Darlene was on the phone with Chet, excitedly going over every detail of the trip. Having never been on a cruise ship, she wanted to know everything, from the island ports where the ocean liner would be docking to what sort of clothes she should bring and how much money she needed to take with her.

Around 10:00 p.m., Todd opened the back door and stuck his head outside. Seeing his wife on the patio with the phone to her ear, he said, "Hey, I'm going to bed."

"Okay," Darlene responded. "I'll be up in a few minutes."

"Yeah, right," Todd said with a slight rising of his eyebrows before ducking back inside the house. He knew better. His wife could talk for hours when she got going, so he wasn't about to wait up. He went upstairs to their bedroom while she stayed outside on the phone with Chet.

Four hours later, Darlene was still on the patio talking with Chet. Her continued excitement about the trip made the lateness of the hour seem inconsequential. It was almost as if she had already put herself on the cruise ship as it moved silently through the dark waters of the Caribbean Sea. In actuality, she was only a few feet away from the sliding-glass door and the cool air-conditioned interior of her house, but she didn't want to go inside. The sticky summer night helped induce the sensation that she was already in the Caribbean, where she wanted to be. It was still months away, but she couldn't get there soon enough.

Suddenly, there was a rustling sound deep in the woods at the back of the property.

The West Hanover Township in Dauphin County was a quiet suburb just northeast of Harrisburg, Pennsylvania. Interstate 81 bisected Manor Drive, where the Ewalts lived.

Their home was well within earshot of the highway, and on quiet nights they could hear the drone of diesel engines rolling east toward Allentown or south toward Interstate 83. The traffic noise would sometimes herd deer and other animals toward their property.

She didn't see what was actually moving out of the shadows, even as it emerged from the woods behind the house. This predator had two legs, and was cloaked entirely in black. As the dark figure approached Darlene, a large knife that had been concealed earlier was now in a gloved hand. He was almost upon her before she finally became aware of his presence, and she was taken by complete surprise by the sight before her.

"Who are you?" Darlene asked.

On the other end of the line, Chet didn't know who Darlene was talking to, but he was chilled by the sudden change in her voice. What he didn't know was that a stranger, dressed like a ninja, was on the hunt and stalking her as his prey.

The patio floor beneath Darlene's feet was a cement slab that sat flush on the ground. It was ringed by a wooden fence, like the kind around a horse corral. It had an open-ended walk-in. And that's just what the stranger did. He caught her and stabbed her repeatedly and viciously in the neck and torso. She began losing consciousness almost immediately.

"Oh my God! Oh my God! Oh my God! Oh my . . ." she said a moment later.

Those were the last words that Chet Gerhart heard Darlene Ewalt say before the phone went silent. He kept calling her name. The longer he stayed on the line without getting a response, the louder he screamed into the phone. But still she did not answer him. He knew something was wrong; he listened and heard nothing on the other end of the open line. He wanted to believe that her husband or her son would be able to work out whatever the problem was among themselves, but another part of him felt that Darlene was in serious trouble. A family emergency of some kind could have abruptly diverted her attention from their conversation, Chet thought, but either way, he could not just forget it and go to bed. Finally, he raced upstairs and woke his wife.

"Something's happened," he told her as she rose with a start.

"What?" Pat asked, squinting from the bright overhead light of the previously darkened bedroom. "What's happened?"

"I don't know," Chet said, sounding confused. "But Darlene's not responding. We've got to go there. We've got to go now."

Pat paused, but only briefly, taken aback by the unfamiliar anxiety in her husband's voice. "Okay, just give me a minute to get dressed."

"Hurry, Pat." As Chet waited for his wife to get ready, he told her what happened and tried calling Darlene from the bedroom phone.

"The line's busy," he announced with a mixture of hope and dread.

"Maybe she's trying to call you back."

"They have call-waiting. It would go to voice mail. The phone's off the hook. Come on. Let's go."

They sped over to the Ewalts. The Gerharts had called the police, but since they were already on the way to Darlene's house, they were told to go check out the situation and call them back. It was a fifteen-minute drive, which they made in ten. As Chet drove, Pat continually tried the Ewalts' number on her cell phone, getting a busy signal each time.

"Keep trying," Chet told her.

Consumed by their own thoughts, they didn't speak. Besides the sound of Pat's dialing, the car was otherwise silent. Even the radio was turned off.

Upon arriving at the Manor Drive address where their friends lived, the Gerharts proceeded around to the back of the house. Chet was walking quickly, ahead of his wife. He knew that Darlene had been outside on her patio while they were talking earlier. He had been trying not to think about the possible reasons she would have dropped the phone so suddenly in an obvious state of panic, but he never expected to discover what he did when he approached the patio. Right up until that moment, he still wanted to believe that everything was okay, even though he'd felt compelled to wake up his wife in the middle of the night and drive as fast as he could to get there.

A light was on in the adjoining kitchen, and in the yellow glow it cast outside, the Gerharts quickly spotted Darlene, seated on a chair near the sliding doors, slumped backward and not moving.

The discovery sent both of the Gerharts reeling. Chet tried to pull himself together as well as comfort his wife.

"Stop," Chet told his wife, turning and gripping her by the shoulders. "Wait here." But Pat didn't have to get any closer. From where she was standing, she could see that her friend's eyes were open and that she was dead. She could see the injuries to Darlene's neck and the blood that was soaked into her clothing and pooled all around the chair, and it just looked like a wet shadow. Pat didn't hear herself when she began to scream, because she had already been screaming in her head.

"Oh my God, Chet! Darlene's dead! What are we gonna do?"

"All right . . . Pat . . ."

"Where's Todd? Oh my God. Where's Todd? We have to get out of here!"

"Pat. . . . We'll call 911."

"Yeah, yeah, okay."

"Where's your phone, Pat?"

"I left it in the car."

"It's okay," Chet said calmly, trying to counterbalance his wife's rising panic. "Let's go get it. Come on. I'm right beside you."

As they went back around to the front of the house, they both experienced the same abject feeling of terror that the killer might still be lurking somewhere nearby, and they feared they would fall prey next. They called for help inside the car with the doors locked, and neither one stepped outside again until the first police cruiser arrived.

A phalanx of law enforcement arrived within minutes of the second 911 call. As uniformed officers and detectives swarmed the Ewalt home, the Gerharts were questioned at the scene and then escorted to the local police precinct to provide additional written statements. It was immediately confirmed that Darlene was, indeed, dead. As police swarmed inside, they did not know what they would find: more victims or the killer.

In the couple's upstairs bedroom, which directly overlooked the back patio where Darlene's body was found, her husband, Todd, was awakened by a sudden commotion as his door slammed open. A heavy sleeper, he was roused instantly by voices coming out of the darkness, screaming at him to put his hands up. In and around the doorway, Todd saw shadowy figures shining flashlights at him. It was too surreal to believe, and all Todd could think initially was that his son and some of his buddies were having some fun at his expense. Then he saw that the figures had guns, drawn and pointed at him, and he realized that it was no joke.

"Is there anyone else at home?" demanded one of the police officers.

Todd responded, "My son and my wife live here with me. My wife's around here somewhere and my son, Nick, is probably asleep in the basement."

At which the officer said, "We looked in the basement and didn't see anyone."

In return, Todd said, "Well look again. Nick is six feet three and 270 pounds. You couldn't miss him. Where's my wife?"

Downstairs, their grown son, Nick, was indeed in the basement apartment, asleep in bed, just as Todd had said. When the police located him, he was ordered out of his bed and onto the floor. As Todd was taken downstairs, he repeatedly asked what was happening and where his wife was, but no one would answer him. When he got to the kitchen he saw his son, who was also cuffed, but no Darlene. When he spotted his wife's purse on the table, along with her car keys and cell phone, he really started to worry. He knew she had to be home because she wouldn't go anywhere without her phone. Without saying anything to him, one of the officers removed his handcuffs and led him to the adjoining dining room while Nick remained in the kitchen and was questioned separately.

It was then that Todd was told Darlene had been killed. At that very moment, he heard the sound of screaming coming from the kitchen. It was his son, who had also just been informed about his mother's death. Later on, after being held at the police station, Nick was finally able to use his cell phone to call his sister and break the awful news about their mother. Sadly, Darlene's mother, Thelma, had to learn of her daughter's gruesome murder by way of the horrifying images of the family's home surrounded by yellow crime scene tape that were splayed all over the local news stations early that morning.

For Todd, the nightmare that was unfolding became a living hell when he realized that the police were looking at him—not as a victim, but a suspect in his wife's violent murder. In police parlance, Todd Ewalt was considered a person of interest in the homicide investigation.

It was not something they hinted at gently. They made it quite clear that they thought he'd killed Darlene, despite the lack of any evidence whatsoever, including a murder weapon.

When Todd was asked what had happened outside, he said he didn't know. He told them he was asleep and hadn't heard anything. No one believed him. They did not think that a mysterious killer walked out of the woods, slashed Darlene Ewalt to death and then just left. As any experienced homicide detective will attest, it just doesn't happen that way. Almost all murders involve people who are well acquainted, and the particularly gruesome nature of this attack led investigators to suspect that Darlene's murder had been a crime of passion.

At that time, motive was the only thing the police had to go on. The facts of the case would bear themselves out in the end. They knew that the forty-two-year-old wife and mother had been killed while on the phone with another man, and that her husband, asleep beside a window mere feet from the crime, claimed not to have heard a thing.

To try to get Todd Ewalt to talk, they had to get him out of the house and into the police station. In that environment, he might feel obligated to tell them more, maybe even confess. They questioned him for hours that night and then again the next day, inquiring about his relationship with Darlene, asking him pointedly what the sore points were in their marriage. They knew that money was a frequent source of friction with any couple, and their line of questioning led him to admit that paying all the bills on time had sometimes been an issue between them in the past. But the detectives knew this already, having checked into the Ewalts' personal finances, and they told him as much. At one point, one of the detectives looked Todd straight in the eyes and said, "You killed your wife because you were having financial problems."

Todd was shocked by the bold accusation, and he thought maybe they were trying to gauge his reaction to determine if he was lying.

He was scrutinized. The police listened carefully to his responses, taking notes and looking for discrepancies in his words as well as his behavior, trying to interpret the subtleties of his body language, the cast of his eyes and the pitch of his voice.

Forced to defend himself, Todd denied killing his wife and informed the investigator that things were actually going well for them financially at that time, having steady work and sufficient savings. That's when police told him that Darlene had been planning on leaving him and that this had angered him into killing her. Todd insisted that wasn't true, and he voluntarily took a lie detector test.

Todd was confident that this test would prove once and for all that he had nothing to do with his wife's murder, and then the police could concentrate their efforts on finding her real killer. When the results came back, however, the police informed Todd that he had failed the test. He could not believe it, especially since he was never actually shown the failed results. He thought it was a tactic to get him to talk and say something incriminating.

"No way," he told them. "It can't be. How can I fail if I didn't do it?"

"You tell us."

"I don't have an explanation."

At that point, Todd refused to answer any further questions without an attorney present. Although he knew that doing so might make him look like a person with something to hide, someone who was guilty, he felt that the police seemed intent on making him out to be a murderer, and he didn't have any other choice.

Although Todd was never formally charged with Darlene's murder, the questions would continue, often and thoroughly, in the days following.

# Chapter 2

## DESTINY

It's difficult for me to recall a time when Kevin and I weren't together. I always knew we were meant to be together, even if other people didn't. We both grew up in Lexington, Massachusetts, and although I won't say we were from "different sides of the track," we *were* from completely different sides of the town. And a couple of years apart.

I was born Jean Hathaway Gilpatric on August 13, 1960, and my family's modest stucco bungalow-style home was in the Meriam Hill section of town, surrounded by much larger and more beautiful Victorian homes. It was an idyllic setting in many respects. Lexington is an old and historic Colonial town, the site of the first battle of the American Revolution. As schoolchildren, we were taught about the battles of Lexington and Concord and Paul Revere's famous "midnight ride" on April 18–19, 1775. Today, on the third Monday of each April, many faithfully observe Patriot's Day to commemorate the events of that day, even though most people might identify this regional day of observance with the Boston Marathon or the Red Sox home opener at Fenway Park. Certainly, there is still a strong sense of community there, and I share fond memories with family and friends of gathering on Christmas Eve for our carol stroll. This activity may sound somewhat antiquated to some, but it was a rejuvenating and peaceful experience to walk through the streets of Meriam Hill, songbooks in hand. In my memories, it always seemed to be snowing. My fingers and toes would be numb from the cold, but it didn't matter—there was such a powerful human connection that occurred. It's hard to find such spirituality and goodwill at any other time of the year. Try going around in a small group ringing doorbells in July and singing on someone's front porch, and see what kind of reception you get.

I was the youngest of four siblings, and there was such an age gap between me and them that not only was I the baby of the family, but sometimes I almost felt like an only child. My sister, Jill, was the closest to my age, and we were eight years apart. The difference in age just lent itself naturally to me being bothersome, especially to her. I would follow Jill around everywhere, so much so that she and her friends started calling me Flea.

My brothers, Bill and Peter, and I were divided by a gulf of fourteen and fifteen years, respectively. They were on the cusp of leaving the house and going off on their own when I was growing up. Since I was essentially the only one left at home, the bond I had with my parents, especially my dad, was very strong. By all accounts, I was a tomboy. Right up through my teenage years, all you had to do was look up and you would probably find me perched in a tree somewhere.

My dad, William Henry Gilpatric Jr., was a dentist, a quiet, gentle man whom people admired and respected. His patients had a fondness for him that still exists after all this time. I continue to run into people I haven't seen in years who tell me that my father had been their dentist and how much they'd liked him. He was only five feet four, but standing across the tennis court at the receiving end of his serve, no one would believe it came from a man his size. The unassuming dignity in which he lived his life may have been due in part to his having fought in World War II and being among those fortunate enough to have returned unscathed, at least physically. He would never talk about his time overseas, but he kept a collection of journals while he was there that were later sent home to my mother, several years after the war had ended. I found them an utterly fascinating glimpse into history from the perspective of one soldier but with the echoing voices of hundreds of thousands. Thinking about it now, perhaps this was the ember fueling the fire in me to document my experiences in my own personal war of sorts.

When I was a little girl, I worshipped the ground my father walked on. But I was only eleven when he was diagnosed with cancer, and I did not fully comprehend how sick he was as he battled the disease for three years before succumbing. I remember the day he passed vividly. It was August 10, 1974, three days before my fourteenth birthday. I was at summer camp when I was suddenly called home with the tragic news. I was devastated, of course, but I was also very angry. As the baby of the family, I was sheltered and protected from the onslaught of life's cruel realities. So although my mother had tried to protect me from the agonizing pain the rest of my family was experiencing, the cold hard fact that my father had been dying before my eyes had somehow eluded me. I was mad at my mother for lying to me, but I was upset with myself for not knowing. How could I not have seen his suffering while he sat quietly in the lawn chair watching as I did flips past him, practicing my gymnastics?

Adjusting to teenage life is difficult enough, but doing so while suffering the loss of the most significant person in one's life seriously compounds the ever-constant struggles of these formative years. Of course, my father's death affected everyone in the family. My mother's days of bridge club and volunteer work were suddenly over; after being a stay-at-home mom and raising four children, she was suddenly thrust back into the working world. I became a latchkey kid, a somewhat new phenomenon at the time. I was left to supervise myself during the after-school hours until my mother got home at dinnertime.

Our house was close to the center of town, which was bisected by a run of old buildings. We lived directly adjacent to a dilapidated printing press, which made up part of what had been dubbed "Blood Alley." If anything, the gruesome name seemed to accurately represent the path of life-altering recklessness that many Lexington teenagers would wind up taking, myself included, and as a result, I was constantly involved in the sort of mischief that ran a little too close to the illicit side. It was probably my first glimpse into the reality of how close the dividing line is between the cozy world of suburbia, where I grew up, and the things that exist on the fringe, the things that our parents wanted to keep us away from when they told us to be home at night before the streetlights came on. Somehow, though, I managed to navigate through those difficult years unscathed. Kevin McDonough had everything to do with that.

Our paths first crossed in the summer between my junior and senior years in high school. I had noticed him around town before then, driving his 1968 Chevy pickup truck. It was baby blue and was always sparkling clean and shiny. But he was the one who had caught my eye, with his incredible head of blond curls and the cutest baby face I had ever seen. I was hooked instantly. I asked around about him and found out that he lived on the other side of Mass Avenue in a house filled with kids—a big Irish family.

It was during this time that my mother met my soon-to-be stepdad, and we sold our house on Oakland Street, packed up everything and moved about a mile away. Shortly afterward, I met Kevin for the first time. It is actually a rather embarrassing story, but something we both still chuckle about. I was hanging out one evening with a group of kids, including Kevin; I knew that Kevin was very shy around girls and that I'd need to break the ice if anything was ever going to happen between us, so I approached him and asked if he'd buy me a beer. I wasn't really a big drinker, but I figured all guys like beer. Or maybe it was just the reckless teen—the Christmas caroler gone bad—coming out in me. Anyway, it worked. He bought me a beer, or three, and we got to know each other. He was a perfect gentleman, so it certainly wasn't a wildly romantic first encounter. It initiated a lifelong bond, however, and I can't help but smile when I think back on those days. Kevin still shows traces of that boy I fell in love with when I first laid eyes on him. The Mac Davis curls are gone, replaced by a sharp buzz that flatters his chiseled features. No more baby face, but I can still detect some of that innocence peeking out from behind those beautiful eyes. Sometimes I'll catch a glimpse of that shy young man, now long since replaced with a razor-sharp wit and offbeat sense of humor, and I wouldn't trade what we have for anything in the world. But it's safe to say that back then even I never would have dreamed that we would be together for life. We weren't the only ones, however, who didn't think we had a future together.

As I got to know Kevin, I realized how different the two of our families really were. He was the fourth of nine children, seven boys and two girls, and his parents were at least fifteen years younger than my mother and father. His Irish Catholic family was considered blue collar, while my Protestant one was white collar. At that time, there was an underlying socioeconomic division in the different parts of town that each of us came from—only his two sisters had gone to college, whereas my father and brothers had all attended prep school, and we'd all gone to college.

The McDonough house was a small cape near the reservoir. His father was the owner of an electrical construction company, and his mother was truly an incredible woman who spent every waking moment raising her children. With enough McDonoughs to make up a baseball team, it's no wonder. But it was a job she took very seriously, instilling in the children the paramount importance of both God and family. The entire McDonough brood would take up a whole pew at St. Bridget's Church on Sunday, with both their parents looking on as their children sat obediently listening to the words of the priest. I can't help but laugh when hearing them recalling their memories of what a project it was getting all nine of them dressed in their Sunday best, hair combed, and behaving appropriately while at church under their parents' close supervision.

Looking back, Kevin and I were both strong-willed

individuals from very different upbringings, so what people saw when we argued were two people prone to volatile outbursts because of our personalities. But there was a constant undercurrent of mutual respect and affection, and what few others saw was that we always reached neutral ground and made up.

To this day, I am convinced that if I hadn't met Kevin, my life would have headed in a vastly different direction. I was blessed when I met him, and have continued to be blessed ever since. However, our future almost dissolved before it ever began. No sooner had Kevin and I met than we were suddenly forced apart when my stepfather quickly grew tired of having a teenage girl around all the time and decided to send me off to boarding school. I didn't want to go, but there wasn't much I could do about it, and I resented my stepfather for that more than anything. But in a way, I was glad to get away. I didn't want to stay at home the way things were; it was a difficult living arrangement for everyone. This man could never replace my father, whom I so cherished. So off I went to Cushing Academy prior to my senior year, excited about the prospect of a better educational experience but sad to be leaving behind my friends and my new boyfriend.

When it was time to decide on a college, I chose Ithaca, in upstate New York, following the same path as my brother Peter. Kevin and I continued to date, though the relationship gradually began to become less serious because of the distance between us. As things became more and more rocky, we broke up for a period of time. Then I had an epiphany of sorts: realizing that I wasn't very happy being so far from home, and so far away from Kevin, I decided to transfer to Simmons College in Boston. Kevin was happy that not only was I closer to home, but I was attending an all-women's institution.

After I graduated, in 1982, we dated for a couple more years before moving into an apartment together on the Belmont/Cambridge line. After a couple of years we thought we had saved enough money to get married and start a family. We tied the knot on September 29, 1985, and we soon bought a condo in Merrimack, New Hampshire, not far from the Massachusetts state line. I began working at Interactive Training Systems in Bedford, Massachusetts, and Kevin settled full-time into the family business, which was also located in Bedford. The fifty mile each-way drive six days a week—we also went back to Lexington every Sunday for dinner with Kevin's family—occupied far too much time, and I wasn't sure how we would ever be able to start a family of our own. It didn't seem as if we had any time for ourselves. Then our son, Ryan, was born on October 12, 1988, and although there were complications with the delivery, making the early part of our son's life a precarious time, the six months that the three of us spent in New Hampshire were a joyous time.

Early in the spring of 1989, we found a house we liked back in Lexington, and we moved in, despite not having sold our condo in New Hampshire. The house in Lexington was a fixer-upper, and Kevin put our entire life savings into doing just that, handling a lot of the work himself. When he was done, it was absolutely beautiful, by all accounts our dream home. It was in a great location, just a few houses down from the town's recreational facilities. It was also perfect because it was centrally situated between both of our parents' homes. It was the happiest time of our lives, despite the fact that by the time our daughter, Shea, was born, on September 11, 1991, we still hadn't found a buyer for the New Hampshire property, and we were carrying two mortgages. The monthly payments were slowly draining us financially. To make matters worse, Kevin and I weren't the only ones in the family feeling this economic pinch—the family's electrical business was also struggling in a down housing market. There just wasn't enough work to keep everyone busy and employed with a steady paycheck. But we had to do something, because we were on the verge of losing everything.

In 1993, after much difficult discussion, as well as tears and heartache, Kevin and I decided to move to northern Virginia, where our best friends had moved several years earlier. There seemed to be some promising prospects in the construction field, and we hoped that the cost of living would be lower. And indeed, Kevin was immediately able to secure a job, so we sold our house in Massachusetts, signed a Deed in Lieu on the condo in New Hampshire, jammed all of our belongings into an enormous U-Haul and off we went. I was emotionally torn by the unknown elements we faced but also filled with hope and the potential for a new life with our closest and dearest friends by our side. It took some time to get used to everything, but we eventually did. We were particularly lucky in that we moved to a wonderful neighborhood where the homes were close together and the people closer, a place where religion and community were central parts of daily life. Our children thrived in an environment that reinforced all the foundational moral elements that Kevin and I valued. We met some wonderful people, some of whom we've remained friends with to this day.

The only drawback to this new living arrangement was Kevin's absence. Working as a superintendent in the construction field required him to travel for weeks at a time. This was not something that the kids and I were used to. It eventually became too much for us to endure, and fortunately it was around the same time that the economy began an upswing, and Kevin's father called asking him to return home so he could help run the business. It was just what we were waiting for; despite the wonderful people and enriching lifestyle in Virginia, I was thrilled and excited to be headed home again. Once a New Englander, always a New Englander, they say—and it's true.

We found a nice home in Chelmsford to settle into, close to Bedford and affordable. Although it needed quite a bit of work and considerable TLC, we figured we had plenty of time to transform it into our dream home, because this was where we were going to be spending the rest of our lives. One of the first things we did was get a dog, Bosco, a beautiful black retriever mix who seemed to complete our family. We all fell in love with the area immediately. There was nothing *not* to love. It was a great place to raise a family. For Kevin and me, it was close to where we'd grown up, just twenty miles from where it all began for us. We had come full circle. It was the best of all worlds for us and where we wanted to be.

By 2007, we had been living in the cozy four-bedroom New England–style cape for eleven years. That June, *Money* magazine listed our town as the twenty-first best place to live in the country that year. It was a proud distinction, but to anyone living there, not surprising—it's a quiet, affluent suburb that boasted a very low crime rate. The type of community where you didn't have to worry too much if you happened to go to bed without locking the door. Downtown Chelmsford is in many ways a picture-perfect postcard of New England life, a Norman Rockwell painting come to life.

Chelmsford, however, is not exactly rural. About a hundred yards beyond our back door, I-495 cuts a path to points south to Rhode Island and north to Boston, just thirty miles away. We never thought much about the possible ramifications of a major highway running directly through our backyard. At the time we bought the house, the only conceivable drawback was noise, which is something that you really do get used to. Little did we know that it was not the vehicles that were moving past us on the interstate that were our biggest problem—it was the ones that were stopped in the rest area a quarter mile away.

# Chapter 3

## HIGHWAY OF DEATH

Tuesday, July 17, 2007

It was about 2:00 a.m., the apparent killing hour for the murderer, who was dressed in black but unmasked as he slipped into the first unlocked door he came across that night.

Thirty-seven-year-old Patricia Brooks was asleep on the couch downstairs in her Bowers Bridge Road home when she was suddenly awakened by a sharp, stinging pain on the right side of her shoulder and across the front of her neck. When her eyes fluttered open, she saw someone standing over her in the darkness. She could not see much more than the outline of a figure clad in dark clothes. Then she detected the swift motion of an object that was giving off a metallic sheen. It appeared out of the shadows, and she instantly felt a strange cold sensation on her upper body and more stinging pain. She was also aware of a warm wetness around her abdomen. Patricia thought she was dreaming at first, but she soon realized that the object was a knife—a very long one. And it was as real as the figure that was lunging at her and slashing her about the throat and shoulder.

She saw the spray of blood that was spilling out of her body onto the white carpeting and instinctively grabbed at her throat, clasping one hand over the torn flesh. She started gasping as she tried to fend off the attacker with her other hand and get to her feet, but he was too big and strong. The man was also wearing a cap, and although his face was exposed, Patricia caught only brief, dim glimpses of him. What was not lost on her was his pungent odor, like a wild animal's.

The commotion downstairs was loud enough to wake her family, who were sleeping upstairs. Within moments, the sound of footfalls could be heard on the floor above and descending the stairs.

Believing he had mortally wounded his victim—the bleeding was heavy and Patricia was now motionless—the killer stepped away from her. He was satisfied that if she wasn't already dead, she would be soon, so before anyone could come all the way down the stairs, he turned and fled the house through the unlocked back door, the same one he had entered through a short time before. He disappeared into the night, leaving Patricia for dead.

She was still alive, however. She had tricked him by playing possum, and it was in this position, as she lay there perfectly still, that she was able to get her best look at her attacker.

She watched him leave, waited a moment until she was sure that he was gone, and then she grabbed her neck and felt the multiple open wounds. She pressed the palm of her hand tightly against her throat to slow the steady flow of blood and tried to get up. Patricia was light-headed from the loss of blood, and she fell back down onto the couch. She immediately tried again to get to her feet, more slowly this time. She managed to support herself as she stumbled toward the stairs. All she wanted to do was get out of that room in case he came back.

"Don't go down there," Patricia mouthed as she met her mother and daughter on the landing. They helped her up to the next floor, leaving a trail of blood behind them.

An ambulance was called, and Patricia was transported to York Hospital. Her injuries were very serious. Several major veins and arteries in her neck were cut, including a nick to both external jugulars. Her esophagus and trachea were damaged as well. She required immediate surgery, but her status was good after she left the OR. Although a full recovery was expected, she was extremely lucky to have survived the attack. Had the blade penetrated a fraction of an inch deeper, she would have died almost instantly.

In a later interview with police at the hospital, Patricia Brooks told them that her attacker "was dressed for the occasion," wearing all black, in an outfit she likened to a prison-guard uniform. She said he was also wearing a dark cap, and a wide "tool belt" was strapped to his waist. She mentioned his bestial smell and described him as a large man with a pot belly that had hung over the belt. He was white, with a stubbly beard and chubby face, and she thought she would be able to recognize him if she saw him again.

---

The Bowers Bridge Road home where Patricia was attacked was located in a rather isolated area of Conewago Township in York County, Pennsylvania, close to Interstate 83. Authorities in the Pennsylvania townships of Conewago and West Hanover, where Darlene Ewalt had been killed four days earlier, did not know what they were dealing with yet. Despite the increased reports of prowlers in these areas around the time of the slashing attacks, police continued to focus on suspects who had been known to the victims.

In Dauphin County, Darlene's husband, Todd Ewalt, remained the focus of the police investigation into his wife's murder. In the absence of any other suspects, he knew that the police believed he was responsible for Darlene's death, or at least knew something about it. Although he understood that they were just doing their jobs, he felt like he was being watched all the time, even as he was grieving the loss of his beloved wife and burying the mother of their two children. He wondered if he had cried enough for their benefit. He was almost afraid to laugh or smile, for fear of how he might be judged. All that in addition to the overwhelming guilt he was feeling for not being awake to save his wife from being killed by a knife-wielding madman who murdered her outside their bedroom window while he slept. The worst part was realizing that the police might never catch her killer if they were focusing all their attention on him.

State police investigators in Pennsylvania, however, soon came to a dead end with Todd Ewalt. With the case growing colder by the day, Dauphin County prosecutors, who had been anticipating an arrest, began to turn their attention to more immediate matters of concern.

By the end of July, there were still no new leads in either case, and neither jurisdiction had yet made a connection between the two attacks, which were separated by a distance of thirty miles. The only similarities between the crimes, besides the type of weapon used, were the proximity of the victims' homes to the interstate. With a network of nearly four million miles of public roadways contained within its borders, the United States has the largest national highway system in the world. Unfortunately, this multilane accomplice had not been fully considered at this point in the investigation, and that oversight would only bring further death.

# Chapter 4

## MURDER ON MAIN STREET

Sunday, July 29, 2007

State police began receiving reports of a prowler from residents of Bloomsbury, New Jersey, around 2:00 a.m. Frightened home owners called in numerous complaints of someone jiggling their door handles and trying to get inside. The picturesque borough in Hunterdon County is home to about one thousand people. Although it is surrounded by farmland, it is situated just ten miles east of the Pennsylvania line and fifty miles north of Philadelphia. Interstate 78 runs directly through it. The massive truck stop at the eastern end of town has always been another world unto itself, part of the community yet separated by an invisible boundary. Truck stops like the one in Bloomsbury provide a safe haven for weary truckers, and unlike more generic rest areas that offer bathroom facilities and food for all motorists, truck stops are generally for truckers only and are all but off-limits to other highway motorists.

There are more motorist-friendly stops all along today's

interstate highways, roadside plazas that feature an assortment of fast-food marts, information centers and tourist
attractions. It is here where commercial truck drivers and
pedestrian travelers often converge. One group pulls over
because it is convenient, another because it is required.
Although travel for private motorists has gotten easier and
more anonymous, the regulations with which interstate truckers must comply have gotten more restrictive, and because
a trucker's stops are mandated, they are also documented.
So when a dark-blue tractor pulling a semi with Virginia
registration tags pulled into the rest area at exit 7 off I-78
in New Jersey earlier that night, it came with a traceable
history. There were gas receipts, logbook entries, bills of
lading and other shipping documents that identified the
truck's origin, its destination, and everything in between.
This particular truck, carrying a variety of nursery and
garden supplies, had left Virginia on July 27, making
deliveries around York, Pennsylvania, before stopping at
the rest area in New Jersey. There was another scheduled
stop, in Uxbridge, Massachusetts, on the way to Nashua,
New Hampshire, where the driver would refill his truck
with goods for the return trip south.

But first, there was at least one undocumented stop
that the driver of this nursery truck was going to make.
He removed a black fanny pack from under the cab's seat
and strapped it around his waist. He didn't have to check
the contents because he had packed it himself earlier and
no one else had touched it. He secured a knife leg strap to
his right thigh and slid a fifteen-inch hunting knife into the
KYDEX pocket sheath. Then he grabbed the hooded mask
and the pair of gloves from the passenger seat beside him
and stepped out of the truck. The mask was brown cam-
ouflage in the front and black in the back, and the black

nylon gloves had leather palms. Wearing a black T-shirt, dark denim jeans and black sneakers, the trucker slipped unseen into the narrow band of trees behind his rig. When he emerged a moment later in front of Route 173, his hands were covered, his face was concealed and he was ready to kill. He prowled through the backyards of the sleepy neighborhood as if they were his own private hunting grounds. Upon finding a locked door, he moved on, also bypassing any house with lights on.

When he came across a two-story residence with a wide front porch at 79 Main Street, the windows were dark, and there was a car parked outside. He peered into the passenger window of the car parked in the driveway on the side of the house. Spotting a purse in plain view on the passenger seat, he tried the car door but found it locked. He had a feeling that this was the one, and he was so confident about it that he didn't even attempt to access the residence from a rear door. He walked straight up the stairs onto the porch and wasn't the least bit shocked when the front door swung open freely.

He quickly entered the ground-floor duplex apartment and paused in the darkness, listening for the sound of a television, voices, footsteps, anything at all. There was only silence. On a low coffee table in the middle of the living room was a set of car keys. He grabbed them and walked back outside. After unlocking the passenger door of the car, he snatched the pocketbook and closed the door swiftly to extinguish the interior light. Right there, he removed the small yellow flashlight he was carrying and started to go through the contents of the purse. He dug out the wallet, which contained several credit cards and some cash, but he looked past these at that moment and pulled out the operator's license, focusing on the picture and the date of birth of the driver. Her name was Monica Massaro. She was blond. Pretty. A beautiful smile to go with it all. She was thirty-eight years old. He could have left at that point, but he felt compelled to stay. And hunt. There was only one car in the driveway, and he figured the woman was unmarried and was alone. He wasn't done yet. He then went back up onto the front porch and stepped inside the house, taking the purse with him and placing it on the floor just inside the door.

Before proceeding any further, he removed the knife from his waist belt. He slowly began to make his way through the ground-floor apartment. He walked down a narrow hallway, passed a bathroom on one side and a closed door directly across, which he opened carefully before discovering it was a closet. He rummaged through it briefly, looking for anything of value among the bath towels and sundry items. Around the corner was a bedroom. He could see the large dresser just inside the doorway. He entered the room cautiously, expecting to find a helpless, sleeping victim. Instead, what he encountered was a terrified woman sitting up in bed, having been woken by the sounds of someone prowling around in her apartment. They were both surprised when he walked through the doorway into the darkened bedroom.

Monica never locked her doors, a habit that concerned her parents as well as some of her friends who were not as free-spirited or trusting. If she had been holding out any hope that this was her upstairs tenant coming in to talk to her about something, or perhaps stumbling home drunk and wandering into the wrong apartment, that thought was short-lived. She had been clutching the remote control for the overhead light and fan, and when she clicked it on, it revealed a hulking figure clad in black, his face concealed behind a mask.

Monica began to scream and jumped out of bed. The intruder raised the knife and charged her at once. He pressed one gloved hand against her mouth to stifle her screams, but she bit his hand and he pulled it away quickly. Angered, he threw her onto the bed and pounced on top of her as she continued to scream. Then he brought the blade of the knife in his right hand across her throat in a smooth, practiced motion. He opened a deep, fatal wound. Her screams were instantly silenced as blood pulsed from the severed vessels in her neck. Monica died quickly, her killer watching, breathless himself with excitement as she bled to death. Then he proceeded to mutilate her body, stabbing and slashing her head, chest, stomach and between her legs.

Before he left, the killer went through her personal belongings in search of a trophy to take with him. Finding a necklace on the dresser, the masked man pocketed it as a souvenir. As he left the apartment, he grabbed Monica's purse, but then went around to the side door at the back of the house to make his escape. After what he had just done, he did not want to risk being seen now.

Stepping outside, he walked behind the victim's house until he reached the railroad tracks. He knew the truck stop was bordered on one side by the tracks, so he headed in that direction. Along the way, he started dumping out the contents of the victim's purse. He tossed out all of the personal effects except her driver's license, credit cards and cash. The bills and loose change he stuffed into the front pocket of his jeans. Before he got into his cab, he tossed the cards and license into a trash can at the Exxon

station and flung the pocketbook up onto the roof of an
adjacent building.

The trucker did not seem to be in any hurry to get
away, as he did not leave right away. He went into the Pilot
Travel Center, which was part of the Route 78 truck stop,
and bought a radar detector. He even had something to eat
and slept a little while before he drove off, continuing on
toward New England and his next stop.

# Chapter 5

UNSUSPECTING

In Chelmsford, July brought the true dog days and everything that came with the sweltering temperatures and
high humidity. I've always loved this time of year, despite
the oppressive heat, but it was the worst time for the air-
conditioning unit in our bedroom to fail. It remained in the
window for several days after it had conked out; we'd been
busy and just hadn't gotten around to fixing it. Instead,
we had been getting by with the ceiling fan circulating
overhead.

The kids' bedrooms were upstairs, but the rooms were
not air-conditioned, and when the weather got like this, it
was simply unbearable up there. As an alternative, Shea
and Ryan would either sleep on the large sectional in the
family room, where there was a ceiling fan and cross venti-
lation from the perimeter windows, or they would crash in
the downstairs guest room, adjacent to our bedroom, where
there were twin beds and a fully functioning AC unit in the

window. It didn't seem to matter much, as the kids were hardly ever home at the same time.

That summer, we planned our family vacation down at Cape Cod for the week of July fourteenth through the twenty-second, an annual excursion we make with our best friends, Lisa and Jay, and their family. We hadn't seen much of our son, Ryan, that summer; he had graduated from high school in June and was enjoying the last of the carefree summer days. In the fall he would be attending Wentworth Institute of Technology in Boston, so he spent most of his time with his friends from high school, who he would not see as often come September. But we had no trouble getting him to join his mother and father and his little sister on this trip. Lisa and Jay had five children, around the same ages as Ryan and Shea, and the kids always have a great time together.

It may have been hot and sticky at home, but it was beautiful by the water. I could stay all day on the beach just soaking up the sun and reveling in the beauty of the surroundings. One morning when the weather was not cooperating, the girls, all the daughters, decided to go into town and pamper themselves by getting manicures and pedicures. The rest of us stayed on the beach. Kevin and I didn't care if it was overcast.

During their "mani-pedis," an episode of *Oprah* was airing on the salon's television. Various experts were discussing what a person should do in the event he or she was attacked or abducted. The girls listened closely to the advice given by previous victims and law enforcement professionals, who all agreed that a person's best chance for survival is to fight back and never go quietly. Although the stories of the survivors and the advice of the guests were at once terrifying and enthralling, the reality of being abducted seemed like a distant concern, something that happened to other people, not to them or to anyone they might know.

The week went by way too fast, and before we knew it, we were back at home, thinking about the workweek and other responsibilities. Shea would be entering her junior year of high school, and she knew how important it was to be ready for the first day of conditioning sessions, scheduled to begin Monday morning, for the upcoming swim season. She was highly self-motivated for a fifteen-year-old. The workouts, scheduled to begin at 7:15 a.m. on alternating days of the week, weren't mandatory, but they were a highly encouraged prerequisite to the official start of practice. For the rest of the summer, Shea would have to wake up early in the morning for a strenuous workout in the pool. We all had to get up early—everyone except Ryan, perhaps—so it was easy enough to tone down our social activities. Most nights were spent around the house, watching television programs, or if a baseball game was on, tuning in to the Red Sox. We were all avid fans.

On Tuesday night, July 24, Kevin and I were transfixed by a tragic and disturbing news story out of Cheshire, Connecticut. The previous morning, two armed men had broken into the home of a prominent area physician as he and his family slept. The report said that two recent parolees had terrorized the family for six hours, raping and strangling the doctor's wife and tying his daughters, eleven and eighteen, to their beds, raping the younger and then setting the beds ablaze. The men bound the doctor in the basement, savagely beat him in the head and torso with a baseball bat, and left him to die. As the house was burning, he managed to escape to a neighbor's, but he was the only survivor. Medical examiners said his daughters succumbed to smoke inhalation, while his wife died from strangulation.

At one point during the home invasion, one of the suspects drove the mother to a local bank and forced her to withdraw $15,000. She somehow alerted a clerk that her family was being held hostage, and the police were notified, but by the time they arrived, the women had all been killed. The suspects attempted to escape in the family's SUV, but they were confronted by a blockade of police cars. They rammed into two cruisers in a desperate attempt to get away, but they were quickly apprehended and arrested.

I was absolutely appalled. It truly was the most heinous crime I had ever heard about. Kevin and I were too horrified to talk immediately after hearing this report. I knew that we were thinking the same thing: if something like that could happen there, it could happen anywhere.

A bit later I turned to Kevin and asked, "Do you think we should look into getting a security system?"

Kevin shrugged and looked at me. "What are the odds of something like that happening here?" he said.

I began to wonder if the doctor's wife had asked him the same question the previous week. A sense of unease had been planted, and I began to question if the feeling of safety and security anywhere was just an illusion.

---

On Saturday, July 28, I enjoyed a night out in Boston with family and friends. I probably overdid it that night, and I knew I was going to pay for it the next day, but none of us were driving and that may have prompted us all to let loose a little bit. We had a great time, and even though it was another exceptionally hot night, and we were still without an air conditioner, I was asleep before my head hit the pillow.

The next thing I knew, our dog Bosco's barking was waking me up way too early in the morning. Kevin had already gotten up and was at the shop. He was an early bird, and a couple drinks the night before didn't faze him in the least. Bosco wasn't stopping, so I got out of bed to see what was wrong. Either his line was tangled around a tree again or he had seen a squirrel or some other creature roaming around. So I went outside, and sure enough, Bosco's line was hung up on some rocks. I could not even count the number of times Kevin or I had gone outside at all hours of the night to untangle the dog's line. I freed him up now, hoping he hadn't been barking too long and disturbing the neighbors. Then I went back to bed, wanting only to wake up again and start the day off on a better foot.

As we were roused from sleep that Sunday morning, Monica Massaro's life had just expired at the hands of a homicidal trucker about two hundred and twenty-five miles away. Our family had no way of knowing that our lives would be the next to intersect with this vicious killer, whose actions were as random as his victims were innocent. Not even he knew who he would target next.

July 29 was a pretty typical Sunday at our house. Shea had been at a party the night before with her friend Ashley, and they were spending the day together, very likely sleeping in. Ryan was camped out at his best friend Ricky's house, where he had been spending a lot of his time that summer. I had been thinking about using my free day to go out and do some shopping, but since Kevin and I had been out the previous night, a lazy day by the pool was just what the doctor ordered.

Kevin came home in the late afternoon, and we hung

out for the rest of the day. We decided to take advantage of the kids not being around and went to grab an early dinner at Filho's, a tasty little bistro about a half hour from our house. Once evening came around, we settled in to catch some of the Red Sox game. They were playing the Sunday night ESPN game against Tampa Bay, when the team was still called the Devil Rays and before they were American League champions. It was a good game, if you like pitching duels. It was scoreless until the bottom of the seventh, when Tampa scored five runs.

After Tampa jumped out ahead, Kevin decided to turn in. Because it was a nationally televised game, it had started later than normal. Add to that pitcher Dice-K's deliberate windup and all the extra commercials between innings, and it was late. Kevin still had to get up at the crack of dawn for work.

"It must be a hundred degrees in the bedroom," he sighed. "I've got to get the unit fixed this week. I can't take any more of this."

It had been hot all week, but that night it didn't seem to cool down at all. I turned up the speed of the ceiling fan and got up to open our bedroom door halfway to try to allow any cross breeze to circulate through. When I noticed Kevin undressing to get into bed, I saw that he had even removed his boxers.

"Kevin," I said, in a chastising tone that he recognized right away.

"What?" he asked, defensively.

I pointed to his boxer shorts, which were now draped on the footboard where he had placed them.

"Oh, come on, Jeannie!"

"What if your daughter chooses to sleep in the next room? That wouldn't be appropriate."

He growled under his breath but put them back on.

A short while later, Shea called from Ashley's house and asked if she could sleep over. Kevin heard me talking to her and got my attention. I looked over and saw him start to remove his boxers again. He was kidding, and he laughed out loud. I turned away and smiled. I urged Shea to come home because she had swim practice early the next morning, and it would be easier for everyone if she was already here. She was disappointed but didn't fight us on the decision and agreed to be home by her normal summer curfew time of midnight.

# Chapter 6

## HUNTING HUMANS

Around 10:00 p.m. Sunday night, July 29, 2007, a blue tractor pulling a semi with Virginia tags was rolling along I-495 North near Chelmsford. The driver was within fifteen miles of Nashua, New Hampshire, where first thing in the morning he would make a pickup from a local plant nursery before heading back. There were no scheduled stops on the return trip, and he was expected back in Virginia by the end of the following day. The seven-hundred-and-fifty-mile return trip could be made in less than twelve hours, so the driver's personal downtime was limited. It was expected that he would pull over at the nearest convenient spot to get some sleep.

When he came up on the northbound sign "Exit 33 Visitor Center/Rest Area," he may have felt the tug of circumstance conspiring and provoking him to pull over. With no other such stops before he reached his final destination, it would have been his last opportunity to indulge a dark compulsion that he likely did not understand himself. He just gave in to it. Whatever compelled him and drove him to such violence, one thing that he had to have been aware of was that this would be his last chance before he headed back to Virginia, so if he was going to do anything, it would have to be now. He entered the rest-stop facilities, where there was only one other tractor-trailer parked. Its lights were dark, though the rest area was well lit. There were no cars around. He pulled into the furthest space behind the other rig and cut the engine.

He didn't waste any time, getting out of his cab much earlier than he had in Pennsylvania and New Jersey. He donned his hunting attire, the exact same set of black clothes he had worn the night before. There were traces of blood on them that had barely dried from the murder he had committed the night before. He hadn't even bothered to shower, despite the stifling and oppressive heat of the past few days. As he set out into the surrounding woods on foot, he could only have been looking to add another trophy to his collection.

Less than a quarter mile south, the figure in black stepped out of the woods at the edge of Woodcrest Condominiums. The three-story, sand-colored brick buildings were bound by I-495 on the north and on the south by Route 110, Littleton Road, which runs parallel to the highway. The trucker began skulking around in the shadows, looking for the right opportunity to enter one of the darkened units. For him, this meant an unlocked door so he could enter quietly. If he could determine that a woman was inside, she had to be alone, preferably sleeping. No situations like that presented themselves. It was only about 11:00 p.m., a lot earlier than usual for him to be out hunting, and there were lights on everywhere. This spelled trouble, but he was determined to try a couple more doors before moving on. Something made him pause outside building 6. For whatever reason, the ground-floor door of apartment 311 stood out among all the others, and he made his move. When he tried the door, however, he found that it was locked. He had also been spotted by the female resident as he approached her unit. She had been watching television in bed beside her sleeping husband when she heard someone trying to get inside through the basement door. She got up and went over to the second-floor bedroom balcony, which overlooked the backyard. Directly below her, she spotted a lurking figure wearing all black in the shadowy darkness. The woman immediately woke her husband and told him what she had seen, then called the police.

Chelmsford is just under twenty-three square miles and retains a fifty-member police department, about thirty of whom are patrol officers. Some nights there might be as few as four units on patrol, but this night, less than an hour before the shift change, there were six. Two of them, Officers Francis Teehan in Car 1 and Shawn Swift in Car 4, responded separately to this suspicious-person call and both arrived at approximately the same time, 11:09 p.m. The woman described the suspect as "stocky" and wearing black clothes, including a dark knit hat. She said she'd been unable to get a look at the suspect's face before he disappeared into the woods in the direction of the truck stop behind the condos.

The officers searched the surroundings, but the suspect was long gone.

---

By 2:00 a.m., the trucker had moved on from Woodcrest Condominiums to the Chelmsford Mobile Home Park, a little farther south on Littleton Road. Based on the time of night that he had been most active in the past, it would seem that he felt much safer at this particular hour. Maybe he even felt invincible. Is that what gave him the brazen confidence that enabled him to enter someone's house in search of a vulnerable woman to control with fear and violence? What appeared certain was that the risks he was prepared to undertake now were not ones that he would have considered earlier. The trailer park was quite large, and the homes were all tightly clustered together, which would have been far too intimidating for him to consider earlier in the night. Now, with his confidence high, he approached the first unit on the left, just inside the entrance of the park. He immediately noticed the glow of a computer screen in one of the windows, and moved quickly out of the shadows.

The residence belonged to Gladys Shea, who lived there with her daughter, Kathy Crowley, and her granddaughter, Michele. Looking inside the window, the trucker observed fourteen-year-old Michele sitting in front of a desktop computer in the small living room. As he moved in for a closer look, the young girl noticed that someone was outside. At first, she believed it was her mother, whom she knew was still up and perhaps had gone out to have a smoke. However, a moment later Michele saw her mother enter the room from the kitchen.

"Mom, were you just outside the house on the porch?"

"No," Kathy Crowley said with a rising sense of alarm.

"Well, I just saw somebody outside the window I thought was you."

Concerned, Kathy stepped outside onto the porch. She looked all around but didn't see anyone, so she went back inside. "There's nothing there now."

"It was probably nothing," Michele said, turning her attention back to the computer.

"It's time to turn the thing off and get to bed, anyway."

"Oh, Mom!"

"Forget *'Oh, Mom!'* Off it goes. You have until I come out of the bathroom."

As the bathroom door closed, Michele sighed and then suddenly spotted something out of the corner of her eye. In the window, right beside her, was a face, though it was covered by what she thought was some type of bag that had been pulled over the head. She screamed, and her mother instantly emerged from the bathroom.

"What?"

Michele jumped up out of her chair. "Someone was in the window again."

Kathy didn't see anything when she looked, but thinking it was a Peeping Tom who she could easily frighten off for good, she rushed back outside without hesitation. A couple of trailers down, she saw something in the darkness. It was a rather large figure, walking farther away.

"Hey, what are you doing?" she yelled at the retreating silhouette.

Suddenly, he stopped and turned to face her, and she knew instantly that she was in trouble. He had a large belt strapped to his waist, and at first she thought he might be a cop or a security guard. But he was dressed entirely in black—like a Ninja, she thought. Kathy did not know what weapons he was carrying, but she was sure that he was not a police officer.

She was temporarily frozen in terror, but as soon as the figure started to make a decisive move in her direction she ran back into the trailer, slamming the door and locking it behind her. At the same time, she screamed to her daughter,

"Close the window! And lock it!" She picked up the phone to call the police, and when she looked back around at the kitchen window she saw the black-masked figure peering in at them. Frantically trying to dial out, she realized that her daughter was still logged on to the Internet using the telephone line, so she was unable to get through.

As soon as she turned and noticed that the face in the window had disappeared, she heard the door handle being jiggled and then a moment later a loud banging. The prowler outside was pounding on the door.

Thinking quickly, Kathy grabbed her cell phone and her daughter, then retreated to the bedroom at the farthest end of the trailer, where her mother, Gladys, was sleeping. She used an ironing board as a wedge under the door handle, bracing it against the floor to reinforce the meager lock.

It was 2:17 a.m. when Kathy reached a 911 operator.

"Please hurry," she begged. "There's someone outside my house looking in all the windows."

"Okay, what's the address?"

As she was talking to the emergency dispatcher, the prowler's violent pounding on the external door was recorded, and the whole trailer was shaking.

"Oh, he's trying to break in! Oh my God! Somebody's trying to break in . . . Get somebody here . . . quick! He's trying to break in right now!"

"Okay, what part of the house is he at?"

"He's at the front door!"

"He's at the front door?"

"He might be in the house! I can hear something now! He's breaking in! Hurry up!"

"Do you know who it is?" the dispatcher calmly asked.

"He's at the front door. Just get the police here, quick!"

There was a sudden explosion of light, prompting all

three women to react in heightened panic, believing the prowler had entered the trailer.

"He's in the house now! *Please!*"

The attacker was still outside, however; he had smashed the outside porch light beside the door. Even as help was summoned and just seconds away, the women remained huddled together, completely defenseless and absolutely terrified.

Officer Robert Murphy of the Chelmsford Police Department had been assigned to Car 1 that night, and he was the first respondent to the scene. Officer Bruce Darwin in Car 4 and Sergeant Frank Goode in Car 9 quickly followed. Hearing the officer's firm knocking on the front door, the female residents thought the prowler had returned. When Kathy confirmed that it was the police, she immediately let them inside.

She explained what had happened, describing the prowler as a heavyset white male wearing tight black clothes that resembled a wet suit. She also described the subject as wearing a belt that "looked like what the police wear" with "things hanging off it."

The officers did not notice any damage to the exterior screen door, but the plastic fixture around the exterior light was busted and the glass bulb had been shattered. Kathy informed them that she believed the man had broken the light on purpose to prevent them from seeing him, and as a result she had not gotten a good enough look to be able to identify him. She also reported that a pack of cigarettes was missing from the outside porch.

Following a thorough search of the area around their lot and elsewhere around the mobile home park, no trace of the prowler was found. The women were so shaken by what happened, however, that they packed some belongings and stayed the rest of the night at a friend's home. They were convinced that the prowler would return, and there was no way they were going to stay there after what they had just been through. The officers remained in the area for more than an hour afterward, patrolling the grounds of the mobile home park, looking for anything suspicious.

---

After leaving Gladys Shea's trailer, the trucker had made his way back through the woods, moving north until he reached Hunt Road, which he followed west. At 3:00 a.m., there were no cars on the road, which would have only enhanced any fantasies he may have been entertaining that he was something of a spirit, moving unseen and unstoppable through the darkness. The road crossed over I-495, less than a half mile south of the truck stop where his rig was parked.

After a short distance, Hunt Road merged into Pine Hill Road, which split off in two directions. To the left was a nursery, and on the other side of the street, at the corner of the intersection that formed a wide-angled Y, was a beautifully restored rambling farmhouse. The trucker took an indirect route toward the large estate, walking among the shadows along the far side of the road before cutting across in the backyard, his steps slow and deliberate.

The property was gated, but he quickly gained access to a large patio area by unlatching the adjoining door. He sidled past an in-ground pool and approached a rear entry exterior door. He tried it. It was unlocked. He stepped into the farmhouse.

As he stepped cautiously through the dark interior, he moved through a narrow hallway into the back end of the kitchen. He immediately spotted an iPod cradled in a stereo dock on a countertop. He reached for it, but in grasping it, he accidentally touched the play button, and loud music began to blare from the device. This home invasion ended at that moment, as the trucker instantly released the iPod and fled, making no attempt to turn it off and leaving the farmhouse the same way he came in.

There were two women asleep in their bedrooms upstairs at the time, a mother and a daughter. Both were awakened by the disturbance, but the daughter got up out of bed and went down to the kitchen to turn her iPod off. It was 3:30 a.m., and she was still groggy as she headed back upstairs through the silent house, thinking that the device had gone off on its own. She then went back to bed and didn't think anything more of it that night.

# Chapter 7

## THE WRONG ROAD

Shea had been dropped off at home at about a quarter to twelve. The first thing she did was come into our bedroom to let us know she was home. Kevin was out cold by then. Usually one of us would wait up until the kids were all in, and as the Red Sox game had only recently ended, I was still wide awake. Besides, the overhead fan had done little to diminish the room's oppressive heat, which was not at all conducive to sleep. Shea told me she was going to sleep next door in the guest bedroom, and I couldn't blame her. She said good night, and as she was turning to leave she started to close the door behind her.

"Shea, could you leave that open a little? Thanks, baby. Have a good night."

Shea wasn't quite ready for bed, however, so she went into the kitchen and grabbed a bottle of water from the refrigerator. As she walked into the family room and turned on the television, she realized that her brother was

not home. Assuming that he would be coming in shortly—
he was older, so he had a later curfew—she innocently
unlocked the back door for him in case he forgot his key,
as he was prone to do. She did not know that Ryan was
spending the night at Ricky's house. Sitting in front of the
TV, she flipped through the stations for a while but quickly
began to tire. She fought sleep, dozing on the sectional
until about 2:00 a.m., when she got up and dragged herself
to bed in the guest bedroom. Even with two twin beds in
there, the room is quite small, and with the AC unit running full blast, it got very cold in there very quickly. Shea
had the blankets piled all the way up to her chin to shield
herself from the chilly air as she slept.

---

Despite having to flee the farmhouse, his fantasy unful-
filled, the trucker felt more charged up than ever. He continued north up Pine Hill, moving through the backyards
of the residences on the northern side of the road. When he
reached a neighboring property, located diagonally to our
home, the neighbor's dogs went wild, barking like crazy,
incensed by the trucker's movement and most certainly the
pungent smell he emitted from his activities over the past
twenty-four hours. One of the neighbors was awakened
and stumbled out of bed, but he saw nothing in the dark
expanse outside his back door. He figured that a passing
coyote had riled up the dogs, which in turn had scared the
wild animal off.

It was around this time that I woke up. Maybe it was
the barking of the dogs, I can't say for certain. And it was
still sweltering. My skin was damp with sweat and my
mouth was dry. I was thirsty, so I got out of bed and went
to the kitchen to get a glass of water. I had a few sips and

then took the glass back with me to the bedroom in case I got thirsty again later on. I went right back to bed, but it wasn't easy to fall back to sleep. I must have wakened Kevin, because I heard him tossing and turning. I eventually dropped off, but it was far from a deep sleep.

Outside, the masked trucker reached Misty Meadows, a narrow dirt road that provided access from Pine Hill for the three homes at the end of the way. Now he was headed directly toward our house.

It was around 3:40 a.m. when he walked up the driveway along the left side of the house. He passed the doghouse, where our dog, Bosco, was on a leash tethered to a line that ran between two trees. The setup increased his freedom of movement to about twenty feet in either direction. He was a friendly, loving dog, but he had always been very territorial. Whenever someone he didn't know came on or near the property, he barked incessantly. But if he barked at all that night, with no air conditioner running and the windows open, we would have heard him. However, for whatever reason, Bosco did not seem to stir as the reeking, dark figure entered the backyard through the side gate and up onto the small back porch to the door, which had been unlocked earlier by Shea.

The trucker entered our house and found himself at the back of the family room facing the kitchen. Shea's purse was on the counter closest to the back door, and mine was on the counter in the kitchen by the phone. He grabbed them both and took them back outside, where he rifled through them, using the concentrated beam of his tiny flashlight to view the contents. He pulled out my driver's license and the cash I had inside. In Shea's bag, he came across a small can of pepper spray, which he tossed into the woods outside the fenced-in backyard. He then checked her wallet and found her high school identification card, which had a small color photo of Shea on it. It was all he needed to see.

*Finally!* he must have thought. *Something was going right.*

This, after all, was what he had set out to find.

He took the small amount of cash from her purse and left everything on the porch table. He was anticipating taking the items with him when he left the house later, confident that he was going to emerge successful. Stepping back inside, he slowly made his way through the dark kitchen, turning left and moving down the narrow hallway. He crept past our partially open bedroom door to his left, ignoring me and Kevin and the wad of cash in plain view on our bureau. Instead, he single-mindedly approached the closed door directly in front of him.

When the masked trucker opened the guest room door and saw Shea asleep, he quickly entered the room and closed the door behind him. The drone of the air conditioner softened any sound he made, and the chill air blowing behind Shea toward the intruder diminished the intensity of his odor. He approached the bed more deliberately, almost a shadow in the cool darkness. The time displayed on Shea's cell phone glowing in the darkness was 3:51. Unsheathing a knife, he clutched it in his gloved right hand and leaned forward over our daughter, who was sleeping soundly on her back, her head turned slightly to the right. He watched her for a moment as she slept, listening to the sound of her shallow breathing. He pulled the covers down to her knees, then reached over and placed his gloved left hand firmly over her nose and mouth.

Shea instantly awakened, but was disoriented at first. Feeling something over her mouth, her first thought was that it was her brother joking around with her, but even in the darkness she could tell that the hulking body leaning over her was not Ryan's. She felt something cold and sharp pressed against her neck, and as her eyes adjusted to the darkness, she could see that the man was wearing a dark mask.

"If you make any noise, I'll fucking kill you," he said in a deep southern accent.

Shea wanted to scream but couldn't. The man's hand was so big that it covered almost her entire face, and it was pressed so tightly against her mouth and her nose that she could not breathe. Her big brown eyes were wide with horror as she peered up at the intruder's own eyes leering back at her from the narrow slits cut out of the mask. To Shea, it was a living nightmare, and she began to panic.

Shea was a swimmer and had very strong legs, and when she kicked them out, it caused the headboard to knock against the wall between the two bedrooms.

I've always been a heavy sleeper, but this woke me up. I could hear soft whimpering and a strange sound of movement coming from the guest room where Shea was sleeping. In my mind, the combined noises could only have been our fifteen-year-old daughter in the throes of a nightmare, but something told me to go check on her anyway, having no idea what real nightmare was awaiting.

As I started to get up, I looked over at Kevin and saw that he was awake. He had heard it, too.

"I'll go check on her," he said as he peeled back the thin sheet covering him.

"No, I'll go," I told him, but he was already on his feet. So we went together.

It was unusual enough for one of us to get up in the middle of the night like this, but both of us going in to check on the kids was not something I ever remember our doing together, even when they were babies. Had either of us gone alone, however, the events that followed would have almost certainly been drastically different. Even more disconcerting, had our air-conditioning unit been operational that night, we might never have heard the sounds of Shea's struggle with the intruder, or her muffled cries.

I didn't even bother to put on my robe; both of us were in our underwear, not expecting to find anything more traumatic than our daughter half asleep in the midst of a bad dream. When Kevin opened the guest room door, however, we walked in on a surreal scene that neither of us could ever have imagined.

There was a large figure in dark clothes leaning over Shea and holding a hand to her face. My first thought was that it was her brother, Ryan, trying to scare her, or worst case, a boy from school bothering her.

"Hey!" Kevin yelled. "What are you doing?"

I could see very little, with Kevin blocking most of my field of vision.

Kevin's voice seemed to startle the intruder, who was not aware that we had been standing in the doorway until that moment. In turning to face us, the intruder grazed Shea's shoulder with the blade, and it was then that I got my first glimpse of him. When I saw that he was wearing a mask and holding a large knife, I knew instantly this was not our son, and it was no prank.

There are few words, if any, to accurately describe the abject horror that I experienced at that moment, recognizing instantly that our daughter was in mortal danger. It was an intensely visceral response, but it provoked a physical reaction *to do something*. I felt that I needed to protect my daughter, and I instinctively started to move toward the bed at the same time that Kevin yelled, "Knife!" and charged the stranger. He reacted so quickly that it seemed to catch the intruder off guard. Kevin grabbed both of the man's wrists and began grappling with him.

"Who are you?" my husband asked him. "What do you want?"

The intruder did not respond.

My husband is not a large man by any means, though he is very strong, with a lot of lean, wiry muscle. However, he easily conceded eighty pounds to the burly intruder, who packed about two hundred and forty pounds onto a six-foot frame. But this did not deter my husband. Despite the size disadvantage, Kevin spun the intruder away from Shea and threw him onto the bed directly opposite her. The intruder was lying prone, partially atop the other twin bed, his head and shoulders pushed against the wall, with Kevin on his back. My husband maintained a grip on the intruder's wrist, trying to prevent him from using the weapon on him.

This bizarre scene was so unfathomable to me that it seemed to be taking place in slow motion.

"Get the knife!" Kevin yelled to me.

Without hesitation, I reached out to try to take the knife away from the intruder. His arm was flailing around slightly and his hand was so big it covered nearly the entire handle. I had no choice but to try to grab ahold of the blade, but he was too strong, and all I managed to do was cut the palms of my hands. I didn't realize how badly I had been cut until later.

Shea up until this point had been thinking that all this had to be a terrible dream until she saw the blood that was now streaming from my hands onto the floor. She took action herself then, alertly grabbing her cell phone and dialing 911. She sounded almost hysterical at first, talking over the emergency operator, who asked her specific questions to try to get her to calm down enough to provide the information he needed to get help to her. Shea quickly regained her composure and told the dispatcher who she was and described what was happening.

"A man came in with a gun and put it to my neck . . ."

In the darkness and confusion, Shea reported that the intruder had a gun as well as a knife.

"And what does he look like?" the operator asked.

"I have no idea, he has a black mask on."

"I need you to stay on the line with me. He has a mask on? All-black mask, he has a gun and a knife?"

"He's big," she said, her voice faltering with exasperation. "He's like a big guy."

"Where in the house is he, do you know?"

"He's in my room, he came into my room and held . . . He put his hand over my mouth and held a knife to my throat and told me if I screamed he'll kill me."

The information was recorded, but as the call was being transferred to the Chelmsford Police Department, Shea thought the silence on the other end indicated that the call had ended. Thinking she had been disconnected, she hung up the phone.

Because she had dialed 911 using a cell phone, the call was dispatched through to the Massachusetts State Police first, which is how the system is set up. Had she made the call from a house phone, it would have gone directly to the local police department. But the information had already been passed on to Chelmsford. At 3:58 a.m., Officer Robert Murphy was told to start heading in the direction of our address.

Shea was about to call back, when suddenly the intruder began breathing heavily and grunting loudly. I turned to see him struggling to get to his feet. In a burst of energy, he stood up fully, with my husband clinging to his back.

"Oh, shit!" I heard Kevin say.

Despite everything else that had just gone on, this was the most terrifying moment of my life. I thought for sure that this imposing figure was going to shrug my husband off his back and kill all three of us. However, Kevin not only managed to hold on, but he was able to wrap one arm around the intruder's neck, bulldogging him as they both tumbled backward. They crashed against the wall between the foot of Shea's bed and the closet. They landed in a sitting position underneath the air-conditioner unit in the window, the intruder in Kevin's lap. It worked to Kevin's advantage, as the intruder could not move to either side, essentially wedged between the footboard and the closet door. Kevin kept his forearm clenched tightly around the intruder's windpipe, yanking on it as hard as he could, sufficiently immobilizing the larger opponent. His other arm secured the intruder's hand that held the knife.

"Shea, quick, call 911 and go get my gun!" her father yelled.

"Okay, Dad!" she responded and walked quickly out of the room, never letting on that we did not keep a gun in the house and going along with the ruse to try to force the masked intruder to submit. As soon as she left, her cell phone rang. It was the Chelmsford police, letting her know that help was on the way. They kept her on the line, asking her questions to keep the officers who were en route updated so they would know what they were walking into. They particularly wanted to know what the intruder was doing.

"Why can't he get out?" the dispatcher asked her.

"Because my dad's holding him down. My parents have to wait until you guys come."

"Okay, they are holding him down right now," the

dispatcher said directly to the officers racing to the scene. "They've got him held down."

The dispatcher instructed her to go outside so she could flag down the police cruiser, but as she was stepping outside onto the front porch she saw the lights of a squad car race past the house. Shea was still on the phone with the dispatcher, who asked her to stand in the middle of the road by the driveway and wait for him to turn back around, which she did.

Although Kevin continued to hold the intruder at bay in a choke hold, the man would not let go of the knife. As I tried again to take the weapon from him, I remained under the impression that this had to be some high school kid, albeit a large one, who was obsessed with our daughter. With this belief in mind, I asked him, "What were you thinking?" I was trying to shame him, like a mother, disappointed that he had taken his obsession to such an extreme and totally ruined his life.

"I just wanted money," the intruder said.

When I heard the southern drawl, I realized that we were dealing with a desperate, dangerous stranger.

Kevin, coming to the same realization, squeezed his arm more firmly around the man's throat, like a boa constrictor curling its body around its prey.

"I'm the one with the money," Kevin informed him. "You should've come to see me, you fat fuck."

"Who are you?" I asked him.

"I'm nobody. Just let me leave."

"You're not going anywhere," Kevin said.

"I'll let go of the knife," he said, barely above a whisper. He could barely get enough air to breathe, and was weakening quickly. "You can take it."

As I took it from him, my fear instantly dissolved and

was replaced by an overwhelming sense of rage, incensed that this person had invaded our home, had just walked right in off the street to terrorize our teenage daughter. Nothing like this had ever happened to me before, and I didn't know how to react. Getting into a dialogue with this person was not something I had planned to do, but I thought engaging him in conversation could create a diversion, and the questions just kept coming out of my mouth. I wanted to understand, even then, how such a thing could have happened, how it was that this person had ended up at our house.

"How did you get in?" I asked him.

"The back door was unlocked," he managed to say.

Continuing with the same line of questioning, I asked, "Would you have come in if the door had been locked?"

"No," he said. "I don't know how to pick locks."

The intruder could sense that it was almost over for him, and with his last bit of strength I could see him struggling to try to free his hands.

It was a dangerous time, I thought. Even though the intruder was all but incapacitated and the police were on their way, if he managed to free himself he could easily inflict serious harm on Kevin and me.

"You're hurt," the intruder said, looking at me. "You should tend to your hands."

I wasn't about to leave Kevin alone in the room with the intruder, believing it to be just a ploy. Shea was outside the house, and with me gone, he would increase his chances of escape significantly. What I didn't realize was that the man was actually trying to free his hands in order to remove the mask from his face. Unlike us, who had no idea, he was well aware that there were much stricter sentencing guidelines for masked home invasions. Kevin held firm, however, and said, "Don't move a fucking muscle, you fat fuck!"

Outside, Shea was waving her arms as the police car came toward the house at a high rate of speed. The police cruiser had missed the house on the first try. Little did we know that having gold numbers on a yellow house made it virtually impossible to read the house numbers at night. This time the driver spotted her and slowed down quickly. Shea got out of the way so the officer could turn into the yard. Officer Robert Murphy drove straight across our circular driveway, over a small landscaped bed of mulch and plantings, stopping just short of the stone wall in front of the house. Jumping out of the vehicle, he unholstered his service revolver as Shea approached.

"Where is he?" he asked her.

"In the house," Shea said. "Fighting with my father."

Officer Murphy was alone at that moment, but with a report of a gun involved and a potential homicide situation unfolding, he wasn't about to wait for backup or waste time calling for a SWAT team to be assembled.

As he charged through the front door, Murphy asked Shea where the bedroom was located, then made his way to us swiftly but cautiously, not knowing what to expect.

"Don't move or I'll blow your head off!" the officer yelled as he stepped into the room behind me.

He momentarily startled me, but I was beyond relieved to hear those words and see his uniform. Murphy told me to drop the knife, which I did. The heavy blade and sturdy handle clattered loudly on the floor, reaffirming to me just how dangerous a weapon it was. It had felt like an eternity as we'd waited for the police to arrive, but it had actually only been about four minutes since Shea had called 911. Now, our ordeal was almost over.

It was hard to believe a scene like this was playing out in our little home. It was as if I was watching a movie. I was standing there in nothing more than panties and a tank top, covered with my own blood from the cuts on my hands. My husband, wearing only a pair of boxers, was still down on the floor with a masked man who he had locked in a choke hold.

The first thing Officer Murphy did was look for the gun. He didn't see the weapon, so instead he kicked the knife I had been holding across the floor to be sure it was well out of reach of the intruder. A moment later, another officer, Sergeant Frank Goode, arrived on the scene. When he entered the bedroom with his gun drawn and ready, it was all over. Kevin and I both felt it.

"Get this scumbag out of here," Kevin said.

Sergeant Goode noticed the hunting knife on the floor and went over to pick it up, placing it on the nightstand, even farther away from the suspect. Then he holstered his weapon and removed his handcuffs. As the sergeant pulled the suspect off Kevin and to his feet, the masked man resisted, straining to keep from being cuffed. Even so, it didn't take much effort for the officer to subdue the suspect and place him in custody. By that time, a third police officer, Officer Bruce Darwin, had also arrived to assist.

"Do you have any other weapons on you?" Sergeant Goode asked as he pulled the mask off the intruder's face. He didn't wait for a response as he searched the suspect. The two patrol officers, their weapons in hand at their sides in case deadly forced was warranted, were amazed at the assortment of bladed weapons that were removed from the suspect.

There were two fifteen-inch hunting knives, one of which was still in its sheath when it was removed from around the man's upper left leg. In the fanny pack around his waist, police found more weapons—including a small knife with a retractable blade, a three-foot length of choke wire and a Chinese throwing star—and a small yellow flashlight as well as a leather mask with cutouts around the eyes and mouth and Velcro fasteners in the back. This was in addition to the pullover cloth face mask that the intruder had been wearing at the time he was apprehended.

As all this was going on, I retreated to our bedroom to put some clothes on. Shea had to help me get dressed because my hands were cut so deeply that I couldn't get my pants on and zippered. I saw the intruder as he was escorted down the hall and out of the house. His mask had been removed, but I caught only a brief glimpse of his shadowy profile.

As Officers Murphy and Goode were loading the intruder into the squad car, I felt an enormous sense of gratitude toward these officers, an appreciation beyond what they had just done for my family but for what they were called upon to do every day in the line of duty. Honestly, the moment they charged into our house, I would have applauded if I had been able.

Paramedics arrived, and I went outside, where they began attending to me, cleaning and wrapping the wounds on my hands. From his seat in the back of the squad car, the intruder shouted from an open window, "She did that to herself!" Nobody reacted to his comment, but we all heard it. He said it again before Officer Murphy raised the back window and drove the suspect away.

The EMTs told me that some of the lacerations would require stitches to close, and they suggested I ride to the hospital with them in the ambulance. They also wanted Shea to come along, so she could be evaluated as well.

They were worried that she might be in shock. It seemed like the right thing to do, so I went back inside to get my insurance card. Shea accompanied me, but when we walked into the kitchen to get our purses, we discovered that they weren't where we had left them. Shea quickly spotted them sitting outside on the back-porch table, and she went out to retrieve them. She noticed right away that her wallet was open and her ID partially removed. An officer had followed her, and he advised her to check to see if any items had been removed. The only things she noted missing were her pepper spray and a small amount of cash.

With this evidence, investigators could conclude that if the intruder's intent truly had been to rob us, as he would later claim, then he would not have gone back inside the house after going through our purses. The intent to commit a sexual assault or kidnapping had been firmly established.

It suddenly occurred to Kevin that our dog wasn't barking. With everything that was going on at the house, it was highly unusual that he would be so calm. "Where's Bosco?" Kevin said, looking at Shea and me. A chill ran through me; I feared he had been killed by this man. I could see from the look on Shea's face that she was thinking the same thing. Kevin went around to the side of the house, expecting the worst. He was relieved when he saw our family pet, quite alive, though utterly engrossed with something down the embankment. Kevin couldn't see what it was that had drawn his full attention, but Bosco seemed okay, and that was all we needed to hear. Although the dog didn't seem quite himself then, and would remain out of sorts for several days afterward, we were never able to determine one way or the other if the dog had been drugged or otherwise incapacitated. He was fine, and that was all that mattered.

When we were ready to be driven to the hospital in the ambulance, the EMTs wanted to separate us, having Shea ride up in the front and me in the back. I pleaded with them to let us sit together. I just didn't want to be far from my daughter, for her sake as well as mine. They relented, even though it was technically against the rules. While we went off to the hospital, the weapons were removed from the guest bedroom and spread out across our front porch so they could be photographed on the scene as evidence. Kevin was asked to stay behind to go over the details of the attack with the police.

---

The Criminal Bureau was contacted to process the crime scene. Detective George Tyros was the on-call detective that night, and by the time his phone rang at home, it was well after 4:00 a.m. His sergeant briefly went over the details of the crime, and Detective Tyros reported directly to the scene. As soon as he arrived, he realized how narrowly disaster had been averted.

Feeling concern for his own safety and following protocol had gone out the window for Officer Murphy when teenage Shea had came running out of the house to tell him that her parents were fighting for their lives with a stranger inside their home. But when Tyros looked down at the arsenal of weapons that the intruder had been carrying, and that were now spread out on our front porch, he was immediately certain that if Officer Murphy had hesitated in any way, or had taken a different approach to deal with what appeared to be a serious hostage situation, it would have resulted in the coroner being called first instead of him.

Detective Tyros understood intuitively that in a situation like that, an officer goes on a gut feeling and worries about the consequences later. Lawsuits take a backseat to doing what has to be done. He had nothing but praise for how his fellow officer had handled himself under the circumstances. Tyros had seen how the fundamental approach to any violent standoff had changed since Columbine. Before that tragedy, police were more apt to wait for backup before going into a potentially deadly situation. These days the protocol was to go right in, weapon drawn, ready to defend yourself and to protect the lives of others with preemptive action. The increasing level of indiscriminate lethal violence in society has altered the dynamic of the police response.

As Detective Tyros photographed and processed the evidence, even at that moment, Kevin, Shea and I were not yet fully aware just how fortunate we had been—or how our lives would be changed forever.

# Chapter 8

## UNMASKING A KILLER

Officer Robert Murphy transported the suspect to the Chelmsford Police Department, where he was booked and afforded his rights by Sergeant J. Ronald Gamache. The arresting officer originally charged the suspect with nine separate offenses, including home invasion while armed and masked, kidnapping, armed assault in a dwelling with intent to commit a felony (three counts), threat to commit a crime, assault and battery with a dangerous weapon, larceny of property over $250, resisting arrest, attempted murder and possession of a dangerous weapon.

Detective George Tyros was still at the crime scene when the suspect revealed his identity to police during his booking. His name was Adam Leroy Lane, and he was a truck driver from North Carolina. He told them that his tractor-trailer was parked at the rest stop on I-495 North. When word filtered through to detectives at Pine Hill

Road, Officer Bruce Darwin was dispatched to the location to secure the rig until the towing company arrived. He then escorted the truck to the Chelmsford Police Department, where the items inside were inventoried so that any valuables and evidence could be documented. The trailer itself was found to be completely empty, but an affidavit had to be filed for a search warrant in order to allow the police to go through Lane's personal effects in the cab. Among the items found inside were another knife, a handheld scouting scope and a portable DVD player with a movie inside, chillingly called *Hunting Humans*. There were other DVDs found in the cab as well, all dealing in one regard or another with the theme of hunting people. Among these other, more mainstream titles were *Alien vs. Predator* and *Rambo*.

A necklace was also found, but because it did not belong to either Shea or me, it was largely disregarded at the time.

The rig itself took up way too much room at the police station and had to be moved. Later that morning it was transported to Ferreira's Towing, which, coincidentally, was practically right across the highway from our house, on Littleton Road, and it was held there in a secured area of the lot.

_____

Shea and I were taken to Emerson Hospital in Concord, where we were attended to right away. The nurses and doctors took great care in treating us both. I needed eleven stitches to close two separate gashes on the palm of my right hand, and eight more were required on my left. None of my fingers had been cut, but I did have a superficial scrape across my abdomen that I discovered later but didn't recall receiving. It was about three inches in length, very similar to the graze the intruder's knife had made across Shea's shoulder, which, luckily, did not require medical attention.

Shea sat next to me the whole time, rubbing my shoulder and trying to comfort me, both of us still quite frazzled by what had happened. When the doctor was through with me, he and the attending nurse strongly advised us, almost to the point of insisting, that we speak with a psychiatric professional. They felt it could only help us to talk to someone impartial and professional before we were released. I've always respected doctors, so I agreed. However, at that time of the morning, no one with those credentials was at the hospital, so they had to call someone in.

While we waited for the psychiatric nurse to arrive, Shea managed to get hold of her brother, Ryan, on his cell phone. He was understandably very shaken by the news when his sister told him what had happened, and he asked her if he should come to the hospital. I got on the phone and reassured him that we were all okay and there was nothing he could do. I told him not to bother coming to the hospital because we didn't anticipate being there much longer, and that we would touch base with him a bit later.

———————————————

After the crime scene had been processed, Detective Tyros returned to the station and immediately went into the office that was being used as an interrogation room to speak with Lane. The detective chatted casually with the suspect at first, trying to earn his confidence.

What struck the twelve-year veteran right away was

the smell: the odor that Adam Leroy Lane emitted was so offensive and powerful that the detective had to leave the door to the room open while he conducted his interview. It was the first time he had ever had to do that, and he had been enclosed in such small rooms many times with suspects who'd given off a wide variety of foul aromas. This one, however, was exceptional. It wasn't the funk of someone who had spent a hot, sticky summer night walking through the woods covered from head to toe in black clothes. Perspiration, especially nervous perspiration, was something that the detective had been exposed to often enough. Nor was this the body odor of the unbathed. The detective had also been around enough homeless to have been able to recognize that. The only smell that came anywhere close to this stench was that of decomposing tissue.

The other thing that struck the detective was Lane's heavy southern accent. It was so thick, the officer often had trouble understanding what the suspect was saying and, frustratingly, repeatedly had to ask him to clarify what he had said. It was apparently a two-way problem, though—Lane paused at one point to comment on the detective's own regional accent, saying, "You guys sure talk funny 'round here."

Although the suspect was passive and restrained at the moment, Lane complained several times about the irritation and swelling of his split lower lip, which he had sustained during his scuffle with the officers. Detective Tyros listened in amazement as the man fussed over the minor injury, touching it to see if it was bleeding and whining about needing stitches. It was apparent that the suspect's concern at that point was entirely for himself and his own well-being. It was almost as if Lane wanted sympathy, trying to pass himself off as a victim. He lamented over his medical woes and the diabetes medication in his truck that he needed. His gripes and grievances, however, fell largely on deaf ears. The Chelmsford Fire Department and paramedics had responded to the lockup area earlier and evaluated Lane's physical condition, determining that he did not require any medical treatment. The prescription drugs in his truck were later removed at his request and placed with his other personal property at the police station.

When Lane complained that he was hungry and needed to eat, however, this was something that the police could not simply ignore. The last thing they wanted was to have the suspect go into some sort of convulsion and lapse into a diabetic coma right there in the police station. Detective Tyros also hoped that agreeing to feed him at that time might elicit a full confession, or at least keep him talking, enough to incriminate himself. Tyros thought that a confession might come easier on a full stomach, so he sent an officer to Burger King to get Lane a couple of burgers and some fries.

---

Shea and I sat down with the female psychologist for about a half hour, discussing the attack and what we were feeling. It was a great way to instantly address the issue and unburden a lot of our fears, but I honestly didn't see the point at that time. We hadn't had a chance to digest any of it yet or discuss it among ourselves, yet there we were, talking about it with a stranger. I'm sure the hospital staff only had our best interests in mind, but all I wanted to do was see my husband and son and get our family all together in the same place.

Kevin came to pick us up when he was done with his

interview with Detective Tyros. It was after 8:00 a.m. by this time, and Kevin told us that the police had requested that we all go down to the station as soon as we could to give formal statements, so we proceeded directly to the Chelmsford Police Department. Detective Tyros wanted to speak with us, but he was still talking with the suspect when we arrived, so we were instructed to write down everything that we could recall about the attack. We were separated so we could not discuss any of the details with each other, but because my hands were heavily bandaged I needed help writing. When Shea was through, I verbally dictated my statement to her and she wrote it all down on paper for me, word-for-word.

---

Detective George Tyros watched as the suspect ate in front of him. It was all he could do to hold back his disgust as Adam Leroy Lane stacked his French fries into a small tower then picked them off the top, one at a time, eating them in silent absorption, the way a child is apt to do. That was his focus, his only concern, and he certainly didn't seem interested in talking even though the detective continued to ask him questions. All the police knew about this individual was that he drove a commercial truck for a living, but not much else beyond that. The detective wanted to get Lane to tell him what he'd been doing with the weapons, the masks, and the rest of his hunting attire, but after Detective Tyros read the suspect his rights and asked if he wanted to talk about what he had done that night, Lane said, "What's it matter anyway?"

Tyros asked Lane to repeat what he said because he couldn't understand him.

"What's it matter anyway?" Lane repeated. "I'm in a shitload of trouble."

"Is that a yes or a no?"

"No," Lane said without looking up, his mouth full of fries. "I want my attorney."

"Ok." Detective Tyros got up and walked out of the room.

There was nothing more they could do with Lane. The prosecutor's office would take over from there. Anything else Lane said would be under oath, in court or through his attorney.

Detective-Sergeant Todd Ahern came in to collect Lane and take him back downstairs to the holding cell, but he didn't seem to want to go. Lane suddenly lost it. The quiet and tranquil suspect Detective Tyros had been talking to suddenly became very loud and belligerent. Maybe the predicament he was in was finally sinking in and he realized that there was no way out. Or maybe he was yelling and screaming like a child because someone took his fries away before he was through with them. Either way, by the time they got downstairs, Lane apologized and went back to being calm and composed once more.

———————————

Detective Tyros came in to see us at that time, along with Detective Jeff Blodgett. They had me temporarily remove my bandages so that they could photograph my injuries. After spending a couple of hours at the police station talking with the police, it was now about eleven in the morning, and I realized that none of us had eaten yet. We were all very hungry, but we weren't ready to go home so we stopped to get something to eat. Shea called her brother, Ryan, and her boyfriend, Adam, and they both met us at the restaurant.

The first thing I did was order a glass of wine to try to help calm my nerves. I was a little on edge, and I felt myself starting to freak out a little on the inside—maybe on the outside, too. The last thing I wanted to do was run into anyone I knew. It was risky going into a popular restaurant so close to home, but it was quiet, before noon on a Monday. Of course, I couldn't count on anything this day, and one of the waiters who was acquainted with Shea and Ryan came over to say hello. When he asked about the bandages on my hands, the kids pulled him aside and told him what had happened.

We sat quietly and ate our meals undisturbed. All of us were in a kind of fog, just going through the motions and in no hurry. We knew we had to go home eventually, but we weren't anxious to face the mess we would find inside, or the media that we anticipated would be camped outside.

When we finally made it back home, though, we found waiting for us our dear friends Bob and Heather Green, who lived a couple of miles away. While Shea and I had been en route to the hospital, Kevin had called a buddy of his who worked at the Lowell Courthouse. He told Mike that a really bad character would be arriving up there shortly and to make sure he was greeted appropriately. He briefly explained to him what had happened to our family and promised to touch base with him later to let him know how Shea and I were doing. Mike then promptly started the telephone chain, beginning with Bob and Heather. They had been circling our house, anticipating our return. They were both such a big help that day. Heather helped me straighten the mess left behind after the vicious home invasion and the bloody injuries sustained in the fight. The guest bedroom, of course, was a disaster, but the adjacent bathroom was not much better. I was shocked by how much blood there was. It was everywhere. Remarkably, Kevin didn't have so much as a scratch. The intruder suffered only a split lip, which hardly trickled any blood, so most of it was mine. I had used a couple of towels to wrap around the cuts on my hands, which at the time didn't seem that bad. However, upon closer inspection afterward, the place looked like a murder scene. There was also a terrible smell lingering in the bedroom. I knew it couldn't have been the blood because the bathroom didn't have that odor. If it had been the intruder, I wasn't consciously aware of it during the encounter. But I also wasn't as close to him as Kevin, and I asked him about it when we were both in the room together.

"Did that guy stink like this?"

"Oh, yeah," Kevin said. "He had some serious BO. I thought I was going to gag."

Kevin removed the AC unit from the window, which we left open all day in the hope that the fresh air would eliminate the stench. After Heather mopped the floors, she removed all the bedding and put it into garbage bags to be thrown out. No one was going to lie down on those blankets and sheets again.

It took most of the afternoon, but once the house was back to normal, our friends left us alone so we could try to get some rest. We all curled up on the couch in the family room and closed our eyes. Even Bosco had come in to join us. I had never felt so exhausted, physically and emotionally, in all my life. But I couldn't sleep. None of us could, except Bosco.

I suspected that we might all have trouble sleeping over

the course of the next couple of weeks, and that belief would prove to be more than accurate.

The very first night at home after the attack I was paralyzed with fear. I couldn't even close my eyes. I kept watching the hall to make sure that no one was coming around the corner. It was irrational and I knew it, but it was awful. The trauma of the first few days was unbearable. Shea wouldn't sleep upstairs, choosing the couch in the family room instead. Adam, her boyfriend, never left her side. He was with her every minute and slept on the couch next to her. He was incredibly supportive and helpful.

Although sleep may have eluded us in the days immediately following the attack, the media did not. It was a frenzy that we desperately tried to avoid, but there was no escape. Television stations were coming from all around, many from outside of Massachusetts. News correspondents would announce they were with such and such a station, and mention the name of a town I'd never heard of before. They all wanted a statement. A quote. A photograph of Shea. Anything. I wasn't ready to speak with anyone outside my family, but even if I wanted to, the police had advised us against it so as not to compromise the investigation. We were told that the less said, the better. Shea's boyfriend, Adam, made this situation a whole lot easier for us. Not only was he there for my daughter, who needed him, but whenever these people showed up on our doorstep, it was Adam who would greet them and very politely ask that our privacy be respected. He was truly a godsend. I don't know what we would have done without him.

As we were trying to keep a low profile, our friends, family and the community were circling their wagons around us in support, and their presence was more than

welcome. Never in my wildest dreams could I have imagined the kind of outpouring of concern everyone showed
us. The calls, cards, flowers and other gifts were just overwhelming.

I've always heard that the goodness in people shines
through during the darkest hours, but I never knew this
to be true personally until that moment. During what was
unequivocally the most traumatic and horrifying time in
our lives, the sun kept shining on our family in the form
of love and compassion from those closest to us. We were
strengthened and renewed with this outpouring, and our
gratitude toward them was felt twofold. Although it is easy
to get caught up thinking about the "random acts of violence" that a few individuals perpetrate against others, I
believe it is more important to focus on the "random acts
of kindness" by so many people in the aftermath of such
tragedies.

One of the kindest gestures I recall was when a man
who lived up the street stopped by the house and gave
us a large bag containing various packages of meat. I
didn't know it at the time, but he owned a butcher shop
in a neighboring town, and he wanted to do something to
show his compassion for what we had been through, as
well as his appreciation for our having aided in the capture of a dangerous predator. I had waved to this man on
the street a couple of times, but I had never spoken to him
before that day. His unexpected thoughtfulness touched
my heart. This man's gift was something that he thought
would comfort us in some small way, and like the offerings
made by so many others at this time, it is something that I
will never forget. Numerous friends reached out to us with
such thoughtful and supportive gestures, but I could have

just cried when our friend Joe Russo unloaded a basket containing a fabulous Italian meal, which our family thoroughly enjoyed for several days. Every single card and letter that we received I have saved in a special box to cherish always.

# Chapter 9

A TALE OF TWO POLICE DEPARTMENTS

Adam Leroy Lane had initially been charged in Middlesex Superior Court, Massachusetts, with a variety of criminal offenses stemming from the masked home invasion, including assault with intent to murder and attempted rape of a child.

From the moment of his capture, Chelmsford Police Chief James Murphy speculated publicly that the incident in our home had not likely been Lane's first. As it turned out, no sooner had Chief Murphy given a statement to the press expressing this belief than the body of Monica Massaro was discovered by New Jersey State Police. Authorities, of course, were still a long way from connecting Lane to Monica's death, or any other violent crime, but everyone in law enforcement who was looking closely at this case was expecting more bad news—and more victims—to turn up in association with the North Carolina truck driver.

Monica ran a house-cleaning business, and when a client

came home from a weekend trip to find Monica's cleaning products there but the house untouched, he became instantly concerned. Monica would often drop off her supplies at his house the day before a scheduled appointment to save time, as it appeared she had on Saturday. But now it was Monday morning, and everything was still right where she'd left them. After checking his phone messages to be sure he hadn't missed her call, her client's concern grew. It was not like her to cancel an appointment, and it was incomprehensible that she would have blown him off completely. He knew she would have notified him if she could not make it. The client then tried phoning Monica several times, and when she did not pick up, he drove to her home. He saw her car parked in the driveway and knocked for several minutes but got no response. At that point, he contacted the police.

The New Jersey State Police officer who responded to Monica's home to conduct a well-being check took note of the address right away. Earlier in his shift, he had received a call from a woman who reported that she had found someone's personal effects scattered along the railroad tracks. In particular, the officer recalled that among the effects had been a pay stub that bore the same name and address that he was now being called on to search. Even before the call from Monica's client had come in, the officer had been planning to follow up on that earlier report before the end of his shift.

At first, it did not appear to the officer that anybody had broken into Monica's residence. There were no signs of forced entry, and nothing appeared to be missing. Everything seemed to be in order—until he walked into Monica's first-floor bedroom and made the grim discovery of her mutilated body.

As a forensic team went to work processing the evidence collected at the crime scene, a multiagency task force was organized to find Monica's killer. Detectives with the Major Crimes Unit of the New Jersey State Police and the Hunterdon County Prosecutor's Office, along with other criminal investigative personnel from various law enforcement agencies, provided assistance to the task force. A New Jersey State Police recruit class was brought to Bloomsbury for the purpose of conducting a grid search of the area surrounding the victim's residence in hopes of locating additional physical evidence.

Early on in the investigation, teams of detectives interviewed many of Monica's friends and family members. In the search for potential suspects, they canvassed her Bloomsbury, New Jersey, neighborhood several times, attempting to gather as much information as possible about the people who knew her. They sifted through the online message boards she frequented. Monica had an active role on a fan website of the rock group Aerosmith. Because of her strong online presence, authorities also looked into whether she could've been targeted by someone who knew her from the site. Monica was also single and actively dating, which created another pool of potential suspects. It was a lengthy and tedious process to locate and evaluate everyone Monica had been acquainted with. She knew so many people it was almost overwhelming.

All possible leads were pursued, but during the initial phase of the investigation, the belief was that Monica had to have known her killer, or at least the killer certainly had to have known her. The mutilation of her body suggested a crime of passion, and the long odds that it had been a random killing were made even more remote when several persons of interest were quickly identified by police. These individuals had been in Monica's personal life and gave strong reasons for investigators to consider them as suspects, from questionable behavior to contradictory statements and other discrepancies. When they became the focus of the murder investigation, these suspects occupied much of the time and effort of the ten detectives working full-time on the case.

---

Police back in Chelmsford, Massachusetts, were trying to learn more about Adam Leroy Lane. On August 2, the search warrant on the truck was executed, and the North Carolina trucker's rig and its contents were scrutinized. Among the items investigators pored over with great interest was the movie in the DVD player, *Hunting Humans*. It was apparent that Lane had been watching the film at some point prior to stepping out of his cab and walking away from the I-495 rest area late on the night of June 29. In fact, he had probably been watching it over and over, studying it.

Detective George Tyros knew immediately what he was in for when he put the DVD in the machine and a cryptic quote from Tim Cahill's book *Buried Dreams*, about serial murderer John Wayne Gacy, was the first thing that appeared on screen. "No one can see murder on your face; there is no brand that sets you apart from the crowd, no outward sign that the dark flower is growing in your soul. People will see you as they've always seen you if you can only bury fear and confusion and remorse along with the evidence."

The gruesome 2002 documentary-style movie is about a fictitious killer who goes about his business of murder, offering tips and advice to the viewer along the way as to how not to get detected. It started out basically as a primer on how to become a successful serial killer, a model that

Lane tried to emulate. It may as well have been titled *Serial Killing for Dummies*.

The killer in the movie is an arrogant young narcissist who leads a double life, working as a mortgage broker by day, and he may very well have been speaking directly to Lane when he cited what he called his personal cardinal rules to follow in order to get away with murder every time. At the very top of his list was to not have a motive and to have no connection to the victims whatsoever; in other words, to choose them at random. Throughout the film, the main character mocks and berates the authorities, who predictably look inward to solve the crimes he commits, focusing on individuals closest to the victims almost to the exclusion of everyone else.

The film eventually goes off in a different direction entirely when another serial killer targets *him*, and the killer becomes the hunted. But the message had become clear to Detective Tyros long before then that Lane hadn't been on the prowl for just the contents of a couple of purses. Only a desperate addict, which Lane was not, would enter a house in the middle of the night for mere pocketbook cash, and there certainly would be no cause for him to go back inside after gaining possession of what he came looking for in the first place. Whatever Lane may have had in mind before he was stopped, there was no way of knowing now. This movie certainly didn't prove anything, but police came away with a much clearer understanding of what Lane's intentions may have been.

———————————————

Kevin, Shea and I were in court on August 6 to attend a dangerousness hearing that was being held for Adam Lane. I wasn't sure what this proceeding was about. I could not believe it was possible that this violent attacker might be let out. I had always thought that only defendants charged with minor first-time offenses were released on their own recognizance, with a promise to return for their court date: the criminal justice system's version of the honor system. The way this hearing was explained to me was that in the state of Massachusetts, in certain crimes involving physical violence and abuse, which elsewhere might be considered bail-eligible offenses, a defendant can automatically be held without bail for up to ninety days before trial. Although a judge typically sets bail based on the defendant's likelihood of returning to court for trial, a dangerousness hearing can be requested by the district attorney to determine whether a defendant is considered a danger to the community at large. The U.S. Constitution stipulates that imprisonment without relief comes only after conviction, so prosecutors must show the court that the risk to public safety is so great as to warrant holding the defendant without bail prior to his trial date.

It was an extremely frightening and anxious time for our family, because up until then we hadn't actually seen the face of our attacker. Kevin had seen the man's bushy moustache in profile when the police had first pulled his mask off, and I had only glimpsed him briefly as he was escorted by police past our bedroom door and was placed into the cruiser.

That day, after everyone filed into the courtroom and we all took our seats, we observed Adam Leroy Lane being taken into the security area. He was shackled and wearing a bulletproof vest over his orange jumpsuit. He wore a beard, though it was not nearly as thick as his moustache, and his eyes had a deranged cast to them. He looked scary and enormous, and at that moment I found myself staring in utter amazement at my husband, wondering how he had ever been able to take this man down so easily.

I had been holding Kevin's hand even though mine were still bandaged, and I felt myself squeezing Kevin more tightly when Lane walked into the courtroom. Lane stood on the other side of a Plexiglas cage, which was clearly there to protect him from us, not vice versa. There he was, a stranger who had walked into our house with the intent to rob us, and probably rape, kidnap or kill our daughter, and *he* was the one being shielded from any harm that might be reciprocated against him. He had police officers all around him, a layer of Kevlar body armor and a wall of safety glass all insulating him from us and the others in the courtroom. I sensed that he found these safety measures every bit as absurd as we did and that he was mocking us as he peered back at us. Lane's very appearance sickened me. The look on his face—like he wanted to crash through the partition separating us and finish the job he had started the week before—was unnerving. Even though I knew he couldn't harm us, I was haunted by thoughts of this man sending someone else after us in retaliation.

The judge that morning, District Court Judge Neil Walker, denied a request that the suspect sit at the table with his lawyer. He remained in the Plexiglas pen like a wild animal with a dozen armed officers serving as his handlers.

Although I had been in a courtroom before, it had been in a completely different role, as a juror. The hearing lasted about an hour, and throughout the proceedings, I had no idea what to expect. It had been explained to us rather precisely what was going to take place that day, but I didn't know how I might react, and I was worried that I would not be able to keep my emotions in check.

Assistant District Attorney Kerry Ahern argued vehemently that Lane not be granted bail based on his actions that night, which included the incidents outside the Woodcrest Condominium and at the mobile home. Several witnesses were called to give testimony. Among them was Kathy Crowley, the woman from the Chelmsford Mobile Home Park who had confronted a man dressed in black and looking in at her daughter while she was on the computer. Several Chelmsford police officers also took the stand, providing sworn statements of their actions that night and the events leading up to Lane's capture.

Detective George Tyros revealed something about Lane that made my skin crawl—based on information that he'd gathered from a sheriff in North Carolina, where Lane resided, Tyros testified that Lane's wife suspected that her husband had inappropriately touched one of his stepdaughters. The detective speculated that this may have been the reason that Lane and his wife were currently separated.

What may have disturbed me the most was when Lane's defense attorney, Daniel Callahan, tried to create a thread of reasonable doubt by calling into question a portion of Shea's 911 call in which she had been unsure if the intruder had thrust a knife or a gun in front of her in the darkness of her room.

"That call you got at 3:55 or 3:58. That call you got indicated a man had placed a gun into the caller's mouth. As far as you know there was no gun, right?" Callahan asked Officer Murphy.

"Correct," the officer responded. "There was no gun."

"So, as far as you know that report was incorrect?"

His lawyer also tried to reinforce his client's innocence by stating that Lane had no previous criminal record and that he had a job and a family. On those grounds, Callahan appealed to have Lane granted a bail of $10,000. He added that he did not feel Lane was a flight risk.

I was told that Lane was fortunate to have drawn Callahan, who was as reputable and solid as any public defender out there. Yet I was appalled, listening to the defense attorney say and do everything he could to get Lane back onto the streets, where Callahan's own wife and family might be at risk. I knew he was just doing his job, but it was difficult for me to imagine anyone defending someone like Lane.

Judge Walker, however, recognized that Lane *was* a danger to society and a serious flight risk. When he announced that Lane would continue to be held without bail pending his trial, I couldn't help but react. I must have been holding my breath in the moments leading up to the ruling, because I gasped loudly. This was immediately followed by an instinctual reaction and I raised my right arm, pumping it in triumph. I looked over at Kevin, who nodded in approval.

---

The same day that Adam Leroy Lane's bail hearing was taking place in Massachusetts, a funeral service was being held in New Jersey for Monica Massaro. It had been a full week since her death, and there still had not been any breakthroughs in the murder investigation. The leads that the New Jersey police had established early on were still being pursued, but with each passing day, the case grew colder, and the less likely it became that the murderer would be identified.

One thing that may have initially delayed the connection between Lane and Monica Massaro's death was the fact that his attack on Shea occurred on July 30, the same day

Monica's body was discovered in New Jersey. Although Monica had been killed the day before, at first glance it might have appeared that the two incidents—Shea's attack and Monica's murder—could not have been related. As far as the timeline was concerned, the Massachusetts incident surfaced before New Jersey, yet the one in New Jersey happened before the one in Massachusetts.

Still believing that Monica had been killed by someone who was known to her, investigators attended her services to observe the mourners up close, hoping to gain some insight and perhaps a few new leads. They tried to be discreet, but there was no mistaking who they were and what they were doing there. It only made the attendees more suspicious of everyone around them. As Monica's family and close friends looked around at the people they would consider her more casual friends and acquaintances, they all wondered if the person who murdered Monica was actually there among them somewhere.

———————————

Back in Massachusetts, the entire Chelmsford Police Department had been working to unearth everything they could about Lane. Calls were made to his hometown and the local police to get a line on him. They talked to his employer. Anyone who could help them sort out who this guy was and what he was about was questioned. They wanted to make sure that nothing was missed so that they could announce what they found about the suspect in their custody to the rest of the country. They were sure that someone somewhere was looking for him, that there had to be a similar unsolved crime somewhere that Lane was responsible for.

They sent word over the National Teletype, essentially

sharing all the information they had about Lane and the case against him with other departments around the country as well as the state. Those departments could then make an effort to determine if it was something that was worth their own investigative time and efforts. The concern Detective Tyros and the other Chelmsford investigators had was that these dispatches might not be received with the same sense of urgency with which they had been sent out. The communication could just as easily wind up buried on a captain's desk under a mountain of files and never be seen again. To avoid this, the Chelmsford police also began making outgoing phone calls to other jurisdictions, notifying them one at a time. They made sure they spoke to someone in order to gain the full attention of their fellow departments on the matter. As it happens, in Massachusetts, the state police handle a majority of the homicides, working in conjunction with the local jurisdictions where the crimes are committed. Larger city departments, such as Boston, have their own homicide divisions, but that is an exception, not the rule. Chelmsford used this to their advantage when they contacted the Massachusetts State Police directly. They also reached out to other state agencies, as far west as the Mississippi River and south down to Florida. They spent days staffing the phones and going down a long checklist, putting Lane's information out there and seeing what it might bring. Like dropping so many fishhooks in the water, eventually, they hoped, they were bound to catch something.

In the meantime, Detective-Sergeant Todd Ahern contacted the local FBI, who advised him that the best thing to do was to file with ViCAP. The Violent Criminal Apprehension Program is a massive nationwide computerized data system, designed to track and correlate information on violent crime, especially murder. The system is particularly valuable in identifying and tracking serial killers. The FBI provides the software for the database, which is widely used by state and local law enforcement agencies around the country.

This was certainly a more effective and less tedious means by which they could alert other law enforcement jurisdictions that they had captured a suspect who might be of interest in open criminal cases. Filing with ViCAP required submitting a considerable package of information to the feds, so Sergeant Ahern immediately began working on that. Even as this process was under way, Chelmsford Police Lieutenant John Roark fielded a phone call from two Massachusetts troopers who had recently attended a ViCAP training seminar in Reno, Nevada. The troopers, Kevin Burke and Mike Banks, had gained new insight into serial killers during the training. Specifically applicable here, they wanted to share the knowledge that Lane's job as a truck driver put him categorically and statistically at a higher risk of being a murderer, not just a home-invading burglar with an interest in young girls. The fact that he didn't have a police record did not necessarily mean that he hadn't killed anyone; it could just mean that he hadn't been caught. Yet.

The ViCAP and its data were somewhat of a revelation to many at the Chelmsford Police Department, including Detective Tyros, who hadn't been previously aware of the program. He quickly discovered that the information in the database pertained not only to unsolved murders, but also "cleared" cases that are left in the system so that investigators could potentially link additional crimes to an active predator. The entries included sexual assaults and missing-person cases linked by highway locations. It was not surprising that the program has been effective in helping to solve both cold cases as well as current killings by serial and spree killers.

Although this information didn't immediately link Lane to any murders, the wheels were in motion, and the Chelmsford Police Department's objective to make other departments aware of Adam Leroy Lane's local transgressions was already paying dividends.

It was actually on August 10, eleven days after Lane's apprehension, that the ViCAP package on Lane was filed. Detective Tyros contacted Jayne Stairs, an FBI crime analyst, who compiled a complete timeline of Lane's trucking route, where he had been and how long he was there.

But now, at least, Lane's name appeared in the FBI's database of murderers and serial killers, even though at that point the North Carolina trucker had not been accused or suspected in even a single death. It was still only a hunch, and whether he had killed before would be known in due time.

The clock was ticking on Adam Leroy Lane.

# Chapter 10

## ADAM LEROY LANE

Although the police did not reveal everything that they'd learned about Adam Leroy Lane to the public, the media showed no such restraint. Journalists, conducting their own investigation and interviews with any witness who was willing to talk, reported everything they gathered, even if it was not 100 percent accurate. Not all of the information circulating in the newspapers and around the Internet was relevant to the case; some of it wasn't even interesting, but even the most innocuous interview with a neighbor seemed to captivate the public, a kind of collective voyeurism that occurs when someone's private life suddenly opens up for the world to inspect.

I found myself drawn to the coverage for more personal reasons, obviously. This, after all, was a man who could very easily have been responsible for seriously harming my daughter, even killing her. It was almost unfathomable to think that such a thing could have happened, but it almost did. I couldn't comprehend why anyone would want to hurt her, but this stranger had seemed willing to do just that. Others may have wanted to know, but I *needed* to know what had provoked this kind of rage in him.

The forty-two-year-old interstate truck driver had grown up in Yadkin County, a small farming community in northwestern North Carolina. I found out little about Lane's childhood, other than that after his father died, his mother remarried, and at age sixteen Lane dropped out of high school. Certainly nothing startling turned up in his background that would have given any indication that he would grow up to commit such acts of random violence.

Lane's current domestic life was the easiest to investigate, and both the police and the press conducted in-depth inquiries with those closest to him. He'd been married twice, the first time in 1988 (no children, and ending in divorce in 1994) and the second time in 2002. As of 2007, he had been living in a mobile home outside the Jonesville, North Carolina, town limits with his second wife, Regina Belle Davis, and three children, all girls. The two eldest were his stepdaughters, and the youngest was his only child. Regina was adamant that she did not believe that her husband could have been responsible for these crimes; at least, that was her public response to the allegations against him, though I found it hard to believe that deep down she didn't have serious reservations about his innocence.

"The man I married is not the man that sits up there in that jailhouse," she told reporters. "I'm just as shocked as everyone else is."

Some of Lane's neighbors described him as quiet and a seemingly good father who "smiled a lot." One stated that he had offered to assist her husband with odd jobs on several occasions. "We thought he was a perfectly nice guy," said Wilda Gayle Spicer, who lived directly across from Lane and his family. Spicer observed that Lane was not home every weekend, but when he was, he usually parked his truck in the front yard.

"The last couple of times he came in," the woman said, "he left his truck running day and night. That truck would run and run and run. He left in it a few times and would come back and leave it running." She added that Lane and his wife were known to burn their trash in a barrel behind the mobile home, usually about once a week. She informed police that soon after Lane's arrest, his wife was seen burning a lot of trash.

Lane would occasionally be seen playing with his daughters in the overgrown yard in front of the family's single-wide trailer, where various dogs also scampered around untethered. A beach towel was hung in the front window for privacy in lieu of a curtain or a shade.

Other neighbors recalled peculiarities about Lane that seemed mundane but were reported as if they were the signs of the apocalypse. Besides a flaring temper simmering beneath an otherwise aloof demeanor, it was corroborated that Lane had perpetual face stubble and wore black all the time, and even in the summer, he usually wore long pants and long-sleeved shirts.

The insights that were perhaps most helpful in understanding Adam Lane came from Miriam Benge, Lane's first wife, who'd filed for divorce in 1993. She did not seem surprised by anything he did. "He thought women were beneath him," she said. Their rocky six-year marriage had been rife with verbal abuse, and about a year into their marriage, she claimed that he'd struck her in the head during an argument. "Old man, you ever hit me again, you're a dead man," she reportedly told him immediately afterward. According to her, he just laughed and said, "I can kill you and play off crazy as a bat and get away with it. They wouldn't do a thing to me."

Lane had been working hanging chickens in a slaughterhouse at the time the couple had first met, at a nightclub. They were married after a short courtship, but according to Benge, Lane was cheating on her within a year. She was aware of Lane's collection of knives, which he never tried to hide. She also revealed that at one time her ex-husband had owned four Chinese throwing stars, which he would toss at the walls inside their rented single-wide trailer. This had always infuriated her, but after a while she stopped saying anything to him about it. She was afraid to. It wasn't worth it. His explosive temper was perhaps his most dangerous weapon, and she didn't want to risk it. Finally, Benge had enough, and her divorce petition was granted in 1994.

Adam Leroy Lane's reputation as a woman-hater was not confined to his ex-wife. Several people who had worked with him came forward to say that Lane could be antisocial, argumentative and controlling, especially toward women.

Jimmy Utt drove cross-country with Lane for about a month in the late 1990s before refusing to get back in the truck with him.

"Adam seemed like he had a bad disposition against everything," said Utt. "He wanted to argue over something, it seemed like, all the time. And when it came to women, he had a bad way with them. One day a waitress come over to him and said, 'Have I done something to you?' and I said, 'I'll tell you what, he's that hateful of a bastard every day.'"

Lane's mother, Betty Norman, who had been living about seven miles from her son, defended him when questioned about his legal problems. One article reported that Norman was a licensed nurse who was keeping more than fifty canaries and parakeets in her basement as part of a home business, and at the time of her son's arrest, she had been working on fixing up a small outbuilding for another home business, Betty's Quilted Handbags.

Despite the fact that Lane's first wife, Miriam Benge, alleged that Lane had abused his mother—"He would cuss her, call her names, [beat] on her," she claimed—Norman went on record saying that she did not think the boy she'd raised was capable of such violence. "Not my son," she told the Associated Press by telephone. When *People* magazine called, she told them, "I don't want to talk about my son."

Benge had much more to say about this man. "They should give him the death penalty," she told reporters. "No appeal, no parole, nothing. They'd be doing everybody on this green Earth a favor."

Lane's second wife, Regina Belle Davis, when pressed for more information by reporters, responded, "No comment unless you've got a big, fat check."

"I hope things work out," the turned-away reporter said as he was leaving.

Regina offered the last word: "I don't think they will."

As far as Lane's work history, he had been regularly employed, either laboring or driving trucks, except during a period after he had undergone back surgery. He was regarded as a loner by his coworkers, someone who was not easy to get along with. Even at Jordan's Country Restaurant, a North Carolina restaurant on Highway 67 catering to truckers, which Lane frequented, the employees noted Lane's unpleasantness. With the cloying smell of grease and the NASCAR models that adorned the interior, the restaurant was much like any truck-stop diner in the south. Most nights Lane would come in alone during the third shift, even if he wasn't working. A creature of habit, he would sit in the smoking area and order the same thing: a Mountain Dew and two hot dogs, "all the way," which for him did not include onions. Sydney Hanson, the manager, would catch hell from Lane if she didn't bring him his drink fast enough after he sat down.

Records indicate that Lane received his commercial driver's license in May 1993, despite his regular operator's license having twice been put on probation, in 1988 and 1992, for speeding violations.

In 1997, Lane began driving for Smith Brothers Trucking out of Ararat, Virginia, hauling household goods and furniture from North Carolina to California and returning with produce on the eastbound trip. He was driving about 5,500 miles over five days and making about $800 a trip. At that time, remembered Dude Smith, whose family owned the company, Lane was partial to western shirts and black cowboy hats. He described Lane as "a little short-fused," and although the trucking company would typically pair up its drivers for the long coast-to-coast hauls, Lane was the only one who went solo. "He was a loner," Smith confirmed. Other drivers who had gone out with him once would ask never to ride with him again.

"Didn't nobody ride with him because he was a little overbearing," was how Smith put it. "He wasn't the easiest guy to get along with."

During that time, Lane had been dating Regina Davis, who usually dropped him off at work. His employers recalled that the couple always seemed to be fighting or arguing about something.

Lane worked for Smith for about eighteen months. At the end of his tenure with the Virginia trucking company, they were hardly using him as a driver because of his attitude. They were hoping that he would quit.

Adam Leroy Lane had no previous criminal history to speak of, at least nothing that might have raised a red flag. In the few years prior to his arrest in Chelmsford, he had been guilty of speeding violations and writing bad checks. In 1992 he pleaded no contest to a trespassing charge, for which he paid a fine and agreed to stay away from the complainant (since deceased).

Until the summer of 2007, Lane's most serious brush with the legal system involved an accidental death. On June 5, 1999, Lane was driving an eighteen-wheeler down North Carolina Highway 104 outside Mount Airy when eighty-one-year-old David Rigney, of Ararat, Virginia, suffered a heart attack while at the wheel of his minivan and crossed the yellow line in front of Lane's rig. Lane could not avoid the oncoming vehicle and struck it head-on. Regina Davis and her daughter Jennifer were both passengers in Lane's truck at the time and were treated for minor injuries. The driver of the minivan, however, was killed.

Soon after, Lane quit work because of back pain from the injuries he'd suffered in the accident. A Salisbury, North Carolina, neurosurgeon gave him a rating of 39 percent permanent disability. He underwent two rounds of surgery to insert screws and a metal rod into his spinal column and to fuse several bones. Because the deceased was uninsured, Lane sued his own employers, Smith Brothers, and its insurance carrier and was awarded more than $130,000 for temporary total disability and medical expenses. Lane initially received more than $60,000 from Smith Trucking, and in 2001 he sued them again for the remaining money that had been owed to him. In January 2002, he settled for an additional $40,000, less attorney fees, according to court records.

A few months after the 1999 accident, Lane fathered a child with his girlfriend Regina Davis, who was still married to another man at the time. A paternity test was administered and proved that Lane was, indeed, the father. By the time the girl was born, in June 2000, Lane and Davis were living together with Davis's two older daughters in Hamptonville, and by 2006, the family had moved into the trailer near I-77.

During the summer of 2007, neighbors didn't see Lane at home much at all. He had been driving for tree farmer Donald Burcham of Fancy Gap, Virginia, traveling up and down the eastern seaboard. He had been driving for Burcham for about six months, making on average about four stops per week.

"His personality was kind of impatient," Burcham told reporters after Lane's arrest. "I had to jump on him a few times for being short-tempered with some people. But there was never anything that would make you think he'd do something like this."

The last time Burcham saw Lane was at noon on July 27, 2007, when Lane left Virginia with a load bound for York, Pennsylvania, with scheduled stops in Uxbridge, Massachusetts, and Nashua, New Hampshire.

# Chapter 11

## CHILLING CONFESSION

On August 20, 2007, with the Middlesex District Attorney's Office and the Chelmsford Police Department having announced the arrest of Adam Leroy Lane, everything changed. That was when the North Carolina trucker drew the attention of the authorities outside Massachusetts for the first time.

Authorities in New Jersey, unable to implicate anyone in the murder of Monica Massaro, had already begun turning their investigative eyes outside of Hunterdon County. Prosecutor J. Patrick Barnes first picked up on the similarities of a murder that had recently been committed in Maryland. He immediately contacted the FBI and spoke to Jayne Stairs, the analyst who was putting the truck-route timeline together on Adam Lane. "How about this case in Maryland?" he asked her. "Could that have been our guy?"

Stairs quickly dismissed that possibility because the killer in the Maryland case had already been arrested by July 29, the day Monica was killed. However, she did inform the prosecutor about Adam Lane's attack in Massachusetts and suggested that the New Jersey authorities call Chelmsford. Barnes passed this information on to the task force that had been assembled to investigate Monica's murder.

It was at this time that Detective-Sergeant Geoffrey Noble of the New Jersey State Police was asked to take the lead in the Massaro murder investigation. The detective had a sister who happened to live in Groton, Massachusetts, a town neighboring Chelmsford, so when the lead came in he jumped right on it. After meeting with the other investigators, who had already been working hard on the Massaro case, the next thing Noble did was follow up on the Chelmsford lead.

At that time, the police station in Chelmsford was a beehive of activity, with the department's resources stretched to the max. All of the legwork, the entire investigation regarding Lane's recent movements and possible connections to other regional crimes, was being handled by the small-town department. Initially, the New Jersey inquiry appeared to be just another call from another department looking for leads on a cold case; calls like those had been coming in nonstop since the investigation began, and none had panned out into anything significant yet.

But as Chelmsford Detective George Tyros listened halfheartedly to the New Jersey investigator, his ears immediately pricked up, noting the striking similarities between Monica's murder and Lane's modus operandi in his own case: the late hour, unlocked door and especially the knife and the proximity to a major interstate with a rest stop nearby.

The nominal connection established, the two men decided

to get back in contact with each other the following day with the specific evidence of their cases at hand. By comparing the Chelmsford and Bloomsbury attacks side by side, New Jersey investigators could determine if Adam Lane was worth the investment of any more of their time. During that follow-up conversation, in a conference call between Detective Tyros and half a dozen officials from the New Jersey State Police as well as the Hunterdon County Prosecutor's Office, in New Jersey, Tyros was asked if there had been anything found in Lane's possession that might have placed him in New Jersey sometime on or around July 29. They were looking for a receipt, map or document, any piece of physical evidence related to Bloomsbury or Interstate 78.

Detective Tyros's wife, Rebecca, also a detective on the force, assisted with the paperwork and the list of evidence while the other detectives were still on the phone, all of them talking at once, telling them what to look for. Finally, Detective Rebecca Tyros came across a receipt that had been entered into evidence, which included the location Bloomsbury. Everyone went silent at once.

"What's the date on it?" someone asked.

"Um . . . July 29."

More silence. Then, "George, we're coming to Chelmsford."

The problem was that after the search warrant had been issued and the evidence in Lane's truck catalogued, only the evidence pertaining to the crime in Massachusetts had been retained by the Chelmsford police. Now, New Jersey needed the rest of the evidence from the truck. Unfortunately, the truck was gone, and its contents cleaned out.

Several days earlier, on August 17, Lane's truck had been moved from the local tow yard to CO & S Towing Garage in Templeton, Massachusetts, where Lane's employer, and owner of the truck, had come to pick it up. Everything that had still been inside the cab at that time had been tossed by the owner into an onsite Dumpster. The trash-removal company had been scheduled to remove the Dumpster the day before the conference call with New Jersey officials. But, serendipitously, they had not, and the container with the rest of Lane's truck's contents was still sitting inside the receptacle at the tow yard.

New Jersey investigators were in Chelmsford by the next morning, August 22. They had to act quickly to collect and preserve any evidence that might connect Lane to the murder of Monica Massaro. New Jersey State Police Detective Nicholas Oriolo, as well as Sergeant Kevin Burd and Lieutenant Jeff Farneski, of the Hunterdon County Prosecutor's Office, made the trip to Massachusetts with Detective Noble. The investigators were greeted and briefed by Lieutenant John Roark and Detectives Tyros and Ahern of the Chelmsford Police Department.

By 1:00 p.m., the investigators arrived at CO & S Towing Garage, where they were met by Templeton Police Chief David Whitaker and patrolman Steve Flis as well as the owner of the garage, who gave his written consent for them to search the Dumpster. With everyone accounted for, Detective Oriolo donned a full-body protective suit and performed what is commonly referred to as a "Dumpster dive." This is just what it sounds like, and every bit as unpleasant, especially when you factor in a sweltering summer day. The four-ton-capacity, thirty-cubic-yard Dumpster was full, and the items that had been removed from Lane's truck were on the very bottom. Some forty-five individual items believed to have come from Lane's rig were recovered. Each piece was meticulously inventoried and placed in a separate package with the seal initialed by Detective Noble.

The Virginia State Police were also contacted by the New Jersey detective, who requested their assistance in the ongoing murder investigation by searching the truck Lane had been operating for possible evidence. Detective Noble spoke with Captain James Miles, Fourth Division Criminal Investigation Commander, who pledged the department's full assistance in forensically processing the truck. Detective-Sergeant James Kiernan prepared a formal letter to Virginia requesting their assistance so that Captain Miles could attain permission from the actual owner of the truck to search his property.

Because of this prompt action, later that same day, Special Agent John Santolla, of the Virginia State Police Crime Scene Investigation Unit, was able to conduct a thorough search of the truck. Sixteen items of evidence were collected and carefully prepared for transport to New Jersey.

Having secured the evidence they hoped would help them build a case against Monica Massaro's murderer, authorities in New Jersey were ready to talk to Adam Lane. The next day, August 23, after spending the night in a Massachusetts hotel, Detective Noble and Lieutenant Farneski went to the Middlesex County Jail in Cambridge, where the incarcerated trucker was being held.

At that time, right up until he sat down with Adam Leroy Lane, Detective Geoffrey Noble was far from convinced that this suspect was responsible for the murder of Monica Massaro. Even though the lead held some promise, and Lane could be physically placed in the vicinity of the crime at around the same time as the murder, there were glaring problems with this suspect that could not be overlooked. For one thing, the crimes were completely different. One of the crimes that Lane had been arrested for in Massachusetts was the attempted rape of a minor. The crime that the New Jersey State Police were investigating involved a middle-aged woman who had been stabbed to death and mutilated, with no evidence to suggest that a sexual assault had been committed and no indication of there having been a sexual component to the homicide. No semen had been found anywhere at the crime scene. Men who commit sexual assaults usually seek out a female in the same general age group. It didn't appear to add up. If fifteen-year-olds were what drove this man's fantasies and urges, he would be a pedophile, as far as Detective Noble was concerned, and in that case, Monica Massaro would not fit his pattern of behavior.

There was also nothing in Adam Lane's criminal history to demonstrate that he was capable of the level of violence witnessed in Monica Massaro's murder. Besides, being killed by a random truck driver who walked into her home off the street was still the least probable of all possible scenarios. This visit to Massachusetts, then, was just another lead Detective Noble had to follow, even if it took him down a dead-end path. That's what police work was. That was how these kinds of crimes get solved. Still, he wasn't holding out much hope. Based on the suspect's reluctance to talk to Chelmsford law enforcement, he expected Lane to lawyer-up quickly.

Adam Lane was escorted into the interrogation room by Captain Daniel Finn of the Middlesex Sheriff's Office. Detective Noble and Lieutenant Farneski were waiting for him there, with both a video and an audio recorder running in plain view. It was 4:20 p.m. when Lane's handcuffs were removed by Captain Finn, and the murder suspect sat down with the New Jersey investigators. After the introductions were made, Adam Lane listened as Detective Noble read him his rights and then he read and signed the Miranda warning form. Before they got started, a DNA sample was collected by Captain Finn, who removed a few hairs from the top of the suspect's head.

With Lane freely consenting to the interview, Detective Noble's questioning proceeded in an intentionally deliberate and methodical manner. He never told Lane exactly why he and the other investigator were there, and Lane never asked. They seemed to discuss just about everything else, each avoiding talking about the real reason for the visit and waiting for the other to bring it up. Adam Lane didn't know it, but his initial lack of interest in learning what the New Jersey detectives actually wanted from him revealed something to the investigators that was as telling as a polygraph needle vibrating out of control. Noble knew that Lane was well aware of the serious underlying nature of the interview. The detective couldn't be certain if the trucker's indifference was out of self-preservation because he figured the law was on to him for Monica Massaro's murder or some other crime, but Noble was certain that Lane was hiding something. Unfortunately, the consequence of this gut feeling was no more admissible than a lie detector test. The police couldn't very well arrest Adam Leroy Lane because he *acted* guilty. Noble was playing a game with Lane, and Lane was playing back. But the detective did not want to be the first to show his hand, and he decided to stick to the game plan. It would be a matter of who could outlast the other.

Beyond Noble's police instincts, he had nothing to go on. In every respect, Lane continued to disguise any outward appearance that he was different from the hundreds of interstate truck drivers that the detective had pulled over during the six years he spent as a uniformed trooper on the turnpike. Many of the truckers he'd stopped had been from the south—North Carolina, Virginia, Texas—and had had strong accents as well. And like Lane, they were always very polite and respectful, addressing him as "Sir" or "Trooper."

The detective casually asked Lane about his life and about the time he'd spent in New Jersey during the weekend in question. It was very conversational, considering the situation. Like any two guys shooting the breeze, sports came up when Detective Noble asked the suspect if he followed the Red Sox.

"If you don't," he added, "you should probably start, because a lot of the guys in here with you are fans, and it might be helpful to you if you knew something about the team."

"Nah, I like the Atlanta Braves."

"Well, I have to tell you, Adam, that's probably not going to cut it."

When the detective started talking about the Patriots, Lane said that he liked the Carolina Panthers, who he mentioned happened to be playing New England that very night in a preseason game in Charlotte.

"That's right," Detective Noble said. "Are you going to watch the game?"

"Nah, on account they got me in solitary confinement. They ain't got no TV there."

The detective laughed. "Oh, that's too bad. I'll sure be watching it later."

As their dialogue continued, Detective Noble continued to carefully avoid any direct questions about Monica Massaro or her murder. If Lane was indeed their guy, Noble believed that he would eventually implicate himself and start talking about some aspect of the crime or the victim that he would otherwise have had no business knowing.

But during their conversation, the bearded, gruff-looking suspect proceeded to portray himself as an ailing, down-on-his-luck truck driver who was just trying to provide for his family as best he could and barely scraping by. He said he had been out of work for a while because of a back injury, which had drained his family's finances, and that he was on various medications for diabetes and hallucinations. He was very proud to be a trucker, boasting of his driving abilities, his knowledge of the road and his punctuality in always arriving on time at his destinations. He even bragged about being able to read and write, and said he had respect for the law.

"I got manners," he told them. "I treat people the way I want to be treated."

After more than seventy-five minutes of this casual interrogation, Lane suddenly seemed to have enough of their cat-and-mouse game. "Sir, if you drove all the way from New Jersey up here, then you have . . . have a reason other than just, I want to talk to Adam Lane."

"You're absolutely right," Detective Noble stated. "We didn't come all the way up here from New Jersey for chit-chat. We believe that the night you stopped in New Jersey, something happened. Something happened that night, Adam. I don't just suspect that something happened that night. I know that something happened that night. We believe you were involved with something that night. That's why we're here. That's what we want to talk about. I think we can help you. But I need to know the truth. By you being honest with us and telling us what happened that night, you'll be helping yourself. You'll get past all this and it will help you. I can tell you that."

"Why don't you tell me why y'all came here," Lane said. "Get down to what it is you want to ask."

For the first time since they began questioning Adam Lane, Detective Noble identified Monica Massaro as a victim in a murder case they were investigating, and Lane was told that he was a suspect in that crime. The detective added that they had evidence that placed him in the vicinity at the time of the homicide.

"See," Lane said, "the thing about this is, just like I told my wife—they're gonna hit me with everything they can find, that they can't solve."

"Adam, what can you tell us about Monica?"

"I didn't do it."

"Did you enter her house that night?"

"I . . . No."

"Can you describe what Monica Massaro looks like?"

"No, sir. My lawyer can answer those questions. I'm done."

"Adam, I just want to be clear here. Are you indicating at this time that you're not going to answer any more questions without your lawyer present?"

"Yes, sir. That's right."

It was 5:35 p.m. Detective Noble felt obligated to stop the interview at that time, which he did immediately. From a legal standpoint, he would be entering into the fuzzy territory of coercion, and he didn't want to jeopardize the case they were making against Lane if it appeared that he was trying to force the suspect to continue talking after he had implied that he wanted to consult an attorney. The investigators promptly gathered their belongings, broke down the audio and video equipment, and were leaving the interview room when Lane called out to Detective Noble.

"Trooper," Lane said, "Can I ask you a question off the record?"

"Sure, Adam. What's on your mind?"

"If you were me, would you talk?"

"Absolutely," Detective Noble told him. "I would talk."

Lane paused for a long moment, seeming to consider the detective's advice, then asked, "Do they have the needle in New Jersey?"

Detective Noble knew Lane was referring to the death penalty. "The state hasn't executed anyone in years."

"Well, how much time am I looking at then?"

"We're not attorneys and we're not authorized to answer those questions, but if there's something you want to tell us, we'll hear you out on it."

At that moment, Detective Noble realized that he was indeed looking at the individual who had murdered Monica Massaro. The last question posed by Adam Lane made him absolutely certain. The detective also saw this as a way to get them back into the interrogation room with the suspected murderer, but Lane had to initiate the interview. Detective Noble was being very cautious, and he wanted to get another opinion to determine the best way to proceed.

"Adam, why don't you take some time alone to think things over," he said, hoping to buy them some time. The detective stepped out of the room to discuss this new development with Lieutenant Farneski. A call was then placed to the first assistant prosecutor of the Hunterdon County Prosecutor's Office, Charles Ouslander, who took the matter under advisement and told the investigators that he would get right back to them.

While the New Jersey lawmen were waiting to hear back

from Ouslander, Detective Noble noticed Lane's face in the small window of the interview room door. Lane was looking directly at the detective and nodding his head, clearly indicating that he wanted to talk. Between this action and the inquiries that Lane had made earlier, Detective Noble interpreted this as Lane's way of reinitiating the conversation, thereby legitimizing the continuation of the interview. After spending more than an hour priming the suspect to confess, he'd been on the verge of going back to New Jersey empty-handed. Now that had all suddenly changed, and the detective felt that Lane was ready to give a full confession. He didn't want to lose him now.

Detective Noble opened the door to the interview room and looked Adam Lane over. "Do you wish to speak with us?"

"Yes, sir."

*That should work*, Detective Noble thought. Lane wanted to talk, so the investigators returned to the room. The camcorder was activated, and after being informed of his rights and acknowledging them by signing another Miranda form, Adam Lane started talking.

"What I'm about to do is stupid," the trucker began, then paused momentarily.

"Adam," Detective Noble interrupted, not wanting to give the suspect any opportunity to rethink his position and wiggle off the hook he'd put himself on. "I'd like to ask you an open-ended question and I'd like you to tell us the truth. It's imperative that you tell us the truth, okay . . . I know it may be difficult, and I understand that. And we're here, we're committed to being here as long as it takes. We're gonna get through this. Adam, tell us what happened on the night when you were in New Jersey and stopped at the truck stop off Route 78."

What followed was a blunt and chilling confession by

Adam Leroy Lane, who took detectives down the path he'd walked on the night of July 29, 2007, beginning at the truck stop, where he admitted that he'd parked his rig before walking into town.

"I know I'm driving the nails in my own coffin, but you wanted the truth. . . . And I'm trying not to die. . . . I was losing everything I had. I don't have much, didn't have much, and now I've lost everything, including my family. You all should get a big conviction off this," he told investigators.

Lane said that he'd been dressed in black and armed with knives and other weapons to use as scare tactics and defense against possible attacks by neighborhood dogs. He said he went on the prowl looking for unlocked homes to rob, crossing backyards and jiggling a number of doorknobs before he stumbled upon Monica Massaro's unlocked door.

"I was walking around, monkeying around like I always do," he told investigators matter-of-factly. "I decided to go for a walk 'cause I was . . . I had lots of time. . . . Went and cut through some yards. I just picked one [house] at random, walking through the neighborhood. How many, you know, if I seen somebody in the house or I seen somebody awake, I'd pass it. I didn't want no confrontation. Couple of houses, they were locked. The door [to Monica's house] was unlocked, and I went in.

"There were no lights on. I was in the house. In the kitchen. Got the keys [to Monica's car] that's on the table. I went out the back door, unlocked her car, got the pocketbook out, set it down, went through it. Then I went in the bedroom."

Lane described how as soon as he walked into Monica's bedroom, she'd sat right up and started screaming. "I didn't even have a knife out," he said, before amending, "I mean, you know, I only had the knife there in case of a big dog."

He went on to describe how they'd struggled, and how Monica "wouldn't let me get away, she wouldn't let me leave."

"I tried to put my hand over her mouth to get her to be quiet . . . She bit my hand . . . I tried to push her back on the bed so I could get out. I fell. I had two back surgeries, I ain't got no strength. I mean, I might look big and mean, but I'm not. I'm weak really when it comes to wrestling around with anybody. Ask the man that put a choke hold on me, because he weighed seventy pounds less than I did."

Actually killing Monica had been "an accident." Lane claimed that she'd injured herself when she rolled into his knife and the blade had accidentally slashed her throat.

"I was leaning on the knife, next to the bed or on the bed, for support. And she rolled, and she rolled over to get away and got cut with it. . . . I thought maybe it was just a little scrape or something. But there wasn't nothing to do. You couldn't . . . I mean, it was gushing out of her. God, there was so much blood. . . . She bled to death. I couldn't do nothing about it. . . . It didn't take very long. Less than sixty seconds.

"I thought if I made it look like somebody murd . . . went in and ravaged her and all that, it'd make it a little better, but they wouldn't look toward me. I wanted to make it look like somebody, like some maniac, sex crime . . . I cut her in a couple places. After she was dead. Between the legs, on her stomach.

"See, this ain't . . . this ain't making it better, this is making me look like a maniac. . . . But I didn't mean to hurt nobody. I didn't want to go to jail for the rest of my life or get a needle stuck in my arm. I didn't have any relations with that woman, before, after or during. I love my wife very much. I ain't out for sexual joys.

"I went out the back door beside the car and up through the yard and back to the truck stop. I took her pocketbook from the car and a necklace I found in one of the drawers. I threw the credit cards and license in . . . in the trash can. Threw the pocketbook on top of a building. I meant to throw the necklace away and never did.

"After that . . . after that happened, I went back to the truck and, and tried to eat, and I bought a radar detector and went somewhere else, laid down and tried to sleep."

---

The interview was abruptly ended at 7:45 p.m., only this time it was by Captain Finn, who needed to get Lane back to his cell because of the late hour. As Lane was hand-cuffed and led away, the suspect strained to turn toward Detective Noble and make direct eye contact. He apparently had more he wanted to say to the investigators, but unfortunately he was not given the opportunity. Detective Noble and Lieutenant Farneski were not about to complain, however. In fact, they could hardly believe what they had just heard. After several hours with the suspect, Lane's detailed confession was more than they could have hoped for. It contained a lot of information that only someone who was at the scene of the crime could have recounted. A probable-cause affidavit was quickly signed, and the following day Lane was charged with first-degree murder.

This was merely the first step in a lengthy process that would bring Adam Leroy Lane to justice in New Jersey for the death of Monica Massaro. The taped confession, however, was not the only evidence that would be used to secure several other charges against Lane. These offenses included second-degree burglary and third-degree possession of a weapon for unlawful purposes. The primary physical evidence was Monica's distinctive necklace, which had been discovered in Lane's cab. There was also the sales receipt for a radar detector that Lane purchased from the Bloomsbury truck stop, dated July 29, 2007, and time-stamped 5:13 a.m. Lane also appeared on a surveillance video from the Pilot Travel Center on Route 173, and it was confiscated by police.

DNA evidence would link Lane to Monica Massaro's murder as well. Not only would her blood be found on the clothes that Lane had been wearing the night he attacked Shea, but it would also be recovered from the same knife he had been holding against Shea's throat.

The evidence against Lane was compelling. The surveillance tape and the truck-stop receipt placed Lane within a half mile of Monica's home. The necklace proved he had been in her house. The blood put him at the murder scene. Together with his confession, it was a rock-solid case. At that point, it seemed just a question of when Lane would be brought to trial for the brutal murder of Monica Massaro.

# Chapter 12

## TRUCK-STOP PERIL

Chief Jim Murphy's initial hunch about Adam Leroy Lane proved to be right on, and he was no longer the only one who believed that there could be other victims of Lane's nocturnal hunting escapades still to be identified. Authorities in jurisdictions up and down the East Coast, heeding the news of the multistate charges being brought against Lane, began checking the details of all their unsolved cases along the highways and truck routes that Lane had used, especially crimes committed near truck stops.

Truckers are required by federal law to keep logs of all their stops, though in the two days prior to his arrest, Lane had not made a single entry in his log. However, now that they knew what they were looking for, investigators could readily gain an exact history of Lane's past and recent movements by combing through the Federal Department of Transportation's databases and then comparing that information with the occurrences of any unsolved violent crimes in those areas where he had traveled.

There are strict federal laws mandating how long a trucker can be behind the wheel each day. After clocking a maximum of eleven consecutive hours on the road, drivers are required to be off duty for ten hours. These regulations may keep drowsy drivers from making deadly mistakes, but at the same time it gives them a lot of downtime. People who spend any time at all on the highways will observe that there are always trucks traveling alongside them. There are so many, they may sometimes be taken for granted. But for every commercial tractor-trailer seen on the road, there are just as many unseen, on duty but off-road somewhere. Accounting for the whereabouts of these truckers became a focus of much discussion in the local Massachusetts media.

As law enforcement was investigating Lane's possible connection to unsolved home-invasion crimes in other states, state police in Massachusetts defended their patrol frequency of Bay State highway rest areas and truck stops, including the ones on I-495 North and South in Chelmsford.

Trooper Jim Burke, of the Concord barracks, told the press that the rest areas and truck stops were all checked a few times a night. "We take notice if there's anybody in the woods, or anything else out of the ordinary," he said. He explained that seemingly empty cabs do not necessarily raise red flags because of the possibility that the driver could be simply using the bathroom facilities or asleep in the truck.

It was discovered that there were actually fewer commercial travel centers with twenty-four-hour restaurants, shower facilities and other amenities in Massachusetts than in other parts of the country, so truck drivers frequently depended on the basic highway-shoulder rest areas for use of restrooms and places to pull over and sleep.

Not everyone, however, was sympathetic to the difficulties faced by long-haul truckers. In the days following the attack, a local newspaper caught up with one Chelmsford selectman, Philip Eliopoulos, who let them know that he had lobbied against having a truck stop constructed on Route 3 long before Adam Leroy Lane came along. As a former member of the Route 3 Project Advisory Committee, Eliopoulos had been one of several opponents who'd fought to have a truck stop permanently removed from the new plan.

"I can see how they benefit the highway," Eliopoulos said of the bare-bones rest stops. "But they don't really benefit the communities that they're in. Just a blanket, no-facilities-type rest area can pose safety concerns. A commercial one is more monitorable."

---

In Bloomsbury, New Jersey, Dan Hurley, the deputy chief of operations and spokesman for the Hunterdon County Prosecutor's Office, said authorities originally withheld information about the Massaro murder investigation because police did not immediately focus on a lead suspect.

"We desperately wanted to be able to give [the residents of Bloomsbury] some relief initially," Hurley said. "The detectives, from the day this task force was first created to today, have worked tirelessly on this." He credited all the agencies involved in the investigation, including the FBI's Violent Criminal Apprehension Program (ViCAP), various state police agencies in New Jersey and Massachusetts as well as local authorities in each state.

"We hope this will bring a measure of closure to the residents of Bloomsbury," New Jersey State Police Lieutenant Colonel Gayle Cameron said. "I'm sure the people of Bloomsbury will rest a bit easier knowing that the perpetrator of this brutal murder has been identified and captured."

However, as more details of Lane's apprehension continued to spread up and down Bloomsbury's wide Main Street, confirming that the murder had been committed by a stranger, the level of concern rose exponentially.

Monica's neighbors were interviewed, and they expressed an overall feeling of unease in the wake of the murder. "Everyone is more in tune with everyday events," said one. "More aware of their surroundings and looking behind them as they walk down the street."

"He could have gone into any house in the neighborhood," said another, who lived just a few doors down from Monica. "It's never going to be the same. . . . If it happened once, it could happen again. Especially something random like that."

Residents may have been relieved that Monica's killer was in custody, but they gave a wide berth to the nearby truck stop, and there remained an overall heightened sense of caution to any stranger. A crime of this nature was unimaginable to many; they did not know how to react.

"We were shocked," reflected Bloomsbury Mayor Mark Peck. "These kinds of things don't happen in Bloomsbury. We're a small, rural community. Before this murder, people used to leave their doors unlocked. They don't anymore."

You could almost hear the collective sound of all the doors and windows being closed and locked every night around the borough.

The mayor went on to say that ways to reduce traffic at

the truck stops where Lane parked would be considered. In particular, he noted that the Pilot Travel Center had faced considerable opposition from residents when it first replaced a similar mom-and-pop facility at the truck stop.

Authorities and citizens alike could at least be satisfied that it wasn't going to be Adam Leroy Lane who would terrorize another truck-stop community like theirs again.

"We have in fact placed a detainer on Adam Lane while he's in Massachusetts facing the charges there," said Dan Hurley, for the prosecutor's office. The detainer prevented Lane's release from custody before he could be transferred to Hunterdon County.

"He will not be coming to New Jersey until the charges are resolved in Massachusetts one way or the other," Hurley said. "There's no way to say exactly when he will be here. We don't anticipate it will be in the next several months and it could be a year. But all of that is just speculation."

# Chapter 13

INSTANT CELEBRITY

Back in Chelmsford, Massachusetts, the reverberations from the news that Adam Leroy Lane was a suspect in the slashing death of a New Jersey woman felt like an aftershock.

Before we learned the news, I was out with Kevin when my cell phone rang. It was Chelmsford Police Chief Jim Murphy. He asked us if we had time to swing by the police station. Realizing this was rather unusual, I didn't ask him what it was about over the phone. I knew it had to be something important. We finished up what we were doing and went directly to the station.

Entering Chief Murphy's office, we were asked to have a seat at the large conference table, and an eerie feeling came over me. Then Deputy Chief Scott Ubele, Assistant District Attorneys Tom O'Reilly and Kerry Ahern, and Detective George Tyros and Sergeant Todd Ahern all began to file into the office. They nodded or whispered greetings to us but didn't say much else. The mood was certainly mysterious, even ominous. Everyone seemed to be waiting for Chief Murphy to speak first.

He did, and this was when Kevin and I learned for the first time that the trucker who'd invaded our home had killed a woman the day before he'd attacked our daughter. The news was startling and horrifying. Even though none of us had believed that this had been the first time Lane had attacked someone, the realization that he had taken a life was chilling. We weren't told any details of the murder, aside from the similarities to his attack on Shea. However, any second-guessing about what Lane's true intentions had been when he'd entered the room where our daughter was sleeping could now be put to rest; it was not robbery, not rape, not kidnapping. It was clear that he'd been planning to repeat the heinous act from the previous night and slaughter our daughter in cold blood while we slept in the next bedroom. I understood then that it *would* probably have happened just that way if the air conditioner in our bedroom had been functioning. Over the rattle and hum of the unit's highest setting, there was no way we would have been awakened by Shea's desperate struggle or her terrified whimpers. That was as horrifying a realization as I could imagine.

Just then, Kevin and I were asked if it was alright if the two lead detectives from New Jersey could come in and meet us, lifting me from my reverie. Kevin and I had no objections, and the men were led into the office, and the door was closed behind them. They introduced themselves as Detective-Sergeant Geoffrey Noble, from the New Jersey State Police, and Detective Lieutenant Jeff Farneski, from the Hunterdon County Prosecutors Office, and stated that they were working on the murder of Monica Massaro.

They told us that they had been in Massachusetts for the past week working with Detective Tyros to build a case against Adam Lane. They also told us about their interview with Lane, and his admission of guilt.

As I looked around at the faces in the room staring back at me and Kevin, the gravity of the moment really hit home for me. I was instantly besieged with conflicting emotions. On one hand, it was a relief to know that it seemed the trucker's confession to the killing would almost certainly ensure that he'd be behind bars for a long time, hopefully for the rest of his life. The home-alarm monitoring system that we had installed soon after the attack could not provide the same peace of mind as would the iron bars and razor wire of the state prison. At the same time, this security came with the steepest of price tags: the life of a vibrant and beautiful young woman. I felt guilty that my relief came at the expense of someone else.

---

We became instant celebrities of sorts. The national media beat a path to our door, somehow getting our home phone number and calling us at all hours of the day and night. Representatives from such programs as *The Ellen DeGeneres Show*, *The Maury Show*, *The Montel Williams Show*, *20/20* and *Dateline NBC* contacted us requesting interviews and appearances.

However, talking about our experience on these syndicated shows would put the pending criminal cases against Adam Leroy Lane in jeopardy, and out of respect for Monica Massaro's family (and those of Lane's unknown other victims), we declined these offers without regret.

All the publicity was personally disruptive, to say the least. For me, Kevin, Shea and Ryan, it made it a challenge to concentrate on our day-to-day responsibilities and obligations. We were all as equally amazed by everything that had happened as anyone else, and felt fortunate and blessed that things had turned out the way they did, but we did not for one second believe that any of us were heroes. Not even my husband, though he'd certainly proved himself to be more than capable of holding his own against a more formidable opponent. I know that the experience had left Kevin with an even deeper appreciation for the police; now he had a newfound respect for what they did on a daily basis. We all did.

Some of the praise, I'll admit, made us feel good. We received many letters and some cards from Monica Massaro's family and loved ones, which helped make our own trying times more bearable. Also, there through all this were Detective Tyros, Chief Murphy, and Assistant District Attorneys Kerry Ahern and Tom O'Reilly, who stayed in constant communication with us during the weeks leading up to Lane's motion hearing. It went both ways, and if they needed us for anything, we made ourselves available.

Additionally, we were assigned a victim advocate, Dora Quiroz, who was always accessible to provide us with immediate information and the answers to all of our questions when everyone else was busy. Victim advocates are specialized counselors who act as a liaison between the state attorney's office and the victims of crime and their families. Dora Quiroz provided our family with much-needed support, which extended onto a personal level, and she greatly aided our ability to cope with the enormity of the strange and unfamiliar situation we found ourselves in.

During this time, our main concern continued to be for our daughter, Shea. She might have appeared fine to outsiders, but we could see that she had been deeply affected by her experience. There would be a natural tendency to rely on alcohol, or other drugs, if she became distressed and felt she needed to escape. Our fear was that it could possibly be a release for her repressed feelings of anxiety stemming from her close encounter with death. Assistant District Attorney Kerry Ahern recommended a psychologist who was affiliated with both the court and the school system. Ahern felt it was important that Shea have a safe outlet and an impartial sounding board who was not her family or friends to express her thoughts and emotions. Kevin and I agreed with this assessment, even though Shea was strongly against it. She didn't feel she had a problem, or would ever develop one, but it was not worth the risk to us. The trauma she suffered could have lasting repercussions, but addressing it quickly and thoroughly was crucial in preventing serious setbacks later on in her life.

There were bumps in the road along the way for Shea, but they were met with unwavering support and guidance from all around the community. We deeply appreciated all of it, particularly the concern expressed by school officials, including Shea's high school principal, Allen Thomas, who personally expressed to us his sincere concern and commitment to Shea's well-being and assured us that her academic needs would be met, no matter what.

# Chapter 14

## PRIME SUSPECT

The picture that was quickly emerging of the forty-two-year-old high school dropout was that of a deadly stalker who used the interstate as his hunting ground. Adam Leroy Lane's modus operandi would be to drive into a truck stop or rest area and park, then drift into nearby towns on foot in search of victims. This pattern of behavior, together with the efforts begun by the Chelmsford Police Department, would help authorities in several other state and local jurisdictions turn their attention to Lane.

Not long after Lane confessed to murdering Monica Massaro, he became the prime suspect in two more attacks, in Pennsylvania. On July 13, a knife-wielding attacker appeared out of nowhere and killed Darlene Ewalt on the back patio of her home while her family was sleeping inside. Four days later, and the next county over, Patricia Brooks survived a slashing attack by a man wearing dark hunting clothes. These crimes of violence had also taken place near interstates, and both involved late-night home invasions where the attacker had used a heavy, bladed weapon. Furthermore, trucking records confirmed that Lane signed for deliveries he made in Dauphin County on July 13 and in York County on July 17, just a few miles away from where the crimes took place on those days. Once these records were verified, officials knew that they had their man, and the announcement was not delayed.

"We found out pretty early on that Lane had made deliveries within miles of where the two victims were attacked," announced Chief Carl Segatti of the Northern York County Regional Police Department. "It seemed to us that this coincidence was not just happenstance."

Lane was also tied to these crimes with DNA evidence. Furthermore, Patricia Brooks had been able to positively identify Lane from a photo array shown to her by police.

A witness who was driving to work along Locust Point Road around the time of Patricia Brooks's attack told investigators that he'd seen a man dressed entirely in black walking in the predawn darkness at around 4:35 a.m. The witness told police he'd thought it was odd that the man was wearing gloves in the middle of summer. He also reported seeing a tractor-trailer parked near the intersection of Locust Point Road and Susquehanna Trail near I-83.

At some point along his escape route the night Lane attacked Patricia, he'd tossed the black gloves he was wearing into a yard a half mile from the victim's home. Investigators later found them both atop an embankment at a home on Locust Point Road. Subsequent testing revealed that Lane's DNA was present on the gloves.

"Our case is going to be made or broken forensically,"

Chief Segatti told the press. Despite the eyewitness account and photo ID by the victim, DNA evidence was still the most reliable.

Prosecutors in Pennsylvania were also confident that DNA evidence would unequivocally show that Darlene Ewalt was murdered by Adam Lane. Although it was not immediately verified, blood discovered on one of the knives that police had confiscated from Lane after his arrest was believed to be consistent with that of Darlene Ewalt. District Attorney Edward Marsico, of Dauphin County, called the potential DNA match "the major part of the evidence gathered so far" in the homicide investigation. Marsico said Lane would be charged in the murder after the homicide case in New Jersey was concluded. "Once we file the charges," he said, "the clock starts ticking."

According to an interstate agreement regarding detainers, Pennsylvania would have to wait until Lane's cases were finished in Massachusetts and New Jersey before he could be returned to face homicide and attempted homicide charges there.

At the time, most everyone was okay with that. Because Lane was already being held, it took away the sense of urgency to immediately file charges in Pennsylvania. The extra time also afforded the police the added assurance that everything would be done right.

In the hope of gathering further forensic evidence that would tie Lane incontrovertibly to the crimes, Virginia State Police were once again called upon for assistance. Both New Jersey and Pennsylvania law enforcement authorities requested their help in processing several other trucks owned by Lane's employer, Fancy Gap Trucking Company, which operated out of Virginia.

Lane had been driving one trailer when he went through

New Jersey but a different one on the route that had taken him through Pennsylvania earlier that same month. It was a long shot that they would find anything of any use in the trucks, but it was more than worth the effort.

In addition to the death toll and the devastation to the victims and their families in the Pennsylvania attacks, Adam Leroy Lane also left in his wake an aura of fear in these two communities, just as he had in Chelmsford and Bloomsbury. Locksmiths and home-security companies may have enjoyed an increase in business in these areas as well, but no amount of crime prevention was going to make the people living there feel safe again.

The quiet York County township of Conewago, in the foothills of the Blue Ridge Mountains near the Virginia line, had been shaken by the attack on Patricia Brooks. Her rural home was surrounded by cornfields and was "not a place you would think someone would come to hunt and find someone to kill," the outspoken Segatti said. "When something like this happens in a rural community, I think people are upset. Ordinary Pennsylvanians who never expect a criminal act of this magnitude go to bed worried."

At the same time all this was going on, authorities in North Carolina began looking seriously at Lane as the trig-german in an eleven-year-old cold case shooting death of a Jonesville police sergeant. Although the manner in which the police officer was killed bore little similarity to Lane's other crimes, a police artist's sketch of a bearded suspect in a red baseball cap uncannily resembled Lane.

In the early hours of October 5, 1996, Sergeant Gregory Keith Martin had pulled over a red pickup on I-77. When he ran the registration, the vehicle came back stolen. The state trooper immediately called for backup, as was standard practice, but as soon as he approached the stolen vehicle, he was shot seven times and died on the highway beside his patrol car. The homicide of the thirty-year-old father of three became a top priority for law enforcement agencies in North Carolina, but frustratingly, no one was ever arrested, and the case quickly went cold. The week of Lane's arrest in Massachusetts, however, the Yadkin County Sheriff's Office suddenly began receiving calls from people who had seen Lane's mug shot in the news and believed he was the person responsible for Sergeant Martin's death.

All around Jonesville, sketches of a man wanted for questioning in the 1996 shooting of Sergeant Martin were still prominently displayed. The walls of convenience stores and other public and civic buildings were papered with images of the unknown suspect. One of the key witnesses was a car salesman from West Virginia who was able to provide a detailed physical description of the murder suspect. He reported that a burly, bearded man was one of two men who test drove the red pickup before it was stolen from the car lot where he was working.

The night that Sergeant Martin was killed, the stolen pickup was found abandoned in the parking lot of Lucia Inc., a clothing manufacturer in Elkin, North Carolina, not far from where Lane was living. A Lucia van was reported missing that same day and later found in nearby Gastonia. Other witnesses had come forward at that time and described seeing a burly, bearded man driving the stolen Lucia van, including one who recounted under hypnosis in 2005 that she saw a man resembling Lane driving the van less than an hour after Sergeant Martin was killed. One other bit of information I was later told was that in Lane's Yadkin County trailer home, police recovered various newspaper clippings detailing the local police officer's brutal murder.

Incidentally, the disturbing DVD *Hunting Humans*, which had been found in the truck Lane drove to Massachusetts, turned out to belong to an Elkin video shop close to Lane's house and Lucia Inc. Lane had previously rented other movies from the store, but he'd never returned the serial killer title and hadn't been back since he'd taken it out.

Although it was worthwhile to take a good look at the local trucker and now double murder suspect, the evidence that North Carolina investigators had against Lane in the Martin case was circumstantial, at best. Prosecutors could not go to trial with any of it. There was never any chance that they would even get a grand jury to *consider* indicting the trucker with what little they had.

With nothing much else to go on, any case against Lane in the Martin murder quickly fizzled out. Some investigators continued to believe that Lane shot the officer, but he was never charged in the homicide, and there remains no significant evidence to prove that he was responsible.

"It's different crimes. It's different weapons. It's different everything," said one FBI agent, summing up the feelings of the majority of law enforcement officials with regard to Lane's possible connection to the murder of the North Carolina state trooper.

# Chapter 15

SERIAL KILLER?

Because Adam Leroy Lane's driving routes over the previous decade took him as far north as New Hampshire, as far west as California and as far south as Georgia, federal authorities tried to determine whether a bona fide serial killer had been captured inside our home on July 30, 2007.

Believe it or not, it wasn't something that could be easily agreed upon.

By this point, I had begun keeping a daily journal, jotting down my feelings and fears as they occurred to me as well as reflecting on what went before. These were my private thoughts and emotions as I tried to make sense of something that was utterly incomprehensible to me, so out of curiosity and necessity I began my own search for some of the very same answers that investigators in a growing number of states were seeking with regard to Adam Leroy Lane.

What I discovered was eye-opening and grotesquely fascinating.

What was in the mind of Lane when he was stalking and killing? We may never know. He might not even know himself. Serial killers account for less than 1 percent of all murders, but they seem to occupy a disproportionate percentage of the human psyche, at least the American psyche. They terrify and captivate us; one reason why they are so scary is that after years of research, experts still can't explain why some people kill, just for the sake of killing, with nothing to gain, without motive or emotion. Just for the sheer act itself.

Studies of killers like him have been conducted by experts in the field trying to shed some light on the subject. Robert K. Ressler is probably the original and foremost authority on criminal profiling. He is a former FBI special agent who might be most famous for coining the term *serial killer* and later advising Thomas Harris on his book *The Silence of the Lambs*. Ressler first began his studies into the minds of killers in the late 1970s. He wanted to know what made them commit such heinous acts of violence. His prison interviews became part of the FBI's Criminal Personality Research Project, of which he was the principal investigator.

After dozens of rigorous and comprehensive interviews, his team was able to uncover patterns of behavior and learning that were common among all the imprisoned murderers. The profiling techniques that resulted from this study were groundbreaking at the time, though they may seem far less spectacular to laypeople today because of the techniques' saturation in movies and TV programs.

In his 1992 book *Whoever Fights Monsters*, Ressler quantified the results of his findings by saying that "there is no such thing as the person who at age thirty-five suddenly changes from being perfectly normal and erupts into totally evil, disruptive, murderous behavior." He goes on to state that the seeds for murder had been implanted in these individuals long before they claimed their first victims, usually beginning in early childhood.

Contrary to the portrayal of fictional murderers, most serial killers do not come from broken or overly impoverished homes. And most do not have intelligence levels that are either below or far above "normal." Their IQs tend to be generally average, like most people. So why, then, do they end up so unfeeling and indifferent to the taking of life?

That's the question that was haunting me about Adam Leroy Lane.

Ressler surmised that although there may have been an appearance of normalcy in the childhood and adolescent homes of these homicidal individuals, there is often a cocktail of dysfunction that simmered just below the surface. At the root, there is often some form of mental illness, physical or sexual abuse, drug or alcohol dependency, criminal activity among members of the immediate family or some combination thereof. But even this cannot fully explain what prompts homicidal behavior; Ressler acknowledges that not everyone who shares those experiences or comes from "dysfunctional families" goes on, as a matter of consequence, to become killers.

However, if there was a commonly shared element among all of the incarcerated murderers, it was the lack of a loving, nurturing family. Ressler found that every single one of the killers he interviewed suffered from severe emotional abuse as a child; all had had "uniformly cool, distant, unloving, neglectful" mothers. More damaging than physical abuse, the lasting psychological harm that results from this emotional torment was what Ressler saw as the crux of the issue.

This in no way blames all mothers for the ills of the world, or even blames Adam Lane's mother for her son's actions. Ressler is quick to point out that even when mothers properly nurture their children, the abuses of the father, or other male family members, can completely undermine all of her best efforts, the resulting damages producing some of the worst killers in history. The absence of a father or father figure, either through death, incarceration or abandonment, at this stage also had a detrimental impact on the burgeoning killers who Ressler interviewed later in their lives. The fathers who stuck around were either abusive or neglectful to the child or the child's mother or both. Ressler simply states that the age of eight to twelve is critical, and in the subjects he studied, it was a time when their aberrant antisocial behavior began to manifest itself.

Ressler also talked extensively about fantasies and the role they play in the mind of someone who is driven to kill repeatedly. He defined fantasy as something that is unattainable in normal life. Whereas a normal male fantasy might be a sexual desire for a movie star, an abnormal fantasy might be to immobilize or slash such a movie star during sex. The fantasies of the deviant, he states, are characterized by themes of dominance, revenge and control.

"Whereas the normal person fantasizes in terms of sexual adventure, the deviant links sexual and destructive acts. Normal fantasies of interpersonal adventure are fused with abnormal attempts to degrade, humiliate and dominate others," Ressler states; abnormal fantasies are substitutes for more positive human encounters.

This depersonalization, he said—making the other person into a mere object—was common among the murderers he talked to in his studies. "Normal people relate sexual activity as part of loving. Deviants feel the sexual urge without having learned that it has anything to do with affection." He classified all of them as sexually dysfunctional. "That is," he suggests, "they were unable to have and maintain mature, consensual sexual experiences with other adults, and they translated that inability into sexual murders."

I felt strongly that this was what drove Adam Leroy Lane to destroy the lives he did. Although he did not sexually assault his victims, his murderous acts are considered sex murders by definition.

Even when the home and social environments are non-nurturing, and seriously violent fantasies develop, Ressler points out, many potential offenders still do not step over the line to commit violent acts. He describes these young men, however, as ticking time bombs, waiting to go off. Murder is always precipitated by some strong precrime stress, so Lane's brief marriage separation could have, in theory, set him off on his murderous rampage, as the indulgence in his fantasies became the solution to his problems.

"Things have been building up to a point where the potential murderer is ready to commit his violent act," Ressler writes, "and then a possible victim appears, one who is in a particularly vulnerable position. And the potential murderer becomes an actual murderer."

For Lane, a woman sleeping alone in a bed was as vulnerable as anyone can be.

The violent act both frightens and thrills the killer, Ressler believes. He has experienced a state of heightened emotional arousal during the crime, and he likes the feeling. Worried about arrest, but at the same time feeling more egocentric than ever, he becomes convinced that he can do it again, with impunity. He is likely to incorporate details of the first murder into his fantasies and begin to construct his future crimes, improving on the methods he used previously to make them even more satisfying.

"Now that the first murder has occurred," Ressler writes, "in subsequent crimes, the life stresses [of the murderer] that preceded the [previous murder] may not need be present. Now that he's over the line, the murderer usually more inconspicuously plans his future crimes. The first one may have had some of the earmarks of spontaneity, but the next victim will in all likelihood be more carefully sought out, the murder more expertly done and displaying more violence to the victim than was evident in the first crime. And the lonely boy from the non-nurturing home has become a serial killer."

That kind of progression is clearly evident in the murders Adam Leroy Lane committed. After he killed Darlene Ewalt on her back porch, Monica Massaro's death was much more brutal. His actions were also bolder; casually striding out of Patricia Brooks's home after her attack and entering Monica's house and remaining in her bedroom after she died clearly demonstrated his belief that he was untouchable. When he got out of his truck in Chelmsford, his fantasies were likely driving him to take even greater risks, and he was probably beginning to believe that he was unstoppable.

For me, all this secondhand research may have done more harm than good. The answers I sought about Adam Leroy Lane only generated more questions. I needed facts but got only theory. I found myself asking a lot of "what if" questions: What if Lane decided to enter another house instead of ours? Would he have claimed other victims and still be on the loose? What if I had gotten up for a glass of water ten minutes later than I did? What if our air conditioner had been working and we didn't hear the sounds from the next room? What if it had been just me who had gone in to check on Shea shortly before 4:00 a.m.? What if the dog had barked, causing me to get up and go outside to check on him like I always did, only to meet with the same fate as Patricia Brooks, or worse yet, Darlene Ewalt and Monica Massaro? What if I had been found lying in a pool of blood the next morning, and *my* husband or son or both became the main suspects in my murder?

These questions plagued me. It was a form of survivor guilt; for some reason, or no reason at all, everything had worked out in our favor, and we had been spared the tragedy and grief that the poor families of Lane's other victims had to endure. I imagined the Ewalts and the Massaros resented us for this, hated us, even. I didn't think we'd deserved to survive more than they had, and I tried to put myself and my family in the other families' shoes.

# Chapter 16

## MOVING FORWARD, LOOKING BACK

The community of Bloomsbury, New Jersey, paid tribute to Monica Massaro with a vigil on September 7, 2007. It was their way of remembering her and what she'd meant to her family, friends and neighbors, some of whom had previously criticized the news media for their limited and shortsighted descriptions of Monica. They printed the information Monica had written on her MySpace page, where she listed among her passions driving fast, reading, and wearing high heels and pink lip gloss. She had been labeled a "rocker chick" who loved live music and worshipped the rock band Aerosmith. To everyone who knew her, however, she was of course so much more. Some of the newspapers later printed apologies along with personal letters from people who wanted to portray Monica more accurately and who provided detailed depictions of the woman they had known and loved. She was roundly characterized as a friendly, outgoing woman who always had a smile on her face.

Many strangers as well as cohorts left messages on her MySpace page expressing their grief over and fondness for the murder victim. Monica had been known as "NJRagdoll" in this cyber community, and on the site, she described herself as an only child who was devoted to her mother and father, and she admitted that she still wondered when she was going to "grow out of it," referring to her carefree lifestyle and devotion to Aerosmith, whom she would follow around the country when the band went on tour.

She liked her Dunkin' Donuts coffee, and the summer. She may have encapsulated her view of life when she wrote, "I don't sit still. I have a lot of fun. I try to always remember to really live and to take every opportunity to have fun and make the most of it."

On this special night, the streets of Bloomsbury were illuminated by candlelight and filled with song as about eighty people walked along Main Street to honor the life of Monica Massaro. A single candle in a vase filled with white roses glowed on the front porch of Monica's duplex.

It was a lively event. Monica's family and friends thought that everything was just the way she would have wanted it to be. There was music, and as people gathered to listen in a grassy area where Route 173 and Main Street bisected, they lit candles, hugged and cried.

"This evening is about recognizing our loss, first of Monica, and also the loss of our innocence and peace as a community," Gina Yeske, a church pastor, told the crowd.

As trucks pulled in and out of the two truck stops nearby, one of which Adam Leroy Lane visited the night he killed Monica, voices sang, "Let There Be Peace on Earth."

At the end of the walking tribute, the pilgrimage of mourners paused at Monica's house to observe a moment of silent prayer led by Father Roberto Coruna, of the Church of the Annunciation.

Jim Bauer, a church member and borough resident, probably made the most poignant comment when he said, "The invisible barrier [between Bloomsbury and crime] has been breached. My kids used to ride these streets on their bicycles. To have that taken away is not fair."

Bauer, who said that he often took late-night walks, also commented that the murder had made him more alert, though he continued to believe that Bloomsbury remained a great place to raise a family.

"We have to be vigilant," he added. "We've seen the face of evil. It's real scary that it's a random act. It could be anybody. That's sad."

It was around this time that an unusual but related story made the news. A woman in Pelham, Massachusetts— only about sixty miles east of Chelmsford—admitted to making up a claim that she had fended off a sexual assault after a man entered her home in the middle of the night on July 29, 2007. Her confession to the hoax came after a ten-day investigation by police looking into the crime. It really came as no surprise to any of the detectives, who from the beginning had noted inconsistencies between the woman's testimony and the evidence. It was an odd coincidence that she had filed her bogus report on the same night that Lane had arrived in Chelmsford, so she obviously didn't know about the trucker's killing spree, but following Lane's capture, the case was taken very seriously in spite of the inconsistencies. She had even sustained undisclosed injuries, which turned out to be self-inflicted.

Copycat criminals are much more common than copycat victims, and early on there were criminologists who suspected Lane of mimicking the brutal killing of Dr. Petit's family in Cheshire, Connecticut. Some of Lane's crimes, however, turned out to predate the Petit family tragedy, and it became readily apparent that Lane's primary motive in invading homes was not to burglarize them. His sadistic nature went much deeper than that.

---

What Monica Massaro's family had to go through was something I could only imagine, yet despite their being consumed with grief, in the days leading up to Lane's court appearance, we received an emotional and heartbreaking card from Fay and Frank Massaro, Monica's parents. I was completely overwhelmed by their words, and I immediately ran out to get them a sympathy card, though picking out the perfect one for this situation proved impossible. I wanted to convey the right sentiment and expression of my empathy to a mother and father whose child had been so tragically and brutally taken away from them. There was no card that could do all this, and although the card I sent to the Massaros was imperfect, with a few of my own words added, I believed it captured my feelings of loss for them, coming from the perspective of a mother who had come close to experiencing the same devastation. This exchange managed to open the lines of communication between us, and ever since then, we have kept in touch, writing and speaking on the phone several times. I determined that I would be there for the Massaro family the day that this monster was transported to New Jersey to answer for what he did to them.

Shea's birthday was also coming up, the day before Lane's September 12 court date. This should have been a joyous time in her life, but Shea was not very enthusiastic about celebrating anything, not even her Sweet Sixteen. She had been born exactly ten years before the terrorist attacks in our country, on September 11, 1991. Her birthdays had been overshadowed to some degree ever since that dark day in 2001, but that year especially, it was a much smaller affair than it might otherwise have been. Kevin and I tried to make it a joyful and memorable event, but it was inevitable that the trauma of less than a month and a half earlier would overwhelm all of our efforts.

The Saturday before her birthday, we rented a limousine to take the whole family to Faneuil Hall in Boston for dinner at a popular restaurant. Shea invited Adam, her boyfriend, as well as his sister and her best friend. Shea's grandfather, Kevin's dad, also joined us. The evening promptly took a downturn, however, when Shea and Adam began to argue during the ride into the city. The rest of the night was filled with tension, which spread like a contagion between everyone. We were walking on eggshells for days afterward, wondering what the end result of this catastrophe of a night would be between Shea and Adam.

Our daughter and her boyfriend rarely disagreed, and for it to become so volatile was extremely unusual. In retrospect, I believe we were all still in shock. It almost seemed like the entire family was in a fog, just going through the motions of normalcy but all the while being acutely aware of how close we'd come to losing Shea. I know in the back of my mind I was thinking what a miracle it was that she was with us at all. Maybe that reality was finally catching up with us.

On September 12, 2007, the day after Shea's sixteenth birthday, Adam Leroy Lane was arraigned in Middlesex Superior Court in Lowell. Kevin and I were there once again. Shea was also with us.

When Lane was brought out, handcuffed and shackled

in an orange prison jumpsuit, his physical appearance was markedly different from the last time we'd seen him. He was now clean shaven, and he had not only lost the moustache and stubble, but had also dropped a significant amount of weight. He seemed exceptionally indolent, almost as if he had been drugged. His appearance was altogether much less intimidating.

"Look at him," I said to Kevin, not with pity, but with even more loathing than I had before I saw him that day. I knew it could only have been a ploy to gain sympathy from the court. Though I wasn't worried that the judge might fall for it, I was angry at the very notion that he might be trying to worm his way out of this. His cowardice and scheming ways became even clearer to us when we were later told that as he was driven to the courthouse for his bail hearing the previous month, he'd bragged to the other inmates riding with him that he was not going to jail because he was going to act crazy. Apparently, that same day he had also intentionally been overheard making threats to kill the judge. Lane's court-appointed attorney, Daniel Callahan, had been allowed up to $5,000 in state funds to hire a psychologist or psychiatrist to evaluate his client. A source close to us also confirmed that Lane had boasted to a fellow inmate at Bridgewater State Hospital, where he was undergoing psychological evaluations, that he was going to be famous, and to just wait and see.

This time, more subdued and pathetic, Lane only spoke to say "Not guilty" to ten criminal charges, including home invasion, assault with intent to murder and attempted rape of a child.

It's standard legal procedure for defendants to plead not guilty to the charges against them at this stage, but it was still disturbing and incredible to hear those words spoken by a man who had been apprehended after he walked into the bedroom where our daughter was sleeping and held a knife to her throat.

Shea was sitting between us, and I saw her shudder when she heard Lane's voice, the same southern drawl she had heard once before coming from behind a masked face in the darkness of her bedroom. I put an arm around her and held her close to me.

Lane's defense lawyer once again argued for his client to be granted bail, despite the new allegations against him in three other states. He imparted the trucker's work history and no prior criminal history as reasons for the grant of bail. He also rebuffed the allegations that Lane had ever behaved inappropriately with his stepdaughter.

It was noted that if Lane posted bail in Massachusetts, authorities in New Jersey would require that he be handed over to them. The state had a detainer on him, and they were anxious to bring him up on charges in the Monica Massaro murder.

Prosecutor Thomas O'Reilly, filling in for Kerry Ahern, stated emphatically that "the Commonwealth has no intention of relinquishing him to New Jersey until our case is over," and he described Lane as a "complete danger to the community."

Lowell Superior Court Judge Chernoff also listened to audiotapes and read documents related to the case before making his decision to order Lane held without bail at Bridgewater State Hospital pending a second dangerousness hearing, which took place the following week with the same result. Lane had waived his right to appear before the court that day, remaining at Bridgewater State Hospital instead. We did not attend that hearing either.

With these rulings, the prosecution was required to bring

the case against the accused trucker to trial within ninety
days or allow some amount of bail to be set.

Three months seemed like an eternity of time to us. We
had our lives to lead, and we tried the best we could to
go on as unusual, but any semblance of a normal family
life went right out the window. The legal system was not
something any of us were very familiar with, aside from
what we might see on television shows like *Law & Order*,
where everything is wrapped up inside an hour. The prosecutors kept us abreast of what was going on along the
way, and from the beginning it was explained to us that
the case might not ever even go to trial, that Lane's lawyers
would likely negotiate a deal. We were informed that any
offer brought to the table would be considered only if it
was in the best interest of the state and the victims, and
that before it was accepted we would be notified. I was still
fully expecting the case to go to trial, and I fully intended
to be there. We all did.

There were other matters that Adam Leroy Lane had to
answer to first. On October 30, a Hunterdon County, New
Jersey, grand jury indicted the trucker in absentia on eight
separate counts, including first-degree murder, felony murder, burglary and weapons charges related to the July 2007
homicide of Monica Massaro. If convicted of first-degree
murder, he was looking at up to sixty-three years in prison
without the possibility of parole. This was the best news
I had heard in a long time, and it made the waiting a lot
easier.

On November 3, Officer Robert Murphy, Detective
George Tyros and Sergeant Francis Goode were honored
for their efforts in the capture and arrest of Adam Leroy
Lane when they were named Police Officers of the Year by
the New England Police Benevolent Association. It was the

first awards ceremony of its kind, involving seventy-two departments in both Massachusetts and New Hampshire.

From the beginning, it seemed that our family had been getting a majority of the attention for bringing Adam Lane to justice, while the work done by the police seemed to be largely overlooked. Kevin and I may have been protecting our own, but they were doing their jobs. They didn't have the same intimate and personal connection to what was at stake, yet they put themselves at risk and fought to ensure that the person who tried to harm our daughter was held responsible. That's what makes their actions so special. I was happy they were getting the recognition they deserved.

A month later, the honor was returned to us when we were presented with Certificates of Appreciation for Heroism and Bravery by the town of Chelmsford. The event took place at the Town Hall and was attended by many local officials, including Chief Jim Murphy and his wife, Kris, two exceptional people whom we had actually known personally prior to this whole ordeal, as well as our friends the Smarts. The formality of this event was more than a little awkward for us, especially considering that we were so thankful to all of them.

"What they did that night is unbelievable," Chief Murphy told the attendees of the ceremony. "Sometimes people freeze, but they reacted. With any hesitation, things would have turned out differently. They refused to be victimized in their own home. By their heroic and valiant efforts, our Chelmsford family not only saved themselves from harm's way, but they also brought some closure and comfort to a family suffering in New Jersey."

The chief credited Kevin's assistance in subduing a deranged individual, who would likely still be at large if not for his intervention. This was something I could not have agreed with more, though Kevin has always down-played his actions that night. In his response to Chief Murphy's tribute, Kevin once again deflected any praise away from himself. "I feel she's the real hero here," he said of Shea. "She had the will to fight, making noise and kicking. A lot of people would have froze in that situation."

Chief Murphy concurred. "Amazingly, she managed to maintain her composure, while guiding the first responding officer to her home," he said.

"She's a tough nut," I added, smiling at Shea. "She reacted and we followed. It was a real team effort in that room."

Like her dad, Shea shunned the praise with a shrug of her shoulders and a smile.

The chief said that many people would always be thankful. "The suspect involved is where he should be, and in all likelihood, where he will be for the rest of his life; in jail, behind bars."

# Chapter 17

LAST STOP: PRISON

Shortly before the start of the trial, Adam Lane agreed to change his plea from not guilty to guilty on the stipulation that the rape charge against him be dropped.

After discussing his demand with Assistant District Attorney Kerry Ahern, we understood that dropping this charge would not affect the severity of the sentence he would receive. Granting the plea change on this condition would also mean that Shea would not have to get up on the stand and relive the events by testifying against the man who had attacked her. Furthermore, we were told that dropping the rape charge would accelerate Lane's extradition, speeding up the process by which the suspect would be transported back to New Jersey to face murder charges for the slaying of Monica Massaro, the only murder committed in Hunterdon County in 2007. In Pennsylvania, where the murder of Darlene Ewalt and the near-fatal attack on Patricia Brooks had also been attributed to Adam Leroy

Lane, there was another team of prosecutors waiting for the Massachusetts case to conclude so they could get the suspected killer in their court. It made sense in every way to have the rape charge dismissed, so it was a stipulation that Kevin and I agreed to grant.

At the time, I did not understand what might have been the real reason behind the request, but it was later explained to me in no uncertain terms that inmates who were convicted of rape, particularly child rape, often had a much more difficult time in prison. Lane seemed to understand that he was going to be incarcerated for the rest of his life, and he did not want to spend it under the constant threat of violence that this stigma provoked. Besides, it was the only chip Lane had left to bargain with.

He had told the prosecutors through his lawyer that he wanted to have the rape charge dropped, not because he hadn't intended to commit the act, but because he did not want his estranged wife to think that he'd been unfaithful. This was the same woman who had recently reported him to the local police and accused him of inappropriately touching one of his stepdaughters. Although no charges were ever filed against Lane regarding this allegation, he and his wife had separated for a period of time shortly after the incident was purported to have happened. They had reconciled just prior to the attacks that summer.

It bears mentioning that the fact that Lane had pulled the bedcovers down below Shea's waist could have been enough to prove intent to rape, though the case wasn't strong, which is why the deal was ultimately agreed to.

Finally, on December 11, 2007, Adam Leroy Lane was scheduled to appear in court to plead guilty to the remaining charges: home invasion while armed and masked; kidnapping; armed assault in a dwelling with intent to commit a felony (three counts); threat to commit a crime; assault and battery with a dangerous weapon; larceny of property over $250; resisting arrest; attempted murder; and possession of a dangerous weapon.

That morning, as we were preparing to go to the trial, I felt sick to my stomach. Ryan had classes, but long after Kevin and Shea were ready, they had to wait for me to get myself together. For a moment I didn't think I was going to make it. With the trial pending, I had been in a dark mood for several days; I had been waiting for this day with dread and anticipation for so long that I couldn't think straight now that it had arrived. I couldn't even decide what to wear. But somehow I managed to pull myself together in time, and off to the Lowell Superior Court we went.

Chief Jim Murphy, Deputy Chief Scott Ubele, Detective George Tyros and Sergeant Todd Ahern escorted us to the courthouse and acted as a buffer for us throughout what was expected to be a media melee. These officers had been through this long process with us from the beginning, and we appreciated it very much. During the entire court proceeding, as Shea and Kevin and I sat close together holding hands, these men remained right beside us, a cocoon of protection from this strange world of criminal justice, which, despite everything that we had been through in the last few months, we still knew very little about.

I had made a personal commitment to stand up in court and address the defendant. As I sat there waiting for the proceeding to begin, I started to get a little nervous, but I never wavered from my conviction. My feelings remained intensely fierce surrounding the events of July 30, and I would not be denied acknowledging them to the man who was responsible for the recent upheaval in my life and the lives of my family. And even though this proceeding involved only those crimes that Lane had committed in Massachusetts when he invaded our home and threatened Shea, I could not help but think about his victims who did not survive, and all the people whose lives he'd turned upside down, not only here in Massachusetts, but in New Jersey, Pennsylvania, and potentially elsewhere.

When it came time for me to make my statement, I got up from my chair but kept my eyes lowered, afraid I was going to miss the step off the raised platform where we were seated. As I started across the packed courtroom my legs were shaking and my heart was beating so hard I thought everyone in the courtroom would hear it. As I took the seat on the witness stand, I adjusted the microphone and cleared my throat, which was so dry I had to swallow several times before I could speak. I took a moment to regain my breath and find my voice. Before I uttered a word, I looked over at Adam Leroy Lane. I tried to catch his eyes, but they were cast off indifferently. He avoided looking me directly in the eye the entire time. He just sat there in a quiet and subdued manner, his orange jumpsuit differentiating him from the rest of the people in the room, the same way his violence and savage behavior differentiated him from law-abiding people everywhere. Even though he now barely resembled the monster who had terrified my daughter on that summer morning, the words I was about to speak were for him, and whether I had his full attention or not, I was determined that he was going to hear them.

"Thankfully, by the grace of God, our family has been spared the devastation that so many other families have been forced to endure because of your heinous actions," I began.

"We will, however, suffer lasting repercussions because of what you put us through. The sanctity of our home and our sense of safety have been taken away from us as a result of your savage assault on our family. The terrifying events of that early-morning attack will be emblazoned in our minds forever, with far-reaching effects we are just beginning to comprehend," I said, and warned him that his actions would be held accountable in more than just a court of law. "All the horrible and sadistic things you have done will ultimately be between you and God. May he be as merciless as you were when taking the lives of all those innocent people. While sadly, the suffering of their families continues, yours is just beginning."

Lane never once looked at me.

He also never showed the least bit of remorse. At one point, when the judge asked him if the prosecution's description of his actions on July 30 was fair and accurate, all he said was, "Pretty much."

Lowell Superior Court Judge Kenneth Fishman promptly sentenced him to twenty-five to thirty years in prison without the possibility of parole.

He deserved more, but the American justice system was not done with Adam Leroy Lane yet. He would be held in a maximum-security prison facility in Massachusetts until his extradition to New Jersey.

Judge Fishman also ordered that Lane submit a DNA sample to the state's database to help determine if he might be responsible for other unsolved murders or acts of violence. In New Jersey, officials provided a search warrant signed by a judge authorizing the procurement of Lane's DNA in the form of buccal swabs, hair samples and fingerprints and palm prints. Now that he had been convicted of a crime, Lane's DNA became the property of any law enforcement municipality where he was suspected of committing further criminal offenses.

At the conclusion of the court proceedings, we were encouraged by District Attorney Gerry Leone to make a formal statement to the press, something we had avoided until then. Now that the trial was over, however, Gerry felt that addressing the media right away would prevent them from swarming around our home later on.

I had been caught off guard by the press a couple of times before, so I had prepared a short statement already. I extended our gratitude to the various law enforcement agencies, our friends and families and especially the Chelmsford community. My comments did not get much airtime, but Kevin provided the media with an irresistible sound bite, which they would replay over and over again in the coming days and weeks ahead.

"I'm a pretty strong guy, but I felt like Hercules that night," he said when asked by reporters outside court how he had managed to subdue Lane, a much larger assailant. The media had been waiting for Kevin to make a comment for more than four months, so when he gave them the "Hercules" remark, they ate this up.

I, however, thought that Jack Harper, a reporter for local News Channel 5, got it right when he referred to Kevin as a "silent hero" through it all. Every man hopes that he will have the courage and strength in a similar situation to react like my husband did, and that's why Kevin will always be my hero, even though anyone who truly knows him would never consider him silent! His quick wit and humor have been making me smile and laugh for thirty years and counting.

Not long after Adam Leroy Lane was sentenced in Massachusetts, Dauphin County, Pennsylvania, District Attorney Edward M. Marsico Jr. publicly announced that DNA from murder victim Darlene Ewalt was, in fact, present on a knife that had been confiscated from the convicted truck driver. Marsico disclosed that Darlene's DNA had been sent to the New Jersey State Police Lab early on after Lane was first arrested.

"State police recognized the similarities in West Hanover and other jurisdictions," he said. "It's great police work."

Todd Ewalt, whom police had initially considered a person of interest in the homicide, was happy that the police had found evidence linking a suspect to his wife's death. "I'm just glad they can get this resolved," he said. "But it's still not going to bring her back."

Todd said that he held no grudges against the police. "[Being considered a suspect] was not a big concern, whether people believed me or not," he commented. "My biggest concern was the loss of my wife. I'm glad they have this guy in custody, so nobody else has to deal with it."

# Chapter 18

## CUSTODY BATTLE

Christmas has always been a special time of the year for me and my family, but as the 2007 holiday season approached, some of the rituals that had typically defined the season lost their meaning. A lot of the superficial aspects of the holidays were stripped away, for the better. Long before December 25, we all felt that we had already received our presents, and just spending that time together was the only thing we could have asked for.

With most life-changing events, I believe that the ability to see the larger picture is relative to the healing process. Coming to grips with the enormity of the past events was challenging for us. Undeniably, the depth of the pain that we were exposed to—our own as well as that of the families and friends of Lane's other victims—changed us.

Although we were all trying to look ahead, it was hard for me to just move on simply because so much was still unsettled with the other families, known and unknown.

But it was right around the same time that we received several holiday cards that really opened my eyes to just how fortunate we were. One was from Darlene Ewalt's best friends, who extended to us heartfelt expressions of appreciation and gratitude. Similar sentiments came from the Massaro family to ours, and the words from both of these families gave light to my spirit during a very dark time. I realized that we would all be forever bound by this tragedy and heartbreak, which none of us would ever be able to forget. I felt that the connection between our families had made us all stronger, and I could only hope that with time we would all find peace in our hearts once again and begin healing.

Just prior to the New Year, as we were getting ready to put 2007 behind us and welcome a brighter, more hopeful 2008, an article published in the *Lowell Sun* named our family among the "25 Most Fascinating People in the Greater Lowell Area." Once again, our faces were splashed on the front page of the newspaper, dredging up all the associated feelings of anxiety and survivor guilt.

The article prompted Gerry Leone, the Middlesex district attorney in Massachusetts, to contact us. He took the time to send a letter congratulating us for the distinction that the *Lowell Sun* had bestowed upon us, and he further noted how pleased he was that our family did not meet with the kind of tragedy that he so often encountered. He also mentioned that if he could ever be of any help, we could simply give him a call. He promised to keep a close eye on Lane's extradition and do everything he could on his end to try to expedite the process. I just thought he was trying to be supportive by keeping us involved. I admit I was naive, figuring Lane would be on his way to New Jersey soon since he apparently was not there yet.

Escaping Lane entirely proved to be a challenge for my family as well. Lane may have been confined to a prison cell, but in many ways he never seemed far enough away. On at least one occasion, he was way too close for comfort.

How terribly ironic it was that shortly after Shea got back to school after the holidays, she ended up visiting the very facility where her attacker was being housed by the state. Her junior sociology class at Chelmsford High School was taking its annual field trip to the Massachusetts Correctional Institute in Shirley (MCI-Shirley), one of the prisons within the Massachusetts Correctional System, just forty miles south of Chelmsford. It was something the class did every winter. All of the sociology students knew about the outing at the start of the school year, and most, if not all of them, were very excited about it. The academic grapevine at the school has consistently ranked it as the best field trip available. Shea, understandably, was not as anxious as her other classmates, but she went along, having little thought or concern about crossing paths with Adam Lane again. She just didn't think about that possibility, and quite frankly neither did I. We didn't know where Adam Lane was being held, but we didn't think that the school would knowingly send her to the same place. The reality was that the school didn't know for sure, either. There was a lot of secrecy as to Lane's exact location, so the possibility did exist that he might be incarcerated in the very same institution that the class would be visiting. In fact, just as a precaution, Shea's sociology teacher advised her beforehand that it would be best if she did not identify herself as Lane's attack victim to anyone at the prison. There was an outside chance that an inmate would be acquainted with Lane, so even such an indirect connection was best to be avoided. MCI-Shirley was a medium- and minimum-level security facility, but Souza-Baranowski Correctional Center, located on the same property, was a maximum-security prison.

Maybe we were all just in denial, disbelieving that any of us, particularly Shea, would have another surprise encounter with Adam Leroy Lane. The next time we anticipated seeing him was in court, with the trucker in shackles and under heavy guard.

The school program was designed to show teenagers what it was really like inside the walls of a state penitentiary while at the same time giving them the opportunity to speak with actual prisoners who participate in the program. The inmates were carefully screened, and the interviews all took place in a highly supervised and controlled environment. The participants were chosen because they best represented the lesson that school is trying to get across to the teens, namely, that otherwise good people can make life-changing, sometimes irreparable mistakes early in life, and that oftentimes these mistakes are made in an instant, without malice or forethought. The students were encouraged to ask questions to obtain a clearer understanding of how their own decisions and judgments can ultimately affect their entire lives.

During this particular trip to the prison facility in Shirley, one of the inmates was speaking to the class and made a reference to a home invasion that had occurred that past summer. The convict knew that the group was from Chelmsford, where the crime occurred, and he revealed that Lane was around the corner in the maximum-security wing. What he did not know was that Shea had been the victim of that attack. Shea never let on who she was, just as she had discussed with her teacher. Her classmates kept quiet as well.

When she told me about this later, I was stunned. I was also angry with the school for putting her in harm's way, but I was more relieved that she was okay. What was even more amazing to me was that Shea seemed unfazed by it, at least outwardly. The extent of any internal or psychological harm this may have had on her was still unknown to us.

Still, although Shea's strength and courage made me proud, at the same time I felt terrible that she had to go through a trauma of this magnitude at such a tender age. It made me want to cry every time I thought about it. It was a harsh realization that no matter how hard we tried, we could not protect her from everything all the time. But just knowing that she was strong enough to survive on her own if she had to was of great comfort.

Ultimately, it seemed that Shea's experience at the prison benefited her immensely and proved to be a pivotal step in her healing process. For her to see the conditions under which Lane had been relegated to live revealed a human aspect of her attacker that provided an invaluable life lesson. In the months that followed, we were kept in the loop regarding Lane's confinement status. We were provided with several interesting facts, and it was gratifying on some level to know that he was not having a good time of it in prison.

Privacy was one of the freedoms Lane no longer enjoyed. All of his incoming and outgoing mail was read. Prison officials would listen in on the conversations he had on the phone. When it was deemed necessary by the court, they would take his hair, blood, anything they wanted. The men Lane shared cell space with were just as apt to report anything they heard him say.

At some point, we were told that Lane had been beaten

rather severely by fellow inmates and had to be moved to another facility for his own safety. Why he was attacked was not known for certain, but it was my understanding that the other convicts were annoyed by Lane's general behavior and nasty attitude. A friend of ours, Kevin Whippen, head of intelligence at the prison where Lane was held, informed us that the other prisoners had likely attacked Lane because of his attempted assault on Shea. It didn't matter to them whether Lane's intent had been sexual assault, battery or murder, nor did it matter that he had not succeeded in harming her. The fact that he was accused of victimizing a fifteen-year-old girl was reason enough. Criminals have their own code of ethics, and this was how they policed themselves. Lane became a target even though he kept to himself and didn't communicate with any of the inmates, usually a given with any new prisoner. He was not from anywhere near New England, so the other cons were even less likely to speak to him. And for what they had to say to him that day, they used their fists and feet to get their message across.

Whippen had not had much direct contact with Lane, but from this incident and what he had been told by the other guards, it seemed that the North Carolina truck driver did not fit the mold correctional officers were used to seeing when it came to violent criminal offenders. Given how respectful and quiet Lane acted overall, to look at him and listen to him speak, they would never have suspected the convicted murderer of such acts. Whippen confided to me that Lane seemed to be a typical, polite and mild-mannered southern truck driver, just as Detective-Sergeant Geoffrey Noble, of the New Jersey State Police, had observed when he interviewed Lane just before the suspect confessed to the murder of Monica Massaro. Whippen also told me that Lane did not display any of the telltale characteristics, such as outward aggressiveness, exhibited by the other sociopathic killers he had encountered through his years on the job.

We had been told at that time that Lane could be transferred to New Jersey to stand trial sometime in February, but that was still uncertain. Again, with my ignorance of the criminal justice system showing, I placed a call to the Massachusetts governor's office, inquiring about the delay. Patrick Marinaro, a special assistant for Governor Deval Patrick's legal counsel, told me that no paperwork had been received yet at their office to initiate the extradition. I immediately called District Attorney Gerry Leone, taking him up on his previous offer of assistance. He was kind enough to look into the matter, and he also asked Assistant District Attorney Kerry Ahern to do the same. After a little digging on their part, it was discovered that the normal extradition process was not being followed. Apparently, the extradition was being conducted through the Interstate Agreement on Detainers, which is handled directly through the Massachusetts Department of Correction and the New Jersey Department of Correctional Facilities. This was the reason there had been no paperwork sent to the governor's office.

After hearing this, my concerns were somewhat minimized, and I felt more confident that things were at least moving along in the right direction, albeit laboriously. It seemed rather unfortunate now that we had agreed to drop the attempted rape charge against Lane, since it had been done, in part, with the understanding that it would result in a quicker extradition. I couldn't imagine it being any slower.

The Massaros were waiting to see justice done on behalf of their daughter, and I felt awful that Lane's incarceration

Ewalt family photo circa 1990s. (*Left to right*: Nicole, Darlene, Todd, Nick and Todd's brother Troy Ewalt.)
TODD EWALT AND NICOLE POGASIC

*Above:* Todd and Darlene Ewalt on their Harley-Davidson, where they enjoyed spending time together.
TODD EWALT AND NICOLE POGASIC

*Left:* A happy moment in the exuberant life of Darlene Ewalt.
TODD EWALT AND NICOLE POGASIC

Monica Massaro, looking radiant as she posed on the arm of her parents' sofa at a family gathering.

FAY MASSARO

Monica Massaro's beautiful home, taped off with yellow crime scene tape after the horrific murder inside. This traumatized the community of Bloomsbury, New Jersey, and rocked the peaceful borough in which Monica had always felt so safe.

NEW JERSEY STATE POLICE

A poignant photo of Monica and
her mother, Fay, in her parents'
home.
FAY MASSARO

Monica sharing a special moment with her dad, Frank, some years back.
Monica's parents, Fay and Frank, were the light of her life and she theirs.
FAY MASSARO

Items confiscated from Adam Leroy Lane after his July 30, 2007, invasion of our home.

CHELMSFORD POLICE DEPARTMENT

*Above Right:* The knives taken from Adam Leory Lane immediately following his assault on Shea.

CHELMSFORD POLICE DEPARTMENT

*Bottom Left:* One of the two masks confiscated from Adam Leroy Lane.

CHELMSFORD POLICE DEPARTMENT

*Above:* Adam Leroy Lane being led into Lowell District Court by Chelmsford Police Officer Steven Doole for his arraignment on Tuesday, July 31, 2007.

SUN PHOTOS, JON HILL

*Left:* Adam Leroy Lane at a dangerousness hearing on August 6, where he was ordered held without bail.

SUN PHOTOS, JON HILL

In court on December 12 for the Guilty verdict. (*Left to right*: me, Shea, Kevin and Chelmsford Police Chief James Murphy).

Following the December 12 verdict, Kevin made his first statement to the media explaining how he subdued Lane the night of the home invasion, saying he'd "felt like Hercules that night". (*Left to right*: Shea, Kevin, District Attorney Gerry Leone and me with my hand on Kevin's shoulder.)

Kevin, me and Shea in our family room during an interview with Dan Phelps from the *Lowell Sun*, explaining how lucky we felt to be alive.
SUN PHOTOS, JON HILL

Kevin during the same interview, giving his view on the recent events.
SUN PHOTOS, JON HILL

Our family with Boston Red Sox pitcher Jonathan Papelbon at the opening Yankees game at Fenway Park on April 11, 2008. (*Left to right*: Kevin, Shea, Jonathan, Ryan and me.)

BRITA MENG OUTZEN

Shea, me and Kevin at the Advanced Homicide Investigation Conference at Princeton University in June 2008 with the Chelmsford police detectives and New Jersey police officers involved with the Monica Massaro murder investigation. (*Left to right*: Detective Justin Blackwell, Detective-Sergeant Geoffrey Noble, Detective Nicolas Oriolo, Shea, Me, Detective George Tyros, Kevin, Detective-Sergeant Todd Ahern, Detective-Sergeant James Kiernan and Sergeant Kevin Burd.)

NEW JERSEY STATE POLICE

in Massachusetts was holding this up for them. Some in law enforcement indicated to us that since Lane was behind bars and held no immediate threat to the public, the other cases against him were not high priority.

I had been wishing I could have done something to speed things up, so when Shea and I were asked to stop by the Chelmsford Police Department to provide DNA samples, I went enthusiastically. The purpose was to rule out our DNA from those of other possible victims who may have been assaulted with the same weapons used by Lane. Since both Shea and I had been cut during the attack, it was likely that the DNA from our blood would be found on one of the seized knives. Kevin accompanied us to the police station to meet Detective George Tyros and two New Jersey state police officers. The procedure only took a couple of minutes. The officers took swabs from the insides of both of our cheeks. The samples were placed in separate plastic bags, labeled and sealed.

While we were there, I couldn't help asking them for an update as to when Lane would officially be transported to New Jersey to face the charges pending against him there. The out-of-state officers were very friendly and wanted to be helpful, but there was no new information available.

# Chapter 19

## LOST INNOCENCE

Adam Leroy Lane's conviction in a Massachusetts court-room may have ended our personal role with the criminal justice system and the man who attacked our daughter, but six months after the attack, the lingering effects it had on our family were not difficult to spot.

For me, the events of July 30, 2007, had inevitably led to my questioning matters of faith and spirit. On numerous occasions I stepped back and wondered if we had merely been a lucky family who had survived a brush with death, or if someone had been watching over us. So many things had worked in our favor as the events unfolded that night; it was terrifying and overwhelming to think that if just one small element in the sequence had been different, the consequences could have been tragic. Ever since the attack happened, when I lay awake in bed late at night, my mother-in-law is among those that I thank. As unusual as it may seem, I often thought about her during the most difficult periods of my life.

Kevin's mother, Mary Lou McDonough, was an incredible woman who had passed away in the spring of 2003 after a long struggle with breast cancer, but during her time on earth, she had touched many lives, including mine, in infinite ways. She had been a mother and a role model to me since I was seventeen years old. She raised nine children and spent every waking hour of every day taking care of her extended family. Never, in all the time I knew her, did I ever hear her utter a negative word about anyone. "If you can't say anything nice, don't say anything at all" was her personal credo. She went to church every day and lived her life with a quiet strength and grace that everyone who knew her couldn't help but be inspired by. When you look at pictures of her, there seems to be an aura of light around her that simply illuminates her being. When she passed away, we were all brokenhearted. It took a long time to pick up the pieces, but she left behind a legacy for all of us to aspire to. I truly believe that she was watching over us that night, along with Monica and Darlene, leading the way for us, giving us strength and whispering in my ear as well as Kevin's to get out of bed and check on Shea together. But never before, or since, have I felt my mother-in-law's presence more profoundly than the night that Shea gave us a real scare of another kind.

It happened the week of school vacation, in February 2008, when all those feelings of confusion and anxiety as a result of the attack reared their ugly heads. After going to a party where she drank alcohol, far more than she could tolerate, sixteen-year-old Shea came home displaying erratic and manic behavior. She even made an offhand comment to her boyfriend, Adam, threatening suicide. It was terrifying and heartbreaking for Kevin and me to witness, and I could only imagine the hell that she was going through, the level of despair and hopelessness that she must have reached.

Whether her behavior was just teenage rebellion or a cry for help, Kevin and I were deeply concerned about our daughter's mental health. As the affects of the alcohol wore off, so did any thoughts and feelings of harming herself, but it ended up being a long, emotionally draining night for us all. Shea's continual assurances that she was "fine" played on my conscience. I couldn't sleep, and I did not want to leave her side. I stayed up all night with her, watching her just to be sure she was okay. I was riddled with guilt, blaming myself for not seeing this coming and for not being better prepared to deal with it. She was so precious; I worried that maybe I hadn't made that clear enough to her, because in my mind I thought that if she knew how much she meant to all of us, she would never have considered harming herself.

Because of this experience with Shea, I was able to more clearly understand and identify with the decisions my own mother had made when I was about Shea's age, and she kept me distanced from the reality of my father's cancer. The summer my father died, she sent me off to camp in New Hampshire as a way to protect me from the heartbreak that was going on at home. I wrote letters almost every day to my father, who would have my mother read them to him in the hospital on the days when he was lucid and the many pain medications he was taking weren't dulling his consciousness. For too many years I resented the fact that my mother had kept me from my father in his dying days, but I finally came to understand that she was just trying to protect her child. It wasn't until much later that I also realized how strong my mom had been. She was a rock, keeping the family together during those difficult years leading up to my father's death. These revelations felt like a delayed loss of innocence for me, and I remember crying, though not mourning the purity of youth but for not fully appreciating all that my mother tried to do for me.

In recent years my mother and I forged a new friendship, a real mother-daughter bond. I have a new appreciation for how frightening it must have been for her, raising a teenage daughter while trying to come to grips with her own suffocating grief. I wish my maturity level back then had been such that I could have provided more support to her instead of posing a constant challenge. I had grown to love my mother more over the past decade than ever before; yet sadly, she now suffers from dementia and Alzheimer's disease. My mom is essentially gone, behind a haze of confusion, yet every time I visit with her I am reminded of what a beautiful soul sits before me. My mother was there during the birth of my children, and she was there through every critical and monumental juncture in my life. I'm glad that she never had to know about the masked killer who invaded our home, or the hell that her granddaughter went through.

The morning following Shea's binge drinking and suicidal threats, I contacted her therapist and made arrangements for her to be seen as soon as possible. Shea did not think it was necessary, and she begrudged my actions as interfering and compromising her sense of independence. However, the loss of innocence that my daughter was experiencing at that time may not have been something she recognized as I did, so all I could hope was that she would eventually appreciate that I had always had only her best interests in mind.

That same day, after I made the appointment, Shea came into the kitchen, where Kevin and I were talking. The television was on in the living room and *Oprah* was just starting. We could hear it from where we were, and the topic—teen suicide—instantly caught all of our attention. When the guests were introduced, I heard Shea gasp. The teenagers had tried to kill themselves in horrific manners, and although they had all miraculously survived the attempts, they had been badly injured as a result. Some of them had been horribly maimed, losing limbs or other parts of their bodies. One young girl laid herself down across a set of railroad tracks in front of an oncoming train, which struck her and severed her legs at the hip. Another young man used a shotgun to try to kill himself. The blast blew half of his face off. It was heartbreaking to watch, yet none of us could look away. Despite everything these young people had gone through and the devastating results of their actions, they were all happy to be alive and wanted to remain on earth with their families and friends. It was utterly remarkable to hear these teens communicate such a profound sense of relief that they had survived, and share an even deeper appreciation for the life they had yet to live.

Their stories were so compelling that after the show ended, Shea, Kevin and I just sat in silence for a couple of moments, looking at one another in disbelief. I could practically see my mother-in-law sitting on the sectional next to us as we were transfixed with the faces and the experiences of these young people on the television. There were valuable lessons to be gained from these tragic experiences, and no one would have known that more than Mary Lou McDonough. I won't say that she turned the channel to the *Oprah* show that day, but she was there with us. Somehow that episode aired at the most critical time for Shea, providing her with a greater understanding of how blessed we were to receive the gift of life and the importance that it never be taken for granted.

I knew that somewhere my mother-in-law was watching over us. Mary Lou McDonough, our guiding light.

Perhaps one decision I made where I should have sought her counsel, or at least exercised better judgment, was when our family granted an interview request by *People* magazine. I had mixed emotions about it from the beginning. The article, which appeared in the March 3, 2008, issue, was titled "How They Caught a Killer." There was nothing overtly wrong with what was written; in fact, I thought it was accurate and tasteful. But the timing could have been better. Shea's meltdown came just a couple of weeks after we granted the interview.

It was the first interview we did with a national media outlet, after turning down all others before out of respect for the families of Lane's victims. In hindsight, I realized we should have held off on the *People* interview as well. But as the end of January rolled around, I mistakenly thought that we were ready to talk about what we'd gone through as a family. Diane Herbst, a journalist with *People* who had been closely following the cases involving Adam Leroy Lane, had shown an eagerness to tell the story from our family's perspective. It was after much urging that we finally decided to sit down with her and revisit what happened on July 30, 2007. She understood our conviction concerning the sensitivity of the content and how her article might potentially affect the families of the other victims. In no way did we want the publication of our story to be the cause of further suffering for anyone.

I remember it was Saturday afternoon in late January when Diane arrived at our home. I felt I already knew her because we had spoken on the phone so many times prior to her visit. She made the four-hour drive from her home in New Jersey, along with her two dogs. They were both beautiful and well-behaved animals, and we welcomed them to share the enclosed backyard space with our dog. Bosco was a gracious host, and the three dogs got along well. This enabled Diane to relax while she conducted her interview. She was warm and personable, and I honestly felt like we were talking to an old family friend.

It felt somewhat redundant to us, especially for Kevin, taking Diane through the sequence of events that night, but it was actually the first time that we'd explained what had happened to anyone outside of law enforcement or close friends and family.

The interview lasted nearly four hours, during which time Diane was also able to meet both Detective George Tyros and Chief Jim Murphy. They were both kind enough to come by our house and answer her questions about the investigation and address the overall safety of our town. We were glad they came as well. Many of Diane's questions were out of our realm of expertise, and we felt more comfortable having representatives of the Chelmsford Police Department there to contribute their views. The input they contributed, along with the answers we provided, gave her a better understanding of how this home invasion affected not only us, but the entire community.

Our son, Ryan, was in the room the entire time during these discussions. Although he hadn't been at home that night, and so did not have a role in the confrontation with Adam Lane, he, too, had been affected by what had happened on July 30 every bit as much as the rest of us. I believe that listening to us replay the sequence of the events that evening for Diane really brought home the reality of the attack for him. Later that evening, long after Diane had left, Ryan was out with friends when he called home just to tell his father and me how much we meant to him and that we were truly his heroes. The emotional tone in his voice made it clear to me just how many lives had been indirectly affected by the criminal actions of Adam Lane.

The following morning, an entourage from *People* magazine descended upon our home to take pictures. I just thought they would be sending a guy with a camera, and maybe a lighting person—I hadn't been expecting a full-scale photo shoot. They brought in a makeup artist and a hairstylist and turned our house into an instant movie studio. We were informed that the first thing we needed to do was pick out appropriate clothes to wear, which they specified meant no black, white or stripes or anything with trademark logos.

Since black and white were essentially the staples of my wardrobe, I had to scramble to find something to wear. We had also been instructed to try to select clothing that was all in the same color family, so that our appearance would photograph complementary to each other. The makeup artist ultimately made the final wardrobe selection, and once that was done, we had our hair styled and then we sat in the makeup chair. All of this took about two hours. By then the photographer and assistant photographer had scouted out the best areas to photograph us and set up their photography equipment and artificial lighting, even though it was the middle of the day.

When everything was ready, the photographer, Grant

Delin, took what seemed like hundreds of pictures of Shea, Kevin and me on the sectional alone. The sofa was right next to the back door, where the intruder had entered. He then took Shea upstairs, where he took several pictures of her in her bedroom. Finally, he had us all go outside and stand at the corner of the house, directly in front of the window of the guest bedroom where the attack had taken place.

It was a very cold, windy and snowy day, and the conditions were more uncomfortable than any of us wanted to let on. The final shot wasn't snapped until around 4:30 that afternoon. It was almost dark, and the temperature had dropped to near freezing by the time they finished. It took them a while longer to get everything packed up, and it was after 6:00 p.m. when the last person left. They were all extremely friendly and very professional, but it was a very long and tiring weekend.

In the days following, I questioned whether we had done the right thing. I was very apprehensive about what the general reaction to the interview might be and how the article would be perceived by others. The last thing I wanted was to have the story depicted in a way that would offend someone or be misconstrued by the public. We regarded ourselves as a very fortunate family, not as heroes. The actions taken that night were not the result of any conscious effort to act "heroically." Anything could have happened in that situation. The facts that came to light about Lane afterward were obviously not something that had any consequence on the actions that Kevin or any of us took that night. We were not trying to capture a serial killer. Truth be told, at the moment, all I thought we were trying to do was prevent a schoolboy who was obsessed with our daughter from throwing his life away.

Initially, we had been informed that the article would appear in *People* on February 8, but the date came and went and our story did not appear. I was more relieved than disappointed, though I was hoping that the article would help people understand the magnitude of our blessings and show them that what we lived through allowed us to tell a story of faith and fortitude. There are many inspiring stories of survival and perseverance in the world, though I realized that what was most appealing for many people was the "good versus evil" confrontation in our story: a deranged trucker whose evil intent was defeated by the ultimate power of a family's love.

When the piece did not appear the following week, I began to think that perhaps the editor had decided that the story was not as newsworthy as they had originally thought. Or perhaps they were just waiting for a more appropriate time, such as after Lane was transported to New Jersey.

The *People* issue finally hit the stands the first week of March, and I braced myself emotionally, anticipating some negative feedback. My main concern was still the feelings of the families of Lane's other victims. I anticipated that Monica Massaro and Darlene Ewalt would be mentioned in the article, along with Patricia Brooks, but I was surprised to see photographs of them also included. When I opened a copy of the issue we received and saw the images of the victims, I immediately wondered how the families felt, even if they did not say anything to us. That worry was somewhat allayed by all the positive feedback we received from day one. The overall response to the article was amazingly supportive of us. I was struck by the resounding sentiment of appreciation expressed by so many. The public reached out to us again, the calls and cards coming from all around the country this time. I was particularly struck by one resident of Colorado Springs who felt compelled to call us after reading the *People* story. In the message he left, he mentioned that he had experienced a similar trauma in his life and wanted to call to extend his congratulations and blessings to us, as well as to communicate his own story, proving that the simple and most basic act of sharing can be cathartic in nature and facilitate healing.

# Chapter 20

## SPRING FORWARD

Eight months later, I still got up every morning and functioned just as I had before the attack. However, impercep-
tibly though it may have been, I had changed. Although
the person who stared back at me in the mirror may have
looked the same, I knew I was no longer that person I had
been before July 30, 2007. This event had come to rede-
fine me as well as Shea and the rest of my family, because
we now deeply understood how incredibly fragile life is.
Every time one of the children left the house, a moment
or two of panic washed over me, and I worried that maybe
it could be the last time I'd ever see them. It was worse
when they weren't home and I heard sirens in the distance.
Sometimes I would imagine the sound of an ambulance
racing toward wherever they were, and I would practically
resign myself to the fact that fate has just caught up with us.
At those times, I'd have to force myself to relax and take a

deep breath. If that didn't work, I'd call their cell phones to make sure they were all right.

A rational fear of the unknown is one thing, but to become obsessed is quite another. Certainly, we parents all have concerns about our children's safety, but I could no longer convince myself that I was overreacting. Bad things had happened once; why couldn't they happen again? I would imagine that the heartache my family had been spared that night might be looming somewhere just ahead of us. Having escaped that fate once before, I couldn't help but feel that it was closing in behind us every moment, unseen, but expected.

---

Late at night I found myself tucking the bedroom curtain behind the corner of the windowsill to provide an unobstructed view of the backyard, feeling that somehow if there was another monster lurking outside, this time I would see it coming. It was one of many rituals I developed in the wake of the attack that I just couldn't seem to break. I wondered to myself just how long I would continue. Sometimes logical thought eluded me when bedtime approached, but nevertheless, this simple routine afforded me not only an added sense of security, but a sense of control.

At the same time, I would ask for a little help by going through a lengthy prayer, asking God to continue to bless my family, just as he had on that hot July night. Most every night I whispered these very personal words with the hope that they would be heard, and each day I knew that they had been. However, I was fearful of falling asleep without reciting this spell in its entirety, believing our luck would run out if I neglected to do so. In a not-too-distant part of my mind, I recognized the absolute absurdity of my fears and superstitions, and I sometimes shook my head in disbelief at my actions. Yet I still continued doing these things.

Along with these unseen fears lurking around every corner, there continued to be a generous outpouring of support from unexpected places and people.

Perhaps the most unlikely of all was a contact we received that March from Boston Red Sox pitcher Jonathan Papelbon and his wife, Ashley. Apparently, the couple had stumbled upon the *People* article and felt compelled to invite our family to be Papelbon's guests at a game during the team's first home stand of the season, a Friday night series opener against the New York Yankees. Because of the relative proximity of Chelmsford to Boston, it must have been assumed that we were Red Sox fans. Their assumption was correct!

The past several months had weighed heavily on all of us, and the invitation created a much-needed diversion. We were all bubbling over with anticipation at the prospect of meeting the Boston closer and the opportunity to watch batting practice prior to the game. It was an experience of a lifetime we could not pass up. I don't know who was more excited, the kids or Kevin and I.

Later, after speaking with Claire Durant, one of the Fenway Ambassadors, we were asked if we would be comfortable appearing on camera as part of the pregame show and being introduced to the sellout crowd of thirty-eight thousand fans in attendance that day. Papelbon's publicity people thought it would help promote the pitcher's image if we were recognized as guests of his and the Red Sox organization. Although we agreed to it, I was relieved that it ultimately did not happen for some reason or other. Still, as the opening series between the two rival clubs approached, I was a little nervous, not knowing what to expect once we got to Fenway Park.

Although we were more than appreciative for having been extended such a thoughtful invitation, it also made Kevin and me feel somewhat uncomfortable. We were concerned that this honor might have made us look like opportunists who were trying to take advantage of our fleeting celebrity status. But we were all such big fans of the Red Sox, who were defending World Series champions, we couldn't pass up the opportunity. And did I mention that they were playing the Yankees?

On April 11, 2008, we went to the game. We met Ann, another Fenway Ambassador, at Gate D on Yawkey Way at 4:00 p.m. She greeted us with four Red Sox home jerseys bearing Jonathan Papelbon's number, 58. They were presented to us as keepsakes of the evening's festivities. We then followed Ann onto the playing field, where we were permitted to watch the Red Sox batting practice close up. It was absolutely amazing to see how big the players were, how much bigger the field looked from this perspective.

Moments after setting foot onto the field, we were graciously welcomed by Jonathan Papelbon himself. He stayed with us for a while, chatting; then he signed all of our jerseys. He was also kind enough to have a professional photo taken with our family. His warm and welcoming demeanor is something we will never forget.

Equally satisfying for Kevin and me, as well as Ryan, was observing the complete awe and joy on Shea's face when she was acknowledged by her favorite player, Jacoby Ellsbury. He went out of his way to make her night special by having a picture taken with her and later giving her a personally autographed baseball. We were also provided with another baseball signed by Dustin Pedroia, who would later that year be named the American League Most Valuable Player for 2008. That ball came our way via Steve Murphy, a Boston Red Sox attendant who also happened to be the brother of Chelmsford Police Chief Jim Murphy. Steve stopped by and introduced himself to us shortly after we arrived at the park and helped make our evening complete.

The whole experience was thrilling (despite the Red Sox loss), and we deeply appreciated everything the Red Sox organization did for us. The efforts of these players, heroes to millions of people including ourselves, went a long way to help a young girl heal from the trauma of a frightening brush with death. To once again see the glint of happiness return to Shea's eyes and watch her experience genuine joy was a source of tremendous satisfaction for her father and me. We were particularly thankful to Jonathan and Ashley Papelbon, who may never fully comprehend the healing power of their very moving gesture.

---

With the weather starting to warm up at the end of April, and the excitement of the visit to Fenway Park fading—but not forgotten—our attention refocused on Adam Leroy Lane.

When a letter from the New Jersey State Police arrived, I hoped that it was notification that Lane's extradition to the state had finally been approved and that he was on his way there already. Instead, we were informed that we had been chosen as "Guests of Honor" at the annual banquet that would conclude the Advanced Homicide

Investigation Conference being held at Princeton University in late June.

Detectives George Tyros and Todd Ahern told us that they would be attending the weeklong series of workshops and would be present at the closing banquet. Chief Murphy was also planning on attending the ceremony, so we were comfortable with the idea right from the start.

Besides being humbled by the invitation and by being considered an integral part of the capture of this multiple murderer, it was a unique opportunity to meet and converse with various people involved in the continuing Adam Lane investigation. There was still so much that was unknown, and I could only hope that within the next few months some additional information would be revealed. Along with the potential for an update on the legal progression of Lane's pending cases, I was very much looking forward to trying to arrange a get-together with Fay and Frank Massaro at some point during our visit to New Jersey. I wanted to express to them in person our heartfelt concern and commitment to the prosecution of their daughter's killer. Kevin and I had always felt strongly about meeting two of the people who are sitting where we so easily could have been ourselves: mourning a beloved daughter.

The reality that we had come so close to losing Shea was something I did not take for granted. In the time since, I have witnessed her blossoming into a young woman before my eyes. Certainly Shea had her own obstacles to overcome since the terror of the previous summer, but I got a strong sense that she was moving forward in a positive direction with more and more confidence each day. At various times I would catch a glimpse of her behaving in a way that seemed mature beyond her years, but then in the next instant the frivolity of the teenage experience would return, and she would act accordingly.

---

Just as quickly as winter had turned to spring, spring was moving on toward summer, and Adam Leroy Lane was still sitting in a Massachusetts correctional institute awaiting extradition to New Jersey, now almost a year since he murdered Monica Massaro.

After another discussion with Detective-Sergeant Geoffrey Noble, of the New Jersey State Police, who sympathized with my feelings, it became apparent that I wasn't the only one feeling irritation in this matter. My impression was that law enforcement harbored similar frustrations toward the tedious bureaucracy within the justice system. Although it was good to know that we were in agreement on this issue, it did not offer any resolution to the problem.

Still, with the days warming and the flowers and trees in full bloom, it was impossible not to find joy in the changing of the season. This kind of weather, after what seemed like an eternity of cold and rainy weather, naturally elevated the spirit. At the same time, it was difficult for me not to think about Monica Massaro and Darlene Ewalt and how unexpectedly life can be cut short. My heart was heavy, knowing that something so precious had been taken from their families. These were the moments of such intense clarity, when I felt the deepest appreciation for all that I have been blessed with, yet the extremes of my mental state could be frightening, and I wondered if something was wrong with me.

Mother's Day provided me with an ideal opportunity for reflection. We spent that Sunday together as a family, and it was then that I realized how my attitudes and emotions regarding Adam Leroy Lane and the justice system were being reflected in my children. I had been harboring extremely negative and destructive feelings about everything related to the July 30 attack, and my moods and words seemed only to have darkened the moods of everyone around me. With this understanding, I vowed to be outwardly more positive and constructive in my judgments, both for my family's benefit and my own.

Adopting such an attitude change couldn't have come at a better time. The gains we were all making individually were not an illusion, but the amount of progress was deceptive. We were struggling as a family. It seemed that every step forward was followed by another backward. We were really getting nowhere.

School had been more of a challenge that year than we had anticipated, for both of our children. Ryan and Shea had always been good students, but now both were failing academically. This was a situation that none of us had ever found ourselves in before, and so we thought they'd be able to get themselves back on track. However, we were mistaken—or in denial.

Shea's academic year had been a wash. She struggled with issues involving her concentration and focus, as well as an inability to sleep at night. To alleviate some of the strain, it was arranged with her school to adjust her course load and reduce her schedule. Following that simple change, I noticed a marked difference in her personality and behavior. Her anxiety diminished, and from all outward appearances she seemed to be happier overall.

But things were difficult even with the reduced schedule during the second half of the year. Being a teenager is difficult enough without adding to that the anxious feeling that everyone was staring and whispering behind your back. At home, Shea was around her family, people who understood what she had gone through; in high school, it was all about fitting in, and I could only imagine how Shea felt every day when she walked through those front doors and was instantly reminded that she was not like everyone else. Who could be surprised that her experience had left her with diminished motivation and a lack of commitment to academic excellence, which she once valued so highly?

The last few weeks of the semester would be pivotal in salvaging what was left of her junior year, perhaps the most critical juncture for any student with college aspirations. It was heartbreaking for me to think of the future limitations that would be placed on her because of a less-than-mediocre academic year.

Ryan hadn't fared any better. The challenges of our son's freshman year at college had overwhelmed him, and after being placed on academic probation his first semester, he was not able to crawl out of the hole he had dug for himself. When we received a certified letter from Wentworth stating that Ryan had flunked out of school, this compounded our already heavy hearts. This had been a complete letdown for us, which led me and Kevin to question some of the choices we had made as parents.

Since the alcohol-related episode Shea had battled through in February, she had continued to visit her therapist regularly, and her therapist felt it could be beneficial for Shea to also see a psychotherapist who could prescribe a low dose of antidepressant and antianxiety medication, which hopefully would stabilize her sleep patterns and increase her motivation.

I was apprehensive about this suggestion because of possible side effects and the unknown long-term implications of prescription antidepressants. Kevin and I agreed that we would only consider this method of treatment if we saw a drastic decline in Shea's well-being.

Measuring that kind of progress is tricky, I realized, and I was afraid we might be making the wrong decision. However, we watched her closely, and luckily, she began to make great strides, and it wasn't necessary to prescribe medication after all.

Although there were many challenges ahead of us as a family, we were still together, and that was the most important thing. After surviving something so profoundly life-changing, no obstacle or difficulty seemed quite as significant. I was confident we would get through this dark time, and things would eventually work out for us, even if not quite the way we had originally envisioned.

# Chapter 21

## ABSOLUTION

Throughout all the personal trials we were dealing with, Adam Leroy Lane's trial status remained in limbo. My impatience and frustration with the legal process led me to search for answers elsewhere. The first place I turned to was the Internet. I wasn't sure what I was hoping to find, or even where to begin looking for it. Thinking that there might be some new or updated information posted somewhere on a public or governmental website, I searched for everything I could think of that was remotely related to the pending New Jersey murder trial. However, there seemed to be nothing new disclosed in anything I came across. It was all the same information, just regurgitated by various news outlets.

Monica Massaro, Darlene Ewalt, Patricia Brooks and their loved ones had been in my prayers every night since I learned that Lane was responsible for the deaths of these two wonderful women and the near death of Patricia Brooks. I wanted to do everything I could to make good on the personal vow I had made to them—that I was going to be there every step of the way to see to it that their murderer was prosecuted and punished for all his crimes.

One day my search led me to a website that had played a significant role in Monica Massaro's life. During her lifetime, only Monica's closest friends and family had known about her affinity for the rock band Aerosmith, but after her murder, suddenly the rest of the world became aware as well. Because of everything our families had gone through, I felt an intimate connection with Monica, so despite feeling a little like I was invading her privacy by surfing onto Aero Force One, the official website of the famed Boston band, I continued to navigate through the site.

Among the other activities and information it provided, the site also hosted a forum for the fan-club base and maintained an extensive online board on which individuals would post information and messages for the use of and review by the other members.

What I came across on the message board was surprising and very distressing to me. Apparently, some of Monica's friends had been upset about the *People* article, specifically regarding the way in which Monica and Lane's other victims had been represented. They felt that Monica's and Darlene's murders, and Patricia's injury, had all been minimized by receiving only a small sidebar synopsis of the crimes against them. Apparently, this had been the source of much discussion on the post for quite some time. I read through each and every post, dreading what I would find written there but unable to stop myself. No one stated it explicitly, but many individuals seemed to feel that the piece had been self-serving to our family. It was just what I had been afraid of.

I could understand how these people could have

interpreted the article that way, given how the piece had centered on us. These people on the forum didn't know us, and they had no way of knowing what was in our hearts or minds. I could have just let it go, and I probably should have, but I became more distraught with each new post I read, and I started to fixate on the need to explain myself and give our side of the story. I essentially wanted to apologize to all of these people who I may have unintentionally victimized a second time by agreeing to the *People* interview. Perhaps I could even clear up some misconceptions, such as any notion that our family had benefited financially from the article, which we had not. I felt that was important for them to understand.

The true purpose behind the article, I'd felt, had been to illustrate that although no one is truly safe in the world today, and the most horrible and unimaginable things can happen to any one of us, having an opportunity to fight back—meaning plenty of luck and the right set of circumstances—could sometimes tip the balance away from evil and in favor of the good.

Did they understand this, and that I had no control over the content of the article or how anyone else would be depicted?

I couldn't be sure, but I decided that I had to say something. I carefully considered how to most accurately articulate my feelings; then I went back onto the website and posted a response.

This is what I wrote:

*I stumbled upon the Aeroforceone website today and after reading several of the messages on the board, I wanted to extend my deepest apologies to those that were obviously offended by the article in* People *magazine. It was never our intention to cause any additional suffering because of our decision to tell our story. I honestly agonized over whether this was a wise choice or not and knew that I would endure some fall-out because of it. We were pursued by the journalist from People, who reassured us that the piece would be done as a public interest story. We were never told that they were going to include pictures and references to the other victims. My hope was to make people real-ize that the unimaginable happens, and happens every day to those who least expect it. I wanted to convey the importance of locking your doors and never ever disregarding the cries of your children, whether they seem pressing or not. It would have been so easy for us to roll over that night and say that our daughter was fine and just having a nightmare because the sound was so faint. Don't for one minute think that I don't clearly understand that Monica and Darlene Ewalt were among the angels that "kicked us in the head" and gave us the ability to overpower that maniac. Not a day goes by that I don't think about both of them as well as the woman whom he so callously left for dead. They are all in my prayers every night and I hope that one day I will be able to watch this guy fry for the pain and suffering and horrible torment that he put so many people through, including but not limited to our family. We were seconds away from having to endure the same awful fate as the Massaros and Ewalts. For those of you that did not rush to judgment about us, I appreci-ate that very much. For the record, as well, in no way did we profit from this story. We were never offered a dime and I doubt we would have accepted it if we were. In closing, this world has suffered a huge loss because*

*of the murder of Monica and Darlene. I am sorry that*
*this sick bastard hadn't come to our house first so that*
*maybe they would both still be alive. Yet I can't help*
*but think that if he had, we wouldn't have had ALL of*
*the angels watching over us and things may not have*
*turned out the way they did because of it. So again,*
*PLEASE accept my deepest apologies to any and all*
*that we have offended in perhaps what may have been*
*a poor choice of judgment on our part.*

*With deepest respect and sympathy*
*The McDonough Family*

I thought I had conveyed everything that I wanted to
say. Once I read through it a couple more times, my finger
hesitated over the Send button. Just as before the *People*
interview, I wondered if I would be better off not saying
anything at this time. However, I knew that these people
had been hurt by something I had done, and I wanted to
make it right by them. Or at least try.

I sent the message, and then shut down my computer.
I knew I had done the right thing, but the rest of the day
I couldn't help thinking about it. I was tempted to check it
every hour, but I waited until the next morning. The first
thing I did when I got up was log on to the computer. I was
positively shaking, fearing that my note would have somehow made the situation worse, turning Monica's family
and friends further against me. To my complete surprise,
however, my post was met with such an outpouring of support that I thought I was going to cry. One after another,
the numerous expressions of gratitude and respect for what
our family had endured and overcome touched me deeply.
I was so relieved. The responses further solidified my

growing belief that the human propensity for love and compassion far outweighs the wicked and destructive impulses acted out by a small minority of individuals like Adam Lane. The gift of forgiveness and understanding that these bloggers extended to us will always remain etched in my mind. Afterward I felt compelled to thank them all personally with a second post of my own.

> *Thank you . . . for your words of encouragement and accolades for my husband and family. Without a doubt, if my husband hadn't gone into that bedroom first and responded as quickly as he did, none of us would be here. He will always be my hero and I thank God every day for our blessings. I will forever work towards getting this psycho held accountable for his heinous slaughter of two beautiful women (and who knows how many others) who did not deserve the awful things that happened to them. When he is finally brought down to New Jersey, and then Pennsylvania to stand trial for his crimes, I will be there! Again, to everyone who responded in such a heartfelt manner, we all are truly touched.*

> *Jeannie McDonough*

More thoughtful and supportive posts followed. It made me feel so good, and so relieved, to hear these sentiments, just being accepted as ordinary people who got caught up in some very extraordinary circumstances.

———————————

I remember lying awake beside Kevin in bed the night before Father's Day, unable to sleep. As I listened to his slow, steady breathing as he slept, I couldn't help thinking that there were at least two fathers who wouldn't be getting cards or calls from their daughters this year. It was sad to think about that on a day when we pay tribute to these men and celebrate their significance in the lives of our children. I realized how incredibly lucky our kids were to have Kevin, that night and every other before and after. I know I was comforted just having him next to me.

In light of the traumatic experiences of the previous summer, that Father's Day, more than any other, had the power to alternately make me smile with happiness and bring me to tears at the same time. I have loved the father of my children for more than thirty years, and feel fortunate to be able to say that. I knew that Ryan and Shea were aware of the curiosity-seekers who would occasionally drive slowly by our house, staring out of the windows in fascination, probably saying to each other, "That's the home-invasion house." Yet were it not for their father's ability to act so swiftly, and with such strength and determination, all those curious people might have instead been whispering, "That's the house where that family was murdered."

Our blessings have been bountiful, and on that special day my only wish was that our children would truly comprehend how much their father loves them. His total commitment to their well-being has given them the opportunity to flourish. Perhaps they already realized this, though my suspicion was that they might not fully appreciate it until the day they become parents themselves.

A week or so after Father's Day, Kevin, Shea and I made the five-hour drive down to New Jersey to be a part of the closing banquet for the Advanced Homicide Investigation Conference. Prior to the evening's event, we sat down at a café with Detective-Sergeant Geoff Noble, of the New Jersey State Police, and several other key investigators involved in Monica Massaro's murder case. Also joining us were Detective George Tyros and Detective-Sergeant Todd Ahern, with the Chelmsford Police Department.

It was initially intimidating to be among so many law enforcement professionals. Both Kevin and I felt more than a little out of place. After only a few moments, however, all of the detectives made us feel welcome and put me quickly at ease. My anxiety began to evaporate as we quickly identified with one another on a personal level, rather than being separated into victims and law enforcement. We talked about marriage, children, a little baseball. When the conversation turned to Monica, it revealed to us just how deeply these seasoned police officers had been affected by the senseless brutality of the case. These men all had families of their own, and they conveyed to us their personal commitment to the ongoing investigation and prosecution of Adam Leroy Lane.

Afterward, we walked over together to the event, which was held at Prospect House, a beautiful and impressive historic hall on the Princeton campus. Detective-Sergeant Noble continued to be the epitome of graciousness, never leaving our sides and truly going out of his way to make sure that Shea and Kevin and I were completely at ease. He introduced us to several of his fellow officers and commanding officers.

We all took our seats and dinner began promptly at 7:00 p.m. We were seated at the table directly in front of the podium so that we would have easy access when called upon to speak. Unbeknownst to us, none of the attendees at our table knew who we were, or that we were not in law enforcement, but invited "Guests of Honor." We were asked not to reveal this secret, and it certainly made for some interesting conversation at our table. When the time came for Detective-Sergeant Noble to make our introductions, a hush fell over the room. All the muffled whispering stopped at once, and all eyes were on our table.

As the New Jersey police detective recapped the details of our July 30, 2007, home invasion, I could sense the chills going up the spines of those listening around us. What seemed honestly amazing to me was how stunned all of these veteran police officers appeared upon hearing the particulars of the attack. At one point Detective-Sergeant Noble's gaze met Kevin's, and I could see both men's eyes as they became clouded with emotion.

We were then invited up to the podium, and the three of us rose to join him. I was absolutely astounded by the level of appreciation extended to us. I looked out at the ocean of faces in rapt attention and my heart was pounding as I began to recite the words I had prepared.

My brief statement was warmly received, and although it seemed to be appreciated by the majority of the detectives, it apparently was met with some disapproval as well. Sitting directly next to me was a well-known FBI profiler who had been scheduled to conduct a criminal linguistics workshop the following morning. Apparently he found my comments somewhat bold, and he took me aside to call me out on them. This individual bluntly asked me if I fully comprehended how my words would be interpreted by an audience full of police officers. I was somewhat confused, because I thought it had gone over pretty well. During the course of our conversation, he made me feel less sure of this, giving me the impression that others could possibly feel the same way he did.

*Here we go again*, I thought, my intentions completely

misunderstood once more. I began to distrust my decision-making instincts entirely, especially when it came to speaking publicly about my family's recent experiences with Adam Lane. I couldn't seem to say anything without offending someone these days, my words coming back to bite me.

At first I wasn't even sure what I might have said to elicit such a response. Then I recalled that in the middle of my statement before the assembly of police officers, I presented the scenario that if Shea had been killed while we slept, Kevin and Ryan and myself would all have been instant murder suspects, at least based upon historical criminology statistics. I simply cautioned investigators to try not to let those statistics alone limit their search for a killer because as the Lane case proves, random violent crimes do occur. I wasn't trying to tell these officers how to do their jobs, but I was thinking about Todd Ewalt and the double tragedy he suffered, first the murder of his wife and then being "accused" of killing her.

In response to the FBI profiler's comment and my perceived indiscretion, I tried to clearly illustrate the meaning behind my words to him and explain that I had been speaking out of a personal sense of fear. I also mentioned that my statement had been reviewed beforehand by the team of detectives assigned to the case and had not been met with any objections. He seemed to accept my explanation, but it left me feeling ill at ease and out of place among these people. Never wanting to offend anyone, least of all these courageous professionals who were only interested in helping me and others who had been victimized, I spent the rest of the evening apologizing profusely at every opportunity to anyone I may have put off by what I said.

At the conclusion of the night, we were left in the

company of our newly made law enforcement friends, in a considerably more casual and upbeat atmosphere. We had the opportunity to spend additional time with one another, sharing our experiences in greater detail. Besides touching on my family's individual torment, we also discussed the elements surrounding the case from the investigator's point of view. The night concluded with a heartfelt commitment on all sides to keep in touch, and we were told we would be kept in the loop with regard to any and all circumstances of the Lane investigation. Detective Noble mentioned several times to Shea that she had a band of brothers in New Jersey who would always be there for her if she ever needed them.

Kevin was inundated with handshakes and business cards from many of the detectives we had been privileged to meet that evening. I later joked to Kevin that now he certainly had people he could call if he ever got into any trouble.

Despite having put my foot in my mouth during my speech, it had been a good night. We were all exhausted by the time we got back to the hotel, and it seemed as though I had barely laid my head on the pillow and closed my eyes when it was morning. We were on the road early, but we were not headed home. We had made arrangements to finally meet Mr. and Mrs. Massaro.

Although we had been in communication with them in one form or another for a long while now, this would be our first opportunity to meet in person. We were not far from where they lived, so we planned to stop by and have breakfast together before continuing our journey back to Chelmsford.

We drove to Frank and Fay Massaro's home, and upon seeing their faces, an impeccable reflection of their own beautiful daughter burnt into their features, I couldn't help but cry. The love and loss conveyed in their embrace was agonizing and uplifting at the same time. The Massaros invited us inside and allowed us to view several family photo albums with them. Looking through the touching and nostalgic pictures of an adorably precious young girl, we saw Monica grow up before our eyes into the exquisite and vibrant woman she became in the final snapshots. The pain and sorrow in the room were palpable, but it was an experience the Massaros wanted to share with us, and we felt privileged that they had opened themselves to us in that way.

Fay's brother, Ronald, and their niece, Susan, also joined us at the house. They both felt strongly about being there to offer support to their family in what was already turning out to be a very emotional visit for everyone. I believe that their presence allowed Fay and Frank a greater level of comfort. Susan conveyed such strong feelings of love and affection for her aunt and uncle that I couldn't help but consider what a terrible tragedy it was that these people would never have a chance to be grandparents to Monica's children.

After a little while, we all moved on to a local restaurant, where the conversation was much lighter and the omelets were satisfying. We were able to focus more on the enjoyment of each other's company, and here the Massaros engaged Shea in an extended dialogue about her active social life. They seemed to really enjoy talking to her, and we all ended up learning a lot about each other during our brief visit. Frank and Fay insisted on picking up the tab, and instead of fighting over it we invited them to come up to Boston sometime soon and we would return the favor. They agreed.

Just before leaving, we took some pictures together to

remember the bittersweet occasion. I only hoped that when the Massaros looked at the photographs, they would realize that even in death, Monica had continued to enrich the lives of others. She'd brought all of us together, and we paid homage to her legacy that day.

On the way home, Shea revealed to us that Fay had given her some of Monica's personal belongings, items that she thought Shea might enjoy. I can only imagine how difficult that must have been for Fay. In a personal tribute to Monica, Shea placed the items that Fay had given her around her room. I know Shea thinks of Monica often, and I believe that Monica will watch over her. I feel very secure in this, even if to some it may seem like superstition.

# Chapter 22

## A DEAL WITH THE DEVIL

In July 2008, we were informed that Adam Leroy Lane was finally going to be transferred to a jail in Hunterdon County, New Jersey, to await trial for Monica Massaro's homicide.

I really didn't know how I was going to feel when I actually received the word, but I was not expecting to break down the way I did. The tears just started flowing and I could not stop them. A message had been left on my voice mail, and I was at work when I listened to it. It actually took my breath away, and I had to sit down. I put my head on my desk and started to cry. Thankfully, I had the opportunity to get it all out of my system before anybody saw me. But it was really only just the beginning.

No transfer date had been specified at that time, only that it was "in the works" and "could happen at any time." Nancy Compton, of the Hunterdon County Prosecutor's Office, had assured me early on that I would be notified as soon as there was any information at all regarding Lane's extradition, and she made good on that promise. Though she may not have fully understood why this was so important for me, I appreciated her consideration very much. It was official, at least, that Lane would finally be going to trial, and hopefully the Massaro family would get some degree of resolution. I knew I would.

Ultimately, the transfer actually occurred on July 29, 2008, exactly one year after Monica was murdered. I remember receiving the news that we had all been anxiously awaiting just before noon that day. Tom Gigliotti, the victim advocate from the Massachusetts Department of Correction Victims Service Unit, called to tell me that Lane had been picked up and was going to be transported to New Jersey sometime that same day.

I think I screamed at first, and then said to Tom, "This is big!" I filled him in on the significance of the date, and he agreed, "Yeah, it sure is."

As soon as I got off the phone with him, I called the Massaros. Frank answered, and he confirmed the news I had just received. I learned that they had been given the same information just a short while before. I could barely contain my excitement, and Frank sounded equally enthusiastic.

I wanted to share this joyous occasion with Fay, and I called her immediately on her cell phone, but she was actually still on the line talking with Hunterdon County Prosecutor J. Patrick Barnes, who had just told her that Lane was on his way to New Jersey to face trial for Monica's death. Fay called me back a couple minutes later, and we spoke at length, sharing our emotions and ultimate hope that Lane would pay the harshest penalty the justice system would allow.

Later that afternoon, I also received a phone call from Detective George Tyros. He left a message for me stating that he had spoken to Detective-Sergeant Geoff Noble, of the New Jersey State Police, and wanted to convey to me the information that Adam Leroy Lane was now officially in the custody of the New Jersey authorities, and had just crossed the state line.

Lane was placed in the segregation unit of the prison because of his attack on Shea, a minor. Given the code of ethics inmates tend to live by—they will often beat or kill prisoners who are known to abuse or murder children—the segregated area kept Lane from being harmed by other inmates.

Although the extradition made some of us want to stand up and cheer, the date of the trial had yet to be determined, and I was told up front that it could still be quite some time before it went to trial. Despite the fact that Lane was in custody in New Jersey, this new wait would be every bit as frustrating as waiting for him to be moved from Massachusetts had been.

I had been in constant communication with Fay Massaro during this period, and I heard the dismay in her voice upon learning that the preliminary hearing had been postponed at least two weeks, possibly as much as a month or more—we'd been informed that the trial might not begin until sometime in September. Fay and I both wanted to scream at the top of our lungs in frustration. It just couldn't come fast enough.

Delays were one thing, but considering how much many of us might have liked to see Adam Leroy Lane put to death by the state, some of us were glad that it was not an option. New Jersey lawmakers had voted to abolish the death penalty in December 2007, becoming the first state in more than forty years to outlaw capital punishment. The bill was introduced in November after a state commission concluded capital punishment does not prevent violent crime, and could lead to innocent people being executed, so on October 31, when Lane was arraigned for murdering Monica, the death penalty was never on the table. Fay Massaro and I were both aware that if the state of New Jersey had still had the death penalty and sought it against Lane, it would be years, not months, before the case against the killer was ultimately resolved. Given the lengthy appeals process sure to follow a capital-punishment conviction, the forty-two-year-old trucker would likely sit on death row for decades until he died of natural causes in prison anyway.

Although we were all disappointed by the delay in holding Lane responsible for his crimes, preferring swift and harsh judgment for this monster, we believed that justice would prevail and the eventual outcome would be satisfactory.

In Pennsylvania at this time, the death penalty was still being considered, and although they had time to decide while they waited for the conclusion of the New Jersey murder trial, prosecutors in the state were busy preparing their cases against Adam Leroy Lane for the murder of Darlene Ewalt and the attack on Patricia Brooks. On July 31, 2008, Northern York County Regional Police in Pennsylvania were so confident they had sufficient evidence to secure a conviction against Lane that they officially charged him with attempted criminal homicide, aggravated assault and burglary in the slashing attack on Patricia Brooks in her Conewago Township home just over a year before.

"It was the appropriate time to charge him," Chief Carl Segatti told the media after the charges were filed before District Judge Scott Gross in Fairview Township, York County. "We have a set of facts we feel are very strong. We can put [Adam Leroy Lane] in the area, his DNA was on clothing found near the scene, and we have a positive identification from the victim."

On Sunday, August 3, 2008, a bench was dedicated to the memory of Monica Massaro at the Borough Park in Bloomsbury in remembrance of the one-year anniversary of her death. I'd sent a flower arrangement to the dedication ceremony, but I wished I could have done so much more.

Just a couple days later, on August 5, 2008, Adam Leroy Lane finally appeared in a New Jersey courtroom, shackled and wearing a bulletproof vest over yellow coveralls. His appearance had changed once again. This time not only his facial hair, but his head, too, had been shaved. He looked softer and weaker than at any time since he'd been taken into custody. He had lost considerable weight, and certainly muscle mass. In appearance, he was no longer the gruff, burly trucker who had been arrested in our home the previous summer. It was as if he had been wearing a costume when we first encountered him, and now it had been stripped away and we were seeing him as he really was. Despite his diminished stature, there was still something frightening and dangerous about him. He seemed completely detached from everything and in his own world. His eyes just seemed to be swimming in their sockets, not focusing on anything, and it gave the impression that his thoughts were just as disjointed. It was frightful. Lane entered a not-guilty plea to the eight counts against him, including the first-degree murder of Monica Massaro. The plea was actually entered on his behalf by his court-appointed attorney on the case, Peter V. Abatemarco, who confirmed that he had not yet had a chance to outline a defense for his client. Abatemarco asked to be given at least four weeks to read through the voluminous discovery files, some seven thousand pages' worth, which he had not yet seen. He added that he might even need to ask for extra time when all was said and done. First Assistant Prosecutor Charles Ouslander confirmed that the material the defense required would be boxed up and brought over to Abatemarco's office that afternoon, and the judge set aside the date of September 4 for a status conference.

If convicted on the first-degree murder charge, Lane could face anywhere from thirty to sixty years in prison under New Jersey's No Early Release Act, with additional years if convicted of any additional charges.

That next day, August 6, 2008, back in Pennsylvania, charges were officially filed against Adam Leroy Lane for first-degree murder in the stabbing death of Darlene Ewalt. It had been more than a year since she'd become the first known victim in Lane's July 2007 multistate killing and slashing spree, and this indictment came as the result of cooperative efforts by law enforcement in all three states. The sharing of evidence collected in the jurisdictions following each crime and the strength of the DNA testing were more than enough to bring these charges against the North Carolina trucker.

Lane, however, who was being held at that time in a New Jersey prison, would not be returned to Pennsylvania to face the charges, which included not only first-degree murder but possessing instruments of crime and loitering and prowling at night, until the case in New Jersey was resolved. Dauphin County, Pennsylvania, First Assistant District Attorney Fran Chardo made that very clear at a subsequent news conference. The announcement indicated that the Pennsylvania district attorney was going to let New Jersey extract its pound of flesh from Lane and not interfere. It did not mean, however, that authorities in Pennsylvania were not going to pursue Lane with everything they had once he was in their custody. Because of the violent and sadistic nature of the Ewalt killing, Dauphin County District Attorney Edward Marsico said he was considering pursuing the death penalty.

"It is terrifying to think a woman like [Darlene Ewalt] was struck down in her own backyard like this," said Marsico. "He is a dangerous individual." Marsico also expressed concern that because of the transient nature of Lane's work as a truck driver, and the manner in which he had randomly selected his victims, there might still be other unsolved violent crimes that he was responsible for.

When asked to speculate what might have been Lane's motivation to commit such acts of violence, Marsico responded that police had no real viable answers at that time. "I think he hates women," the prosecutor added bluntly. "He is targeting women."

A month later, the killer was back in court. On September 4, 2008, wearing his yellow prison jumpsuit and ubiquitous bulletproof vest, Lane was escorted into New Jersey Superior Court by Hunterdon County sheriff's officers for a brief status conference. He sat quietly at the defense table with his attorney. The public defender, Peter Abatemarco, addressed the court, confirming that the state had provided him with discovery material for the case, including the *Hunting Humans* DVD and the statement that Lane had made while incarcerated. He then asked the court for more time to discuss the material with his client, a request to which First Assistant Prosecutor Charles Ouslander agreed and State Superior Court Judge Roger Mahon granted, ordering another hearing for Lane on September 29.

It might have been just another few weeks to the court, but to the Massaros, it was hell. It was twenty-five more days they would have all this hanging over their heads.

———————————

Before Lane's next court date, Shea turned seventeen. It was a gloriously beautiful crisp and clear fall day, not unlike the world-changing September 11 seven years before. Just as it is for all Americans, for me this date will forever be marked by tragedy and the reflection of how in an instant our nation was stripped of its innocence and sense of security. For me, however, it will also be a day of celebration. On that day in particular, I looked at my daughter with overwhelming gratitude that her life hadn't been snatched away, and with a sense of awe that she continued to stand before me strong and resilient. No doubt, I will always take pause on this day for all those innocent lives that were taken on 9/11, and with my next breath, I will give thanks to God that this day will also be celebrated by my family for the immense joy that it brings to our lives by marking Shea's entrance into the world.

Kevin and I also had two reasons to celebrate on September 29 that year. Not only was it our wedding anniversary—we had gotten married exactly twenty-three years before—but it was also the day that Adam Leroy Lane changed his plea to *guilty* for the July 2007 murder of Monica Massaro.

We were not in the courtroom for this announcement,

but I was glued to my computer, checking the Internet for up-to-the-minute trial updates all day long.

Monica's family was all there, along with many of her friends. Fay Massaro sobbed throughout the proceedings, which were at times graphic. It was extremely unsettling for me to think about them being subjected to this kind of torment, and reliving the agony of losing a child.

I had previously become aware of Lane's gruesome admissions through the Middlesex County Prosecutor's Office and from Detective Geoff Noble, but Monica's family was now being forced to endure the details of their daughter's murder in a public courtroom, some of it directly from the mouth of the killer himself.

---

Lane admitted to parking his truck at a nearby truck stop off Interstate 78 and then walking into the quiet Hunterdon County neighborhood where Monica had lived, forcing his way into her home and purposely killing her. Monica's mother completely broke down when Hunterdon County First Assistant Prosecutor Charles Ouslander confirmed that the victim's throat had been slit, and that Lane had sat and watched her bleed to death.

"You did take a knife and cut her throat from ear to ear?" Lane was asked.

"Yes, sir," he answered, his southern-accented voice completely devoid of emotion. Lane also said that there had been a lot of blood after he cut her throat, and that he'd watched her die before inflicting further injuries upon her body.

Throughout the proceedings, Lane sat calmly before Hunterdon County Superior Court Judge Roger F. Mahon, with four court officers surrounding him. Clad in a yellow jumpsuit, bulletproof vest and shackles, he never once turned to face his victim's family. Nor did he look at the investigators who had caught him and were present in the Flemington courtroom. He gave no final statement.

"Putting him to death would be too good for him. I hope that he will suffer every day for what he has done and never taste freedom again," Fay Massaro told the packed courtroom in one part of a prepared statement that was read for her in court by a victim advocate. "My husband and I will never have another happy day for the rest of our lives. Life has lost its meaning for us."

First Assistant Prosecutor Charles Ouslander stated that Lane had intended to kill that night, and he had shown Monica no mercy. "I ask that the court show no mercy toward the defendant now," he said, in a comment clearly directed at the judge.

Judge Roger Mahon agreed with the prosecution's assessment, noting that he had seen no remorse whatsoever from Adam Leroy Lane, except for the fact that he had been apprehended. Mahon commented that he did not understand how Lane, a father of young girls himself, could inflict such "evil" upon women. Lane's own lawyer, Peter Abatemarco, admitted that he could offer no explanation either, though the public defender said that his client's guilty pleas had been entered to spare "everyone involved the trauma of a trial."

Under the terms of the plea deal, in exchange for his admission to murder in the first degree, Lane was spared the possibility of serving a life sentence. However, attorneys on both sides expressed confidence that Lane would not outlive the state's recommendation of a fifty-year state

prison sentence, which would be served consecutively with
the twenty-five years he had already been given for his
conviction in Massachusetts. Lane's lawyer said his client
had resigned himself to spending the rest of his life in jail,
with the understanding that his diabetes and other health
issues would likely cut his life drastically short. Regardless of Lane's health issues, Judge Mahon accepted the
plea agreement that was on the table. Lane also agreed to
waive his right to an appeal in exchange for the prosecution agreeing to dismiss seven other counts related to the
murder. Furthermore, New Jersey's No Early Release Act
required that Lane would need to serve 85 percent of his
sentence, or forty-two and one-half years, before becoming eligible for parole and without probation. Along with
the twenty-five-year term he had already begun serving for
his crimes in Massachusetts, this meant that Lane would
spend at least the next sixty-seven and one-half years in
state prison. He would be eligible for parole when he was
one hundred and eleven years old.

With the plea bargain all worked out and accepted by
both sides, all that was left was for the judge to consider
the deal and either impose the sentence agreed upon or rec-
ommend his own. The sentencing date was scheduled for
October 23, 2008.

---

I planned to go to New Jersey for Lane's sentencing hearing. Kevin agreed to join me, knowing how deeply committed I was to lending support to the Massaro family. I
was greatly anticipating the satisfaction of seeing this evil,
coldhearted killer brought to justice.

Fay Massaro credited the law enforcement officers for
the effort they put into building a case against Lane.

"Without them, he might still be hunting humans," she said, referencing the DVD movie found in Lane's truck.

That same evening as Lane's September 29, 2008, New Jersey trial, as our family returned from a dinner out together, Fay called me. I told her that she and Frank had been in our thoughts all day. I had almost called her several times earlier, but refrained, not wanting to have her recount the tormenting events that occurred in the courtroom that day. When she told me that she had been fielding calls from family and friends nonstop since they'd returned from court, I was glad not to have added to her burden, though I was relieved to hear her level and composed tone of voice. She said she very much wanted me to be aware of the outcome, and I didn't mention to her that I already knew what had happened.

Something that I found equally disturbing was a comment posted online in response to an article that highlighted the killer's guilty plea:

"He's my father. He's a loving and caring man, he just made a few mistakes. He's human. Why can't we just forgive and forget. Everyone makes mistakes. God be with you, dad. May you get out soon."

It had supposedly been posted by one of Lane's daughters, though it was also suggested that it might have been the work of a troll. If it had been from one of his children, perhaps she was too young to understand the magnitude of her father's crimes. Either way, the statement left me in a state of emotional turmoil. Although I was not without empathy for what Adam Leroy Lane's family must have experienced, particularly his innocent daughters, the casual and dismissive tone of this comment utterly floored me.

But the justice system was not through with Adam Lane

just yet. Brad Winnick, Lane's public defender in the Darlene Ewalt murder trial, reminded everyone that the Dauphin County district attorney in Pennsylvania was still leaning toward seeking the death penalty against Lane if he was convicted of murdering Monica Massaro.

We could only hope so.

# Chapter 23

## SENTENCING A MONSTER

In the days leading up to Adam Leroy Lane's October sentencing hearing in New Jersey, I began quietly gathering the strength I would need to make the trip. The connection was real and very personal. I relished the thought of seeing Lane squirm as his life was reduced to the number of years he would spend in a jail cell. At the same time, although I was anxious about the hearing, I was also disheartened—no trial meant that we might never know what had prompted him to indiscriminately take the lives of innocent people, without any conscience whatsoever or fear of reprisal in this life or the next. There was no guarantee, of course, that a trial would have provided this kind of insight and knowledge, but it was at least a possibility. I still hoped to someday learn the mysterious motivation that prompted Lane to these random acts of violence, but it did not seem likely that it would be this day.

We had been told that Darlene Ewalt's family was also

planning to attend the sentencing hearing. Although I didn't share the same level of personal communication with Darlene's family that I had with the Massaros, I felt their loss deeply as well. I knew that the pain Darlene's husband and children were feeling could very well have been our own. I desperately wanted to wrap my arms around them and express how deeply affected I was by what they had to endure. I imagined that the Ewalts wanted to be in New Jersey that day for the very same reasons that I did, though the degree of their suffering would have prompted a much stronger need to see this killer held accountable for his crimes.

Actually, the only reluctance I had about making the journey myself stemmed from a feeling that my family's level of loss did not come near the devastation that the Ewalts had endured. These people had suffered so much. Part of me felt that I somehow didn't deserve to be in the same room with them, in that sense. But I knew I had to conquer these feelings of survivor guilt, and God willing, I would also see Adam Leroy Lane prosecuted and sentenced for the crimes he'd committed in Pennsylvania, as well as any others yet to be discovered. As far as I was concerned, I was going to follow this path wherever it led. The sense that my convictions might be somewhat unhealthy did occur to me, but it is difficult for people who haven't experienced this kind of trauma to understand the driving need for complete closure. I felt strongly that because our family had been fortunate enough to survive Lane's attack, we needed to see this thing through for those people who had been lost. I also recognized this need as a means to an end by which I could finally take back control of my life and restore some of the sense of security and trust that was taken away by Adam Leroy Lane.

Kevin and I left for New Jersey the afternoon before the hearing. It was a relatively somber ride through very light traffic, and we made the trip in just over four hours. Neither of us spoke very much. I know I was consumed by introspective thoughts and speculation about the forthcoming events. The emotional undercurrent surrounding this visit was slowly simmering with each progressive mile.

We arrived at around 6:30 p.m. and then made plans to meet Detective-Sergeant Geoff Noble for dinner. He recounted for us the specifics of Lane's confession, some of which we had not been aware of previously. He described the tactics that he had used on Lane to coax an admission out of him and extract the details that had been necessary to get a conviction to stick. We were both riveted by Detective Noble's explanation of how and why he felt his approach had worked so successfully with Lane. He precisely answered every question we had and addressed each of our concerns with an impressive measure of confidence that marked his many years of experience. We called it an early night, all of us needing our rest for what was sure to be a long, psychologically draining day. Before we parted, we made a firm commitment with Detective Noble to continue to foster the friendship we had developed.

The following morning, to describe myself as a bundle of nerves walking into the Hunterdon County Justice Complex would be a gross understatement. We arrived at 8:15 a.m., and I wondered what I could possibly say to Todd Ewalt, or the rest of Darlene's family, to adequately convey my feelings of empathy for their loss. I wondered what they looked like, and I scanned the faces of everyone who entered the courthouse, trying to pick them out. Would they be in a recognizably fragile mental state? Their emotions could easily run the gamut from infuriation to despair to complete and total despondency. Even if the passage of fifteen months had diminished the appearance of outward suffering, this court proceeding would invariably reopen all the raw emotions that may have been forced down inside by the requirements of day-to-day existence. Everything could all come bubbling back to the surface.

Without knowing it, however, it later turned out that we had walked right past Todd Ewalt outside the courthouse just before we'd entered the building. Thinking back, I can recall noticing an attractive, lost-looking man milling about in front of the building.

Before the hearing got under way, we were called into the library of the prosecutor's office for a brief and cordial meet-and-greet. This was where Kevin and I were introduced to Todd Ewalt and his family for the first time. Though this was an informal gathering, we did not get a chance to talk or interact the way I would have liked, but I still put my arms around Todd and gave him a hug. I truly hoped that he felt the emotional conviction of my embrace. I wanted to explain to him how strongly I felt that his wife was joined with Monica Massaro and my mother-in-law among the angels that had orchestrated the successful outcome of our actions the night Lane was apprehended in our home. I wanted to tell him how I believed that his wife was as much a part of that event as Kevin, Shea and I had been. I wanted him to know that the heart-wrenching circumstances behind our families' connection would have a deeply significant impact on my life forever.

As I watched him and Kevin shake hands, I couldn't help but wonder if Todd had been entertaining any disparaging thoughts about why our family had been so fortunate, while his family had been left with an irreparable hole. However, it was evident to me that Todd, and his parents, who were there beside him, held no such bitterness or resentment toward us. Their expressions and smiles bespoke only their overwhelming gratitude for the role we'd played in apprehending Darlene's killer.

We barely had a chance to say hello to Frank and Fay Massaro in the courthouse library before it was time for all of us to be escorted into the courtroom to take our seats. Kevin and I were situated directly behind the Ewalts and two rows in back of the Massaros. From our location, we had a clear view of most of the people in attendance, and it was especially gratifying to see so many facets of the law enforcement community represented, particularly those detectives with whom we had become familiar and who had been directly responsible for the successful outcome of this investigation, from discovery to conviction. Today's sentence would be representative of a triumphant conclusion for all parties whose painstaking effort and dedication had culminated in this final disposition, though for the Massaros, it could only be at best bittersweet.

Before the trial got under way, a gentleman seated behind us tapped Kevin and me on the shoulder and introduced himself as Chief Dan Hurley of the Hunterdon County Prosecutor's Office in New Jersey. He told us how pleased he was that we had decided to make the trip down and that he was honored to meet us. We were flattered, and when he referred to us as heroes, we didn't know how to respond. He stated that law enforcement was indebted to us for taking a serial killer off the streets and saving the lives of countless innocent people in the process. This kind of unsolicited recognition from this man was obviously gratifying to hear. Although I would like to have offered him the simple truth that our actions were primarily the result of a basic instinct to protect the life of our daughter, and that we were lucky to be alive, I just shook his hand and thanked him. Kevin, naturally, did the same.

As Adam Leroy Lane was led inside, Fay Massaro immediately broke into tears. He was heavily chained and surrounded by extra security, and once more wearing a bulletproof vest. The very idea that he was being so well protected from harm must have frustrated the Massaros as much as it did me. Every time I saw him that way, I couldn't help but think how backward the whole judicial system could be at times.

On cue, the judge entered the courtroom from his chambers and took his chair behind the bench. As the hearing began, I harkened back to the previous December and my first experience with the criminal court system. I was comforted by the feel of Kevin's arm draped around my shoulder. However, I could feel his body tense when First Assistant Prosecutor Charles Ouslander described Monica's murder in chilling detail, saying that Lane "deliberately, purposefully and brutally" cut the victim's throat first and then began cutting her all over to "make the murder look like it had been done by a maniac."

The prosecutor's words pounded in my ears over and over again as he described how Lane had sadistically inflicted knife wounds to Monica's body, stabbing her breasts, abdomen and genitals, even after he had mercilessly watched her bleed to death. It was extremely difficult to comprehend the vicious manner in which Lane had mutilated this beautiful woman, and then left her to be found that way. My heart was aching as I imagined the horror and devastation the Massaros must have been experiencing at that same instant. Almost as unsettling to me was the realization that Todd Ewalt was likely imagining the tragic last moments of his own beautiful wife's life at the hands of this monster, and how she must have suffered. The bravery and restraint he showed in not lunging across the courtroom but sitting in solidarity with the Massaro family was commendable, and must have taken every fiber of his self-control.

"This defendant needs to be incarcerated for the rest of his natural life," Ouslander said. "I ask the court to show the defendant no mercy."

Lane's attorney, Peter Abatemarco, stood before the judge with a straight face and argued that except for the assaults in three states within days of the Massaro slaying, Lane had lived an otherwise "law-abiding life."

Lane alternately stared down at the floor and up at Superior Court Judge Roger F. Mahon. He never once looked over to meet the gaze of the Massaros or the numerous investigators scattered around the courtroom.

Before the sentence was imposed, when given the opportunity, Lane declined to speak on his own behalf. The court, as always, had the final word. "This sentence," Judge Mahon declared, "is intended to keep the defendant incarcerated for the rest of his life." Then, as expected, he sentenced Adam Leroy Lane to fifty years for the death of Monica Massaro, under the terms that had been agreed upon a month earlier. Short of putting Lane to death, this was the limit of the earthly punishment that could be imposed on him for taking Monica's life. Fay and Frank Massaro could at least take some satisfaction in knowing that their daughter's killer would never have the freedom he once enjoyed or the opportunity to destroy any other lives.

As we were exiting the courtroom at the conclusion of the proceeding, in a long and somber procession, we streamed past a gauntlet of detectives and state troopers, many of whom we had come to know and admire. We were led back upstairs to the library, and as the room slowly filled up, we were provided an opportunity to become acquainted with some of Monica's closest friends and other family members. It turned out that I had previously unknowingly been communicating with several of these women on the Aero Force One website. It was wonderful to be able to meet them in person. It gave me an even greater understanding of how special Monica had been and how influential she had been in the lives of those fortunate enough to have known her. Her zest for life, her love of music and dancing and her indomitable optimism were all reflected in the many friends she had surrounded herself with. We were all in agreement that Monica and I would likely have been drawn to each other if we had had the opportunity. Unfortunately, it was her death that had brought us together.

As we began to depart, members of the prosecution team stepped forward to ward the reporters away from family members and provided statements. Chief Dan Hurley, of the Hunterdon County Prosecutor's Office, was among them.

"This was a tragic case," he said. "The successful conclusion of this investigation that shocked everyone in Hunterdon County is a testament to each and every police officer, state trooper, detective, crime scene personnel, assistant prosecutor and the prosecutor himself. Additional lives have been saved by putting him away for life."

In a touching show of appreciation to law enforcement, as well as to Monica's many friends, the Massaros had arranged for a luncheon at a restaurant nearby immediately following the sentencing hearing. Kevin and I were honored to be included in the invitation. It was such a thoughtful and courageous gesture on their behalf to put aside their pain and anguish to extend their appreciation to everyone who had been there for them in their time of need. It also afforded all of us an opportunity to interact in a more relaxed setting. It turned into a relatively large gathering of friends, family and law enforcement officials, all paying homage to a woman who had been struck down in the prime of her life.

Being with Frank and Fay Massaro that afternoon, I could easily envision the loving relationship they must have had with their daughter. She had flourished with every year of her life spent in the care of this kind and generous couple. How truly sad it was that this love would no longer manifest itself in a physical sense, though she will live forever in their hearts and in the spirit of everyone who knew her.

A reporter from the *Lowell Sun* called us at home the day after we got back. When I was asked what I thought of the sentence that Lane had received, I said, "We are glad justice has been served on behalf of Monica and the Massaro family. My hope is that [Adam Leroy Lane] suffers miserably for the next fifty to seventy-five years. He deserves no less, and yet so much more."

# Chapter 24

## COMING TOGETHER

The beginning of the holiday season was marked by Adam Leroy Lane's sentencing hearing, the second time in as many years. And it was not over yet for him, or for any of us. There were still charges in Pennsylvania that Lane had to answer to, both the attack on Patricia Brooks and Darlene Ewalt's murder.

The stress of the season was compounded further by a *Dateline NBC* producer who contacted us, as well as the Massaros and the Ewalts, in the days prior to Thanksgiving about setting up an interview.

When we were first asked if our family would be willing to participate in the filming of a segment to be aired as part of their story on Adam Lane we declined the interview outright. My primary concern was the other families, but when we learned that they were at least considering participating themselves, we began to rethink our own decision. If they were interested in cooperating with the show and having our family participate with them as a unified group, then we would consider it.

We had been informed that the producers intended to go ahead with the story about Lane's path of death and destruction in July 2007 whether or not the families played active roles in the piece. This complicated our decision, which instinctively was not to talk to any more national media until all of the cases against Lane had been resolved. However, if we refused to be interviewed, we would have absolutely no control over the content.

I was still skeptical, even after I had been told that Todd Ewalt and his children had agreed to the interview, considering that the cases against Lane in Pennsylvania were not concluded. I knew that Frank Massaro was vehemently against any involvement. He felt that *Dateline* would only sensationalize and exploit the memory of his daughter and the manner of her death. But Fay felt that perhaps our family's participation might be the best means to represent both of our families' interests. All I could do was advise her not to push Frank into doing something with which he wasn't completely comfortable.

*Dateline* gave us until November 18 to decide, at which time we would all meet—the families who chose to be involved and the producers of the show—to come to some sort of understanding regarding how they would proceed with the story. With the Ewalts being the only family committed to *Dateline* at that time, our participation would require us to travel to Pennsylvania for the meeting. The uncertainty surrounding our involvement, as well as the potential ramifications of the interview itself, made me very uneasy. It consumed my thoughts and distracted me from everything else I had to do.

Creating additional pressure was the fact that Shea was

then in the middle of her college-applications process. Distracting her from the tasks at hand could prove to be a major disruption. For all these reasons, I was hoping we could postpone this meeting until after the first of the year. Trying to unite three, possibly four families in one place at one time, particularly during the holidays, was no small endeavor. Flexibility would be necessary to accomplish this at any time of the year.

After speaking again with Fay at length one evening, we decided to defer the matter with *Dateline* to Janet Kerr, the Massaros' victim advocate. Janet had provided strong support for the family, helping Fay and Frank make informed decisions throughout the lengthy legal process. Since her primary role was to safeguard the Massaros from various forms of harm and to ensure that their best interests and well-being were always considered, it made sense to consult with her on this issue.

In the end, the Massaros decided not to participate and that the best course of action was for our family to go without them, just as Fay had suggested to me earlier. At the same time, Fay cautioned me that there was a strong possibility that what we understood to be a purely informational meeting had the potential to result in much more, including unsolicited camera time. This meant that they could have surprised us by sticking a camera or microphone in front of our faces and asking us questions we may not have been fully prepared to answer. The results could have ranged from making us look bad to harming the criminal cases still pending against Lane, or both. The prospect of a media ambush, along with the subsequent pressure of an interview without prior preparation, ultimately influenced us to choose not to attend the meeting in Pennsylvania after all. We determined that if the *Dateline* producers were truly interested in our input, they would have to come to us on our terms, not theirs. That was what we told them in so many words, and I was somewhat surprised when they agreed to it.

When the date for the Pennsylvania meeting arrived, I couldn't help but wonder if the Ewalts had actually met with the people from *Dateline* and how it had gone. My secret hope was that the NBC news program would be able to use its extensive investigative resources to provide some answers to the countless questions regarding Adam Leroy Lane's motivation to kill and his careless disregard for human life. At the same time, however, I felt that if all those professionally trained investigators and police officers in multiple states and jurisdictions could not solve that dark mystery, I didn't think *Dateline* correspondent Hoda Kotb and her team would be able to crack it.

Meanwhile, we scheduled our own appointment with a *Dateline NBC* producer. Marianne O'Donnell arrived at our home late in the afternoon on December 2, 2008, for an informal interview, the purpose of which was to attain the necessary background information and facts about our shared experience with Adam Leroy Lane. There was no cameraman, no makeup or lighting people, just Marianne and a little notebook. After a few minutes of initial pleasantries, the conversation quickly turned to July 30, 2007, a time that seemed simultaneously so long ago yet still fresh in our memories. Marianne also ended up enlightening us herself by asking some probing questions we did not expect. I was surprised to find my curiosity piqued, awaiting the answers my family was going to give her.

For example, one of the things the producer asked Shea was, "Do you feel vulnerable around your neck area in any way?"

I found it interesting that she raised the subject, because I had been wondering the same thing myself, except with regard to Patricia Brooks and the impact of the assault on her. Patricia had been left to bleed to death by Adam Leroy Lane, with life-threatening slashes to her throat and all along her upper body. Not a day went by that I didn't think about how narrowly our daughter escaped the same fate. I was relieved to hear Shea respond that she did not think much about it anymore, though the question certainly seemed to give her pause. Shea had come a long way in such a short period of time, and her resiliency and ability not to allow the experience to completely consume her life continued to astound me. But Shea did mention that she felt anxious when fumbling for her keys and trying to get into the house late at night, which was news to me, but I could certainly understand her anxiety.

The mutual exchange of information between us continued as various facts about the Pennsylvania cases that we had not been aware of previously were revealed to us. Kevin and I were both enraged to learn the extent to which Todd Ewalt had been pursued as a suspect in his wife's murder. Marianne informed us that it has been her experience that no faction within the justice system ever goes out of its way to extend an apology to any of the individuals who have been falsely accused of a crime. As a consequence, Todd had been forced to defend himself and hire an attorney. The resulting exorbitant legal expenses had placed a serious and undue financial burden on the family. This was on top of the painful emotional toll that they had already been subjected to after this loving wife and caring mother had been taken away from them forever. Much of what Marianne revealed about the Ewalts substantiated my own fears that had things turned out horribly different for Shea on

July 30, then Ryan, Kevin and I would all have been looked at with a similar amount of criminal suspicion.

The meeting was closed with a commitment from Marianne that she would be in touch with us regarding the details of how exactly *Dateline* intended to proceed, or more specifically, the logistics of the filming and final decisions regarding the material content.

After she departed, I could not stop thinking about Todd Ewalt. I recalled that shortly after our own experience with Lane, we had been notified about a fund that had been set up through local police jurisdictions to benefit the victims of violent crimes. These funds were intended to assist victims with medical expenses and lost wages stemming from their injuries. Hopefully, this was information provided to Patricia Brooks, considering the condition that she was left in and the amount of unwarranted medical expenses that must have surrounded her recovery. However, it seemed only right to me that there also be a fund available through the individual states or the federal government to provide for legal fees incurred in cases of wrongful arrest and prosecution.

Todd Ewalt's plight spurred me to research the possible options available to those who have been falsely incriminated. To my surprise, I could not find a single place where these people could turn for help. Even the Innocence Project, originally founded in 1992 by Barry Scheck and Peter Neufeld, is devoted to freeing people who have been wrongfully *convicted* of crimes, typically by using the latest DNA testing methods to prove their innocence. I was shocked to learn that, up to the time of my research, statistics indicated that some 232 defendants who had been previously convicted of serious crimes, predominantly sexual assault and murder, had been exonerated by DNA testing. The Innocence Project also performs research and advocacy related to the causes of wrongful convictions and is a member of the Innocence Network, which brings together a number of innocence organizations from across the United States. What the Innocence Project does is nothing short of heroic—however, the individuals they save had already been convicted. I went on to place calls, only to have my suspicions confirmed: short of bringing a civil suit against the accuser, there was no means in place by which to recoup one's financial losses if subjected to an erroneous criminal accusation.

A short while later, we received our plane tickets and an all-expenses paid trip to New York, including hotel accommodations at the Waldorf Astoria. We would be flying out on February 25, 2009, but with each passing day, I remained skeptical about how the *Dateline* piece would be presented. I continued to have these concerns despite the fact that I felt very comfortable with Marianne. I knew that she found our story compelling, and I was confident that she would do all she could to ensure that it would be presented in the right manner. I just did not want to be party to the further sensationalizing of the murders or exploitation of the families' misfortunes. Our family may not have been through exactly the same thing as the Massaros and the Ewalts or Patricia Brooks, for that matter, who was violently attacked and survived, but we understood how important their right to privacy was at that time. To say anything out of turn would be disrespectful and hurtful.

After our experience with the *People* article, I feared that the story might end up being slanted more toward our good fortune in having overpowered Lane and minimize what I felt should be the central focus of this story, the devastating loss of the victims at the hands of a brutal and sadistic killer and their families' subsequent suffering. If the piece was edited in any way that would dishonor the memories of Monica Massaro or Darlene Ewalt, or offend Patricia Brooks, I would have been terribly disappointed.

---

It was on a Friday the 13th, of all days, that February of 2009, when our faithful Lab and retriever mix suffered a stroke while Kevin was out walking him. We were forced to have him put down. He was twelve years old but had otherwise been healthy and alert right up until the day he died. We'll all miss him. For Shea, it seemed as though she had not known a day without Bosco, and she was particularly devastated by the loss. Recently, he had become her personal protector and bodyguard. She had been making tremendous progress in handling the terror she sometimes felt, but she still had trouble sleeping on occasion, so Bosco began staying in her room, giving her some much-needed comfort.

It was because of how much Bosco had meant to all of us, but Shea in particular at that time, that we went out rather quickly and got a new family dog. It was something we all agreed on, and we wound up with a beautiful little boxer pup, which we named Nitro. The kids just adored him, and even though he would follow them both around and keep a close watch on them, he was not there for protection. We still had Kevin, who watched Shea like a hawk these days, for that. We all watched out for each other a little more.

Then, right around that time, in mid-February, out of the clear blue I received a phone call from Middlesex, Massachusetts, District Attorney Tom O'Reilly. Upon hearing his voice, my heart automatically skipped a beat, as I knew immediately the subject matter of his call; Lane was headed to Pennsylvania to face trial for Darlene Ewalt's murder and the attack on Patricia Brooks.

Throughout the duration of this entire legal process, Tom had always managed to bring a sense of ease and clarity to the extremely unsettling and unknown circumstances that we found ourselves in. His experience within the justice system and his overall professionalism in dealing with the various facets of law enforcement facilitated an instant bond of trust between us.

After a brief exchange of pleasantries, Tom informed me that Lane's extradition to Pennsylvania had been initiated and that the paperwork was in progress. He said he needed to obtain authorization from Kevin and me specifying that we would be willing to give up the legal right to retain Lane in the state of Massachusetts. It struck me as peculiar that something like that required our approval, but I wasn't about to hold this process up any longer, and I gave our consent, even if I didn't fully understand it. At the time, Lane was still being housed within the Massachusetts Department of Corrections, which only temporarily gave up custody when he traveled to another state to stand trial. Pennsylvania had already requested permission to keep him there permanently, so that he would either serve a life sentence there for killing Darlene Ewalt or possibly face the death penalty, which the state enforces in capital murder cases. It was my further understanding that should Lane be tried, convicted and sentenced in Pennsylvania, if my family insisted that he be returned to Massachusetts to serve out the twenty-five- to thirty-year sentence he'd received for attacking Shea, then his sentence in Pennsylvania would not be applied until after that sentence had been completed. In actuality, the Pennsylvania sentencing wouldn't come into play until after Lane had also served the additional time he'd received in New Jersey for the murder of Monica Massaro. The severity of Pennsylvania's punishment would be undermined if it could not be enforced for one hundred and eleven years, the sum of the Massachusetts and New Jersey sentences. If that was the case, then any sentence would merely be additional years tacked onto what was essentially a lifetime sentence already. In such a scenario, there would be no impact on Lane whatsoever, and the feeling was that justice would not adequately be served on behalf of Patricia Brooks and Darlene Ewalt or their families.

I felt, as I'm sure the Massaros, the Ewalts and Patricia Brooks did as well, that Lane deserved the most severe punishment: death. I knew that he was afraid of the death penalty, as are most murderers. I was particularly aware that this final courtroom showdown could potentially be the last chance to uncover the possible existence of other victims who had not yet been identified. Just the threat of the death penalty might be all that was needed to force Lane to cooperate and provide authorities with information relating to all his past crimes. However, there were definitely at least two cases that were going to be heard, and on January 6, 2009, the district attorneys from York and Dauphin counties in Pennsylvania suddenly decided to join forces and combine their cases against Adam Leroy Lane in order to bring the serial killer to justice. Stanley Rebert, the York County district attorney, announced that York County would be transferring the Patricia Brooks stabbing charges to Dauphin County, where Lane was charged with murdering Darlene Ewalt. It was hoped that trying the two cases together would reduce the complications of two separate trials and get them both concluded in half the time.

The news came as a bit of a surprise to me. It was not something I would have suspected, but judging from the reaction I noticed from others involved in the case, it did not seem to be shocking or in any way detrimental to the criminal cases pending against Lane.

"This is an aggravating circumstance," said District Attorney Rebert. "The York County case is an aggravating circumstance for the Dauphin County case. So, Dauphin County is in a better position to seek the death penalty."

Rebert also stated that one trial would save both time and money as well as avoid putting the victims and their families through twice as many criminal proceedings. The decision to pursue a capital-punishment sanction against Lane, though it pleased many people, would not be decided by public outcry. In the state of Pennsylvania, a capital punishment can only be brought against a defendant if one or both of two specific criteria are met. The first is that the crime must involve a repeat offense. Either that or the crime that the defendant is being accused of committing must have occurred during the commission or act of another felony. With the Ewalt case, this would be the second homicide that Lane had been accused of committing. The New Jersey murder conviction paved a clear path for a death-penalty trial against Lane in Pennsylvania.

As for Patricia Brooks, she had managed to stay out of the glare of the media spotlight from the very beginning. I'm sure the press doggedly pursued her. Newspaper reports confirmed some time afterward that she had moved from the home where she had been attacked by Lane as she slept.

"She's doing as well as can be expected," said Chief Carl Segatti, of the Northern York County, Pennsylvania, Regional Police Department. In a rare mention of Patricia

Brooks at a news conference, Segatti added that he was not sure what might have pushed Lane to attack these women, and Dauphin County District Attorney Ed Marsico admitted that authorities still wanted to know why the killings took place.

"We are struggling to figure out what could motivate a person to commit these sorts of crimes," Marsico said. "Obviously he has some animosity toward women. He sought out women randomly."

# Chapter 25

## NUMBERS GAME

By the end of February 2009, our family was en route to New York City to participate in an interview with Hoda Kotb, a correspondent for *Dateline NBC*. Unfortunately, Ryan was unable to accompany us because of his scheduled midterm exams at college. Having entered a new school with a fresh slate, Ryan knew how important it was that he focus more seriously on his schoolwork. Although he wanted to join us, he thought better of it, not willing to let even the smallest of distractions jeopardize his future again. I thought it was the right thing to do, and we all supported him. I was still apprehensive. I didn't know what to expect or what questions we would be asked. I admit that I also harbored some other, more superficial concerns, such as how I might appear on camera. I was not looking forward to the entire country seeing me with ten extra pounds courtesy of the NBC television cameras, not to mention the twenty extra pounds I had packed on over the previous two tumultuous years.

Also weighing on my mind at the time was an e-mail that I had received the day before. It was from Todd Ewalt's victim advocate, Jennifer Storm, who requested my assistance in pressuring the governor's office to expedite the signoff on Lane's impending extradition to Pennsylvania. A few weeks earlier, Kevin and I had already given an authorization that gave Pennsylvania our consent to keep Adam Lane in that state to serve the entire length of his prison sentences after they tried him. However, Lane had still not been moved, and the Pennsylvania prosecutor's office was hoping I might be able to remedy whatever red tape was holding up his extradition with a phone call. Since I had previously contacted the governor's office and inquired about the same issue almost a year and a half earlier with regard to the New Jersey case, and was rewarded with only further frustration and failure, I wasn't sure it would do any good. But I agreed to try it once again to see if I might have an impact this time around. I made some quick phone calls and got ahold of E. Abim Thomas, a member of Governor Patrick's legal counsel, and left a message. I made my case as best I could, but I didn't know what might come of it, if anything. However, after we landed in New York and arrived at the hotel, I received a call on my cell phone. It was Thomas. She was as helpful as she could be, given the circumstances, and promised me that she would contact me personally once the governor had signed the grant. We agreed to reconnect the following week. It was very encouraging news.

Marianne O'Donnell had gone to great lengths to make sure our stay in New York would be a positive and

memorable one in every way. The accommodations at the
Waldorf were exemplary; the food was simply outstand-
ing, and the entire dining experience was unlike anything
I have ever had before. All of this was something that most
people may never experience. Having become friendly with
Marianne, I'm sure she just wanted to put us all at ease and
try to offset some of our anxiety at having to recount our
horrific experience during the summer of 2007 in front of
a national television audience.

The next morning, Marianne met us in the lobby, and
from there we proceeded to our interview by limousine.
Interestingly enough, the filming took place in an obscure
loft tucked away in SoHo and not in the NBC studios as
we had been expecting. The atmosphere was laid-back and
comfortable, which helped to reassure us that our decision
to sit down with *Dateline* had not been a mistake.

Hoda Kotb immediately put us further at ease with her
friendly demeanor and even the way in which she shook
our hands, holding them firmly but gently as she greeted
us. She introduced herself to Shea with a warm, "Hey,
girl," which left an immediate and lasting impression, not
only on our daughter, but Kevin and me as well. At that
moment, we looked around at each other, feeling confident
that she would portray our experience in a positive and
sincere manner. She made it easy to answer the questions
posed to us, and before we knew it, it was all over. It was
like a dreaded trip to the dentist that you fret and worry
about all week, but once you get there, it is not as bad as
you thought.

As we spilled out onto the street afterward, a cameraman followed us, like our own private paparazzo. *Dateline*
wanted to get a few casual shots of our family in motion. It

was rather comical to think about seeing ourselves in such a scenario, trying to act as if it was normal for the three of us to be walking along the crowded streets of New York City like this every day. And trying to do it while someone was taking pictures of us made it difficult just to keep a straight face. Some people on the street stopped and stared. You could see them trying to figure out who we were. I laughed out loud, wondering what they may have been thinking. The stars of some reality show, perhaps? We had our fun with that, but I became much more sober-minded when I considered how these pictures might be perceived by those who did not know us.

Our flight back was scheduled for early that evening, which left us with plenty of time to take in some of the sights of the Big Apple. Marianne had even arranged an impromptu tour for us at Rockefeller Center and lunch at the Rock Center Café. We had something to eat with an excellent view of the skating rink and the Prometheus statue. It was a beautiful day. The entire trip was something none of us will ever forget. Later that night, however, my feet firmly planted on Massachusetts soil once again, I felt an incredible sense of relief even though I had enjoyed our brief visit to New York and felt that the taping had gone well. I only hoped that now life would go back to normal for the McDonoughs.

---

In my continued need to grasp some kind of understanding of Lane's motivations, I started Googling "truck drivers" and "truck stops" and "truck stop crimes," or anything that was directly or indirectly related to these topics. It wasn't that I thought I might find something that law enforcement officials had missed, but I was curious about how unusual a crime spree like this might be. I thought perhaps there might be some insight I could gain about the life of a truck driver. Maybe something about the job was conducive to homicidal behavior, like being a postal worker, as the joke goes.

I was shocked by what my search turned up. I simply could not believe how many truck drivers have been suspected or convicted of highway murders through the years. In fact, after what I found out, I'd think the phrase "going postal" should be permanently replaced with "going trucker."

There was horror and grief splashed all over the Internet, like the blood of the victims at the hands of these truckers who made the towns around the interstates their personal killing fields. It was not quite a daily event, but it appeared to happen often enough to make my family's situation less exceptional than I first thought. I felt all the more fortunate as a result.

*Los Angeles Times* journalist Scott Glover wrote an interesting article in the Sunday, April 5, 2009, edition of the newspaper. Citing an ever-growing database of female murder victims, Glover reported that the FBI suspected that serial killers working as long-haul truckers were responsible for the slayings of hundreds of prostitutes, hitchhikers and stranded motorists whose bodies had been dumped near highways over the last three decades.

In 2004, law enforcement officials identified a pattern of homicides involving the deaths of prostitutes who worked in and around truck stops in the south-central region of the United States. These killings had taken place over a number of years and initially involved the states of Oklahoma,

Texas, Arkansas and Mississippi as well as Indiana and Pennsylvania. In 2009, the FBI launched the Highway Serial Killings Initiative to track suspicious slayings and suspect truckers.

In the years following, federal as well as state and local law enforcement agencies began meeting for joint case consultations, resulting in the identification of more than two hundred truck-driver suspects. Timelines have been compiled on more than fifty of these individuals to date, with more in progress. These timelines, which cover the entire United States, are available to departments that have rape and homicide victims meeting the following description: prostitutes working from truck stops, hitchhikers, transients, stranded motorists, unidentified dead bodies, and any other victims at risk where the suspect is likely to be a long-haul truck driver.

Many of these crimes remain unsolved, but in other cases, the suspected truckers are still at large. One such trucker had served fifteen years for a previous murder in Illinois and was paroled early; then on March 16, 1996, he offered a Denver, Colorado, woman a ride home. Her body was discovered the next day, beaten, strangled and raped in an alley adjacent to railroad tracks. The trucker was quickly identified as a suspect, but he fled when he realized a warrant had been issued for his arrest. He abandoned his tractor-trailer at a truck stop in Sioux City, Iowa, and has not been seen since.

In another example, a California trucker-murderer turned himself in to authorities one day in 1998 by walking into a Humboldt County sheriff's station with a severed breast inside a Ziploc bag and telling a deputy that this was just "the tip of the iceberg." It seems the handsome, clean-cut trucker, who kept his rig impeccably clean, had a penchant for prostitutes and hitchhikers. He was convicted of killing four women, their mutilated and dismembered body parts found scattered throughout the state. And in a more recent case, a fifty-six-year-old independent trucker from Illinois was implicated in the deaths of six people in four states throughout the South.

There is a map of the United States in the FBI office near Quantico, Virginia, covered with more than five hundred red dots, each one representing a murder victim in the Highway Serial Killings Initiative database and spanning thirty years of time. Despite all the red on the map, one FBI supervisory agent believes that the number of such offenses has been "grossly underreported." Some estimates say that as many as eighty thousand unsolved, apparently random violent crimes, not limited to murder, have taken place and continue to take place all across the country. With more than fifty thousand miles of highways connecting American cities and towns, it would seem that no one is really immune from this kind of thing.

The database is filled with information on scores of truckers who've been charged with killings or rapes committed near highways or who are suspects in such crimes, but authorities do not have statistics on whether driving trucks ranks high on the list of occupations of known serial killers. Investigators could only speculate that the trucker's mobility, lack of supervision and access to potential victims, most of whom lead high-risk lifestyles that leave them particularly vulnerable, make it a good cover for someone inclined to kill. Painting with a broad brush, one investigator described the trucking community as a "mobile crime scene."

The FBI had not publicized the existence of the program

to the public until just prior to Glover's article. Working in relative secrecy, the information that these FBI analysts gathered had helped solve dozens of cold-case killings, and making the database available for law enforcement agencies to submit additional case information helped locate numerous suspected offenders. With information and data gathered from local police departments on seemingly random killings, sexual assaults and other violent crimes, the analysts can use the system to spot patterns that might otherwise go unnoticed. The Highway Serial Killings Initiative was designed to help local police "connect the dots" to slayings outside their jurisdictions. Unfortunately, even with all the progress and success of the program, there is still a long way to go, with many of the dots remaining unconnected to any known suspect.

It makes the whole thing seem like a numbers game. But all these dots have names.

Hunterdon, New Jersey, County Prosecutor J. Patrick Barnes credited the FBI with helping them eventually solve the Massaro case.

"We're so busy looking at cases in our own towns, our own counties and our own regions that we sometimes miss what's going on around us," said Barnes. "You can't connect the dots if you don't know what the dots are."

It is frightening to think that there are others like Lane in the world, but there are many more like him out there. This is by no means meant to disparage all truck drivers. There are far too many good ones, who abide by the laws, both moral and man-made, to make any kind of critical judgment against the profession as a whole. The harsh reality is that there are people in all walks of life and in many lines of work who are capable of hurting and willing to hurt other people for no reason. These are dangers you cannot spend too much time worrying about because you have to live your life. Everyone, however, should be aware that these dangers exist and minimize them at every opportunity. For the rest, I guess, that's why we have police departments and police officers. If it is all just a numbers game, I am glad we have officers, like the ones we have in Chelmsford, on our side.

# Chapter 26

## A FRIEND IN PENNSYLVANIA

Finally, on May 21, 2009, Pennsylvania State Police took Adam Leroy Lane into custody and transported him from the Massachusetts prison where he was being held to face charges in Pennsylvania for the July 13, 2007, murder of Darlene Ewalt and the brutal attack on Patricia Brooks four days later. He was arraigned around 3:00 p.m. at a Linglestown district court in Lower Paxton Township before Judge William Wenner. Troopers noted that Lane was fully cooperative during the trip from Massachusetts. Once in the Pennsylvania courtroom, he appeared quite at ease, speaking freely with troopers.

Lane was charged with first-degree murder, possessing instruments of a crime and loitering and prowling at night in Ewalt's murder, and attempted homicide, aggravated assault and burglary in the attack on Brooks. After the hearing, Lane was committed to the Dauphin County Prison, his new home, where he would be held without bail to await a preliminary hearing for both crimes. At a press conference immediately following the arraignment, Dauphin County District Attorney Ed Marsico remained tight-lipped on whether prosecutors would seek the death penalty against Lane. They were not showing their cards, and Lane's attorney had not revealed whether his client was going to plead guilty to the charges to avoid a possible death-penalty trial.

Then, on June 9, 2009, against the advice of his attorney, Lane decided to waive his preliminary hearing, basically deciding not to challenge the county's case, so the case would instead head directly to the trial phase. That day, prosecutors were busy lining up their witnesses to testify against the North Carolina truck driver when First Assistant Public Defender Brad Winnick informed Senior District Judge Edward Harkin of his client's request.

It was a pleasant surprise for Marsico, who said, "I'm very pleased he exercised his right to waive the hearing. It saved Miss Brooks from having to testify and relive the horrific events of 2007."

This paved the way for Marsico to make the formal announcement that they would be seeking the death penalty against Adam Leroy Lane for the murder of Darlene Ewalt.

"If any case calls for a capital prosecution," Marsico said, "a case like this does."

"The Ewalts were in agreement with our decision to seek the death penalty," said prosecutor Fran Chardo. "The death penalty is appropriate in this case more than any other I've seen. We have put forth evidence that we believe shows this is a true serial killer. It's hard to believe something like this could happen . . . that this sort of crime, this sort of serial crime would occur. It's awful."

_____

In July 2009, as the two-year anniversary of this whole tragic ordeal approached, and with the end of the legal aspect of this nightmare seemingly coming to an end, I took a step back emotionally, disbelieving how quickly the time had passed. Although in many ways the incident in which we came face-to-face with a violent intruder whom we learned afterward was a serial murderer seemed so long ago, but in recent nights I had experienced episodes in which I found myself paralyzed with fear. It was the very same feeling I had experienced early on, during the days and weeks immediately after the attack. Although these kinds of anxious moments had tapered off slowly over time, I discovered that I had not fully divested myself from the unnerving symptoms of post-traumatic stress.

One particular evening, I had been lying in bed when I happened to glance out of the bedroom window and saw what I thought was a man standing in my backyard. It seemed so real, and all I could do was hope that my eyes were playing tricks on me because I was frozen in terror, unable to move. I wanted to wake Kevin but I couldn't speak. I felt my heart skip, and I started to get that familiar black pit in my stomach. He had come back to finish the job, I thought.

I soon realized that it was just a shadow from one of the tiki torches set out for Shea's high school graduation party—and the very fact that we were able to mark the two-year anniversary of that horrible day with our closest friends and family by celebrating Shea's graduation only made the occasion even more momentous. One late night, later that same month, I was seated in front of our desktop computer, poring over a very full e-mail in-box. I hadn't been able to get to e-mails for almost a week because of the focus on planning Shea's party. As I was deleting what was unimportant and opening what appeared to be relevant, I came across a Google alert, one of many that had been sent to me over the past two years. My Google archive for Adam Leroy Lane was admittedly quite vast, even though I had begun discarding many items that were either redundant or bore no real relation or significance to us. This one, however, I discovered was different. In an article dated July 10, 2009, PennLive.com stated, "Dauphin County prosecutors to seek death penalty against North Carolina truck driver."

In all reality, I guess I had been waiting for this exact news item since the beginning. My gut reaction was to jump up and cheer. At the same time, the report renewed my hope that the complete truth about this killer would ultimately be revealed, including his motivations and information that might lead to the discovery of any other victims whom he may have been responsible for murdering in the past. An impending death sentence could very well become the catalyst for him to finally disclose these insights. Would he talk if it was his life being used as a bargaining chip? Would he confess to other crimes—if it meant saving his own ass? It remained to be seen.

Still, it was just more death hanging over the head of everyone whose lives had become entangled with Adam Leroy Lane's. Nevertheless, there was nothing for us survivors to do except get on with living.

Several months later, however, something happened that I don't think any of us could have anticipated, and it had the potential to change everything. Out of the blue, on the evening of October 19, 2009, I answered a call on my cell phone and heard the voice of an emotionally distraught female on the other end of the line. I didn't recognize who it was when the woman first began to speak, but from the context of her conversation, I quickly realized it was Nicole Ewalt, Darlene and Todd's daughter. We had not spoken in some time, and I was somewhat surprised to hear from her. I could tell she was choking back tears as she went on to inform me that it had been leaked to her that Lane was in a medically induced coma.

"What did you say?" I asked, unsure I had heard her correctly.

"He tried to kill himself," she told me. "He's in a coma."

"Oh my God. Did you hear about this from Jennifer?"

"No," Nicole said, "I know someone who works at the medical building near the prison where he was taken for treatment. She said it was him."

Nicole had been told that Lane's prognosis was not good and that he was, in fact, clinging to life by a thread. She did not know much more than that at the time, but apparently this was information that she wanted to share with me, and I thanked her, telling her that if she ever needed someone to talk to, she could always call me.

I hung up the phone, stunned by what I had just heard. Could this be how it all ended? I almost didn't want to believe it, and I actually hoped that it wasn't true. It wouldn't be fair. Lane's fate was supposed to be in *our* hands, or at least in the hands of the people. *We* were supposed to take his life. Now he was taking yet another life away from us. And the Ewalts and Patricia Brooks would not get their day in court with Lane. Justice would've been preempted.

I needed verification, so I immediately made some calls to my police contacts, George Tyros and Geoff Noble. I related to them what I had been told and they promised to look into the matter and get back to me with any information they gleaned.

I could not help but notice how markedly different their reactions were to the possibility of Lane's death than Nicole's and mine had been. Where we felt anger and disappointment upon learning of Lane's suicide attempt, they took a certain professional satisfaction in the news that such a dangerous individual would be gone from this earth. I knew both of these men to be empathetic and caring people, but it was simply much more personal for us, especially Nicole. I understood how Nicole had essentially put her life on hold pending the outcome of Lane's upcoming trial. Everything hinged upon this murderer facing the death penalty and being held accountable for taking her mother's life. Until then, there could be no moving on. She was suspended in time, merely going through the motions of life. I sympathized, knowing that had things turned out differently for my family, I don't think I could have functioned in any normal capacity until our daughter's killer had been punished to the fullest extent possible. Under such circumstances, how could one *not* become consumed with avenging a loved one's death? Having Lane off the streets, even dead by his own hand, was somehow not good enough. He needed to be judged. He needed to be publicly condemned. And we all needed to be there to witness it.

I felt much closer to Nicole because of these shared emotions, and I knew by how she'd reached out to me that she felt the same way. I wanted to do all that I could to

help her get through this. And whether Lane survived the
suicide attempt or not, I knew it wouldn't be the end of it.
Like me, law enforcement authorities involved in the case
all concurred that Lane was probably responsible for other
murders that had not been linked to him yet, and it was
almost inevitable that more gruesome discoveries would
follow. If Lane were to die now, the identity of these victims might never be known. I wondered whether Lane had
left behind a suicide note, and whether he had provided
some information, such as names, descriptions or whereabouts of those unknown victims, in an attempt to clear
his conscience before he died. I knew that was an unlikely
notion, and entirely predicated on the concept that Adam
Lane actually had a conscience, so I was not holding out
much hope. How anybody could do what he had done and
possess a full complement of human emotions did not
seem very realistic. Still, I waited to hear back from the
police on this matter.

   In the end, it turned out to be untrue. Lane did not
attempt to kill himself. Nicole had been given inaccurate
information. An inmate from the prison where Lane was
being held *had* been admitted to the medical facility where
a family acquaintance of the Ewalts was employed, but it
turned out not to be Lane. That the information was false
did not actually surprise me. Adam Leroy Lane was a coward, and I knew he did not have the guts to take his own
life, even as he so indiscriminately took the lives of others. To prowl through the darkness of night and victim-
ize women as they slept was the epitome of cowardice. As
much as I did not think Lane deserved to be breathing the
same air as everyone else on this planet, I was actually glad
that he had not taken his own life. Now, at least, we would

get to face him in open court. Whatever terrible things happened to him after that, I was all for it.

───────────────

As 2010 began, Adam Lane was still sitting in a Pennsylvania prison cell awaiting judgment. The delay, I was told, was because of the "discovery process" at work, part of the slowly grinding wheels of justice. I could only wonder how a case that seemed so cut-and-dry to us laypeople could take so long for the lawyers to prepare. And knowing how these continued delays were so exasperating to *me*, it must have been nothing short of torture for the other families. Given the uncertainty and anxiety of the pending case against Lane, every day that passed could only have been a sad reminder to the Ewalts and Patricia Brooks of what was missing from their lives, what had been forever taken away from them by a man whose rights were being so carefully considered in preparation for this final court proceeding.

March 2010 roared in like a lion, bringing with it another late-season winter storm that buried Chelmsford and the surrounding communities under more than a foot of snow. After digging out on the morning of March 2, I got to work late and saw that I had missed a phone call from Nicole Ewalt. She had left a message, saying she was in the area and wanted to take the opportunity to pay me a surprise visit. From what I understood, Nicole and her fiancé, Suntorn, worked together delivering medical supplies to hospitals and clinics along the eastern seaboard, and today they had purposely chosen a delivery route that would bring them up to New England, in the hope of finally meeting me and my family.

I immediately called her back and discovered that she

was in New Hampshire and less than thirty minutes from
our home. I was instantly excited, though I wished she had
contacted me much further in advance. My coworkers had
always been very understanding when it came to the needs
of my family with regard to our run-in with Lane, but I
could not get out of work at the last minute without causing
a significant disruption.

Nicole agreed to wait for me, and I was glad. She and
her fiancé had driven all through the night, though, and
they were exhausted, so she asked if it would be all right if
they parked in our driveway and crashed in their truck until
I got home. I would have liked to be there to greet them,
and I felt terrible that no one was home to let them inside so
they could rest in comfort. There was no way Kevin could
do it with his work schedule, and Shea and Ryan both com-
muted to college, so they were out of the house most of the
day. I texted Shea, knowing that she would probably beat
me home, and asked her to let Nicole and Suntorn into the
house and make them comfortable.

My daughter was as surprised as I was to hear from
Nicole so suddenly that morning. I knew it would be somewhat awkward for Shea to meet a young woman whose
mother had been killed by the same man who almost certainly would have killed her as well if one of any set of circumstances had been different, but she, of course, agreed
to welcome them as soon as she arrived home.

The very circumstances that brought our families
together would undoubtedly make for an emotional meeting for all of us. For the better part of a year, Nicole and
I had been in contact, speaking briefly on the phone and
texting each other with updates and developments in the
case as well as sharing personal information. She had
called me in excitement one day and told me all about her

recent engagement. Another time, she'd reached out to me in aguish when her travels had taken her past the home where Monica Massaro had been killed. I was happy to be there for her on both such occasions, in joy and sorrow. These were times when a girl really needs her mother, and in some small way if I could provide a measure of comfort or relief to this young woman whose mother was suddenly and mercilessly taken from her, then I felt it was my duty to do just that. As mothers, I think we all feel a sense of responsibility to step in and help another's child if we can. I felt it was imperative Nicole understand that as alone as she felt, given the terrible loss she'd suffered, people cared, *we* cared, and we empathized with her anguish and all that she had been through. I only hoped that I could convey the depth of my emotion and sorrow to her somehow.

When I pulled into the driveway a little before 4:00 p.m. I saw that Shea had come home to let our guests inside to rest. They were asleep on the sectional couch in the family room, so I tiptoed around the house for a while, not wanting to disturb them. Before too long Nicole awoke, and the first thing I did was give her a great big hug. It was as natural as if I had embraced my own daughter. She seemed comfortable with me from the very beginning.

Nicole and I sat down at the kitchen counter, chatting quietly so as not to wake her fiancé, who was still asleep only a few feet away. We talked about her trip, her job, what had brought her out this way and just about everything else, skirting around the topic of her mother's murder. All I could think about was saying the wrong thing and causing her further pain. The psychological effects of this visit to our home alone could have detrimental effects on her already fragile psyche. She had already confided in me that she still had very little appetite and slept fleetingly, waking to the slightest sound.

Sitting before me, I saw a beautiful young woman who could no longer fully experience all the joy in her life because of the senseless and destructive actions of a psychopathic trucker. It was heartbreaking to look at her that way, and I could not help but see myself in this lost woman's image, realizing how easily it could have been me if I had lost Shea to Lane's violence. The fact that Nicole had recently gotten engaged and was making plans for her wedding was a positive step forward, but if there was unresolved grief, I knew it could just as easily compound her feelings of loss. What should have been one of the most wonderful and joyous times of her life was suffused with sadness and grief.

"Would you mind if we take this conversation outside?" Nicole asked. "I could use a smoke."

"Not at all," I said. "Our dog looks like he could use a little time out himself."

As we stepped out onto the front porch, Kevin drove in and came over to greet us. Following a brief introduction, Kevin excused himself, citing a desperate need for a shower.

"Nicole's fiancé, Suntorn, is still asleep on the sectional," I reminded him.

"Okay. I'll be extra quiet."

"Thanks. We'll be outside for a while."

The streets had been plowed, and it was a lovely evening, so we decided to go for a walk. It was cold, but the sun was setting and it was peaceful and calm. Nicole had a smoke while I kept pace beside her with the dog on a leash. When we reached Misty Meadows, I broke the silence by explaining how Adam Leroy Lane had walked up this very road on his journey to our back door more than two and a half years before. By bringing this up, I figured that if she wanted to talk about anything related to Lane, it would provide the perfect opportunity. It would be her choice.

Nicole did speak then about her mom, telling me how Darlene had mentioned to her in the days just prior to her death that she had experienced a strange feeling that she was being stalked. This eerie rumination sent chills up my spine. Although I knew that Lane picked his victims at random, I began to wonder if he had, in fact, planned his attacks more carefully, even casing the homes around the truck stops beforehand so as to pinpoint the best targets for his nocturnal bloodlust. It had always seemed too much of a coincidence to me that Lane could have repeatedly stumbled upon the homes of sleeping females who happened to have left their doors unlocked. Though police investigators all agreed that the home invasions were arbitrary, with the unlocked doors providing him with the simple opportunity, I was still haunted by the very thought that he might've watched us for days, lurking around our property and peeping in the windows.

Nicole also admitted that she, too, often played the "what if" game.

"You know, I was supposed to stop by my parents' house that night," she explained. "I should have been there. I planned to go, but . . . something came up . . . I don't know . . . I got busy doing something and I didn't end up going."

"Nicole, don't do that to yourself."

"No," she said, "it's true, I would have been outside on the patio with her. Don't you see? She wouldn't have been sitting out there all alone. He would have seen both of us. He wouldn't have attacked *two* women. Maybe he would have moved on to another house and hurt someone else, and that would have been terrible, but he would have left us alone."

I could hear the palpable regret in her voice, and I witnessed firsthand how underlying guilt emanated from her with this confession. What a terrible burden to bear, I thought. I knew it would not matter what I, or anyone else, said. In her heart, she'll always believe her mother would be alive today if her plans to visit her parents that Friday the 13th had not changed.

I urged her not to focus on the countless "what if" questions and drown in the depths of endless speculation, but suggested that she instead look ahead to the day that the murderer would pay for what he did to her mother and her entire family.

"What's important is to keep focused on the future," I told her, realizing how clichéd that sounded as soon as I said it, but still hoping to get the message across to her somehow. I just knew that I could not bear the thought of my own children having to experience what Nicole had been forced to endure when she buried her mother, and to have them go on and torment themselves with guilt for the rest of their lives would have been just too much.

"As a mother myself," I told her, "I know that your mom would want nothing more than for you to be happy and to move on with your life."

That seemed to strike a chord with her, and she fell into silent thought for a moment.

When we got back to the house, Suntorn was awake and hungry. We made plans to go to dinner and chose Vincenzo's, one of our favorite restaurants, which was just down the road. Nicole, Suntorn and Kevin and I enjoyed some fine Italian food and buoyant conversation. In broaching the subject of what had brought us all together that day, I wanted to be sure that Nicole fully understood our feeling of certainty that Darlene, along with Monica Massaro, had been with us in spirit the night Shea was attacked and that her mom was a factor in our daughter surviving that night and being with us today. For that, I thanked Nicole on behalf of her mother. She was grateful, and in continuing the inevitable discussion about Lane, one of the things she brought up was the horrible position her father, Todd, had been forced into because of the unusual nature of her mother's murder: namely, that it had come at the hands of a stranger. Todd had been suspected, if not officially accused, of his wife's slaying. As far as the Ewalt family was concerned, however, law enforcement had had tunnel vision with regard to the perpetrator of this crime. Authorities had taken great liberty in assuming that various marital issues, such as financial troubles and their recent disagreement over an upcoming cruise, were motivation for Todd wanting his wife dead. The police even went so far as to cite a failed lie-detector test as affirmation of his guilt, instantly casting him under a dark cloud of suspicion and generating harsh public scrutiny, even though Todd was only told by the police that he failed and was never actually shown the results. Regardless, this had devastated her father, Nicole revealed, and made things that much more difficult for her and her brother at the same time. She expressed her gratitude to us for capturing Lane, which provided irrefutable proof of her father's innocence.

We ended our dinner with a promise to keep in touch and to meet again when the trial date had been firmly established. We told them that Pennsylvania authorities had informed us that we would be receiving a subpoena to testify and thus would be expected to be there. However, I told her, as far as we were concerned, we planned to be in the courtroom regardless the day that Adam Leroy Lane was scheduled to face judgment for the crimes he committed in Pennsylvania.

Because of the late hour and the light snow that had begun falling outside, I suggested to Nicole and Suntorn that they stay overnight rather than take the chance driving at that time and in those weather conditions. My only hesitation was that they would have to stay in the room where Lane had attacked our daughter just a few days after he'd killed Nicole's mother. I was concerned about how this might affect Nicole, not just that night, but in the future, and I apologized profusely about the circumstances surrounding the sleeping arrangements. Nevertheless, Nicole accepted our offer of hospitality, which I gave her a lot of credit for. I don't think I could have done it if I was in her shoes. As it was, I had a difficult enough time falling asleep, tossing and turning all night.

The next morning, Nicole and Suntorn were up early and on the road by 8:00 a.m. Before they left, I asked Nicole how she'd slept. She told me that she'd cried herself to sleep but that it had nothing to do with the violent history of the room; it wasn't any different from most nights since her mother's death. Then we hugged one last time, our hearts heavy with regret for all that had transpired over the past few years. We were happy for the opportunity to spend that time together, but I knew that when we looked into each other's eyes, we both wished it hadn't come to this. We would both gladly have traded Darlene's life for any friendship the two of us might develop as a result of our family's connection to her mother's murderer. I told Suntorn to take care of this young woman who would eventually be his wife and urged him to be patient with her, which I could tell he had been all along. With the trial in Pennsylvania looming, I wasn't sure about anything, but Nicole and her fiancé and her entire family remained in my prayers, with the hope that someday they will be able to find peace in their lives again.

# Chapter 27

## TRANSITION TO TRIAL

The dread and anticipation of the upcoming Pennsylvania trial seemed to grow more and more each day after Nicole Ewalt and her fiancé, Suntorn, visited us. We still did not know exactly when it would begin, but we sensed that we were getting down to the nitty-gritty. From what our sources were telling us, it could be announced at any time, and it would likely come without much warning. So when a call came in from Nicole late in the evening on March 19, 2010, I thought this was the news we had been waiting for. However, she informed me that earlier she had received a disappointing voice mail from her father pertaining to Lane's date with Lady Justice.

"The trial's going to be delayed indefinitely," she said. "My dad found out that Lane made threatening remarks about possibly harming one of his defense attorneys ."

"Oh my God! What happened?"

"One of his lawyers was a woman. I'm not sure of all

the details, but I understand that he made a comment to someone else which made her fear for her safety, and she requested court permission to withdraw from the case."

Nicole was in a near panic, fearful that having to get a new defense lawyer up to speed on the case would mean basically starting all over and that it would be another three years before the trial began.

By this point, I felt it had become utterly ridiculous that the crimes in Pennsylvania hadn't been resolved, but I tried to reassure Nicole that everything would work out and that she needed to take a deep breath and not let her dark thoughts get the best of her.

Making matters worse, the prison where Lane was then incarcerated was within sight of where Nicole was living. She admitted to me that with every setback such as this, her frustration level would rise so high that it would push her one step closer to actually going over to the detention facility to confront Adam Leroy Lane in person. She was not exactly sure what she would do or say if she found herself face-to-face with her mother's killer, but if the courts weren't going to do something soon, she felt she had to take some kind of action herself.

It was difficult to impress upon her how futile and possibly harmful this approach would actually be if she went forward with it. She was fuming with anger, and I could hardly blame her. However, I told her that with every flame of rage that consumed her, or any time she had so much as a bitter thought about him, it gave Lane further power over her and her life. I tried to convince her that he was not worth it and that the legal system would take its course, and in the end Lane would get what he deserved. What Nicole deserved was to live her life; her mother would want nothing less for her.

The following day I reached out to Jennifer Storm, the Ewalts' victim advocate, who confirmed exactly what Nicole had told me, though providing further detail and perhaps an even bleaker outlook on the future of the case. In her e-mail, Jennifer stated, *"The PD's office is requesting removal from the case based on the threats and the President Judge agreed—apparently it was bad. This means a new attorney must be appointed. We are pretty sure who it will be and it won't be good for the Ewalts. The individual is a real showman in the courtroom and will do everything he can to discredit the Ewalts and most likely attempt to pin the whole murder on either Nick or Todd or both. It will be a very hard trial for them, but if they are up for it, Ed will move forward with the death penalty. I let Todd know that we will do everything we can to advocate for their family once the case goes to trial. This will, however, set us back months as a new attorney will need to get acquainted with the case, hire another psychologist for an exam, etc. The other option is to allow a plea of life without the possibility of parole, which Lane will take. District Attorney, Ed Marsico, will ensure that he serves his time in PA."*

This was very worrisome. I realized that Lane could have intentionally threatened his lawyer just so she would dismiss herself from the case and thus create a delay while the system reset itself. What was to stop him from doing this over and over again, permanently delaying the trial and keeping the Ewalts from ever moving on with their lives? It amounted to nothing short of cruel and unusual punishment for this family. This bothered me a great deal, and I could only imagine what it would be like for Nicole, her brother, Nick, and her father, Todd, when they learned all this from their victim advocate. Not to mention what

Patricia Brooks, Lane's other Pennsylvania victim, must have felt.

Not content to follow my own advice and do nothing, essentially what I'd told Nicole to do, I sent a text to Detective-Sergeant Geoff Noble, the lead detective in New Jersey who'd handled the Monica Massaro murder investigation. I wanted to talk to someone who had experience in this area and could explain to me how something like this could happen.

I vented my frustrations to him, as I had so many times before. I told him how disturbing I found it that Lane could so easily manipulate the legal system in this way.

"What makes absolutely no sense to me," I began, "was how the Public Defender's Office, knowing Lane's history with women, would assign a female attorney to defend him in the first place."

Geoff Noble listened to everything I had to say and then offered me his usual cool and calm counsel. He reminded me that in the interactions he'd had with Adam Lane, the trucker's behavior and attitude had been one of resignation, not aggression.

"The only time Adam Lane became combative," he said, "was when he was asked about any sexual gratification he may have gotten before, during or after the attacks, so it is feasible that he could have been naturally provoked to violence by his lawyer if she asked him something that made him uncomfortable."

Noble also expressed some concern that the trial could be significantly delayed, and he worried that after what had happened with the Public Defender's Office, the judge might feel the need to bend over backward to ensure that Lane received fair representation, which could slow things down even further. Though he was not privy to what was being discussed in the Dauphin County Prosecutor's Office, he referred back to the line in Jennifer's e-mail that read: *"The other option is to allow a plea of life without the possibility of parole, which Lane will take."*

Detective Noble's implication that such an offer was likely already on the table stopped me in my tracks. It would not be the best-case scenario, but it was an ending that was in sight.

----

During the months following Nicole Ewalt's visit to our Chelmsford home, we tried to arrange another such encounter, since her travel routes continued to bring her through Massachusetts. Finally, on June 1, 2010, we were able to hook up again when Nicole had a delivery scheduled in the vicinity. It would be just the two of us this time, and our luck was such that I had the day off from work, which enabled us to relax for a couple of hours and chat about where things were with our lives. It was comforting for both of us to share our thoughts and time this way.

Nicole expressed her uncertainty about the final decision the court would render if it went to a jury trial, and this was very troubling to her. Although District Attorney Edward Marsico had been vocal about pushing for the death penalty, Nicole was afraid that it may have been a political ploy, a scare tactic by prosecutors to take some of the fight out of Lane and his defense counsel. Most all of the people we talked to in law enforcement told us the same thing, reiterating just how unlikely it was that Lane would ever actually face a capital-punishment trial. In fact, I would learn later on from Marsico himself that although there had been two hundred and twenty-five people on death row in Pennsylvania since 1976, only three of them had been executed. That fact alone would have had a significant impact on the family's decision to avoid a lengthy trial and accept a plea bargain.

Further complicating the matter, if a death-penalty trial *was* pursued, then all jurors would have to agree beyond a reasonable doubt on the existence of "aggravating circumstances," specific conditions that tended to increase the seriousness of a given crime and its corresponding penalties, criteria that needed to be met to pursue a capital-punishment case in the state of Pennsylvania. Enhanced punishment could be applied to offenses involving murder for hire or other crimes for profit such as arson; extreme cruelty or depravity; substantial prior criminal record; failure of rehabilitative efforts; particular vulnerability of the victim because of advanced age, extreme youth, or disability; and many other factors that may be considered by the court. In Lane's case, his crimes were made worse, in the eyes of the law, because they were committed with a dangerous weapon in conjunction with another serious crime—home invasion. Lane's criminal actions seemed to clearly meet the aggravating-circumstances criteria required for a death-penalty case, but as Nicole expressed, the outcome of any trial was not guaranteed.

In further considering the additional personal trauma that the family would have to endure, not to mention the media circus that such a trial was sure to generate, and the unlikelihood that Lane might ever be put to death by the state, Nicole explained to me that her family had decided to forgo the trial and accept Adam Leroy Lane's plea of guilty in exchange for his life.

"It will just be a lot easier," she explained. "If we accept the plea he'll get life in prison without the possibility for parole and that will be the end of it. So that's what we're going to do. Patricia Brooks has agreed as well. There won't be any trial."

"I completely understand," I told her in all honesty. "I think that's the best decision for everyone." I was just glad that the Ewalts and Patricia Brooks were willing to put all of it behind them and move on.

"That bastard will suffer longer, rotting away in a cell for the rest of his natural life, every day having to think about what put him there."

That made her smile slightly, and she gave me a hug. Then it was time for her to go.

As Nicole backed out of our driveway in a large truck, the irony of Nicole's job was not lost on me. Not only had the two of us become close because the truck driver who had killed her mother had also tried to kill my daughter, but she was also driving a truck to make a living, and the roads and highways that had brought her here from Pennsylvania were the same ones that Adam Lane had traveled upon to get to our house.

Pulling away, Nicole looked so fragile inside the steel-framed cab, but I realized she was a lot stronger than her slight image portrayed. As a testament to her strength, Nicole harbored no resentment toward truckers in general. In fact, it was a profession that was taken quite seriously within her family, her own grandfather having supported his family in that same manner. I remember her telling me once, "Not all truckers are bad. It's unfortunate that they are often given a bad rap because of the actions of only a portion."

As we waved good-bye, neither of us was certain when or what our next encounter would bring, but I knew she would be all right, and that she and Suntorn would find a way to get by and find happiness for themselves and their own family that they would start someday—grandchildren that would have made Darlene very happy.

---

Good fortune arrived sooner than I anticipated in the form of an e-mail from Jennifer Storm on Thursday, June 10, 2010. With the words "sentencing hearing" in the subject line, I opened the message eagerly to find a very brief but satisfying update. The Ewalts' victim advocate wrote, *"Dear Jeannie, It appears we have a resolution in this case. Ed has offered a sentence of life imprisonment plus consecutive time for the York County case (Lane's attack on Patricia Brooks) transferred here for prosecution. Lane has agreed to this. Both Patricia Brooks and the Ewalts are in agreement to this as well. He will plead guilty and be sentenced on the same day. It will be the last week of June either the 28th, 29th, or 30th. I am waiting to hear back from the Ewalts and from Patricia to determine the best time for them. Regards, Jennifer."*

The following Monday morning, June 14, 2010, just a month short of three years from the date of Darlene Ewalt's murder, her daughter, Nicole, called to let me know that a date had, indeed, finally been scheduled. She was crying with tears of both joy and sorrow when she told me that in two weeks' time, they would finally be given a chance to face down the monster that had torn their lives apart. It had been a long time coming, for sure.

When I got off the phone with Nicole, I did not know what to do first. There was no question that Kevin and I would be present in that Pennsylvania courtroom, sitting alongside the Ewalts, Patricia Brooks and her family, and probably the Massaros as well. We would all be present to hear the verdict and see Lane's face when the judge read the sentence.

There was a lot that needed to be done before we could begin to make our travel plans, but before anything else, I did the first thing I needed to do: I cried.

---

The days leading up to the Pennsylvania hearing were oppressively hot, not unlike the extreme temperatures we'd all experienced three summers earlier during the more than two weeks of terror when Adam Leroy Lane burst into our homes and our lives on a killing rampage. There were plenty of other reminders of what we had been through as well, and they seemed to be everywhere. I suppose it would never completely go away for any of us.

I had spoken with Monica Massaro's mother a couple of days prior to our departure to shore up the travel plans we made together. Fay Massaro was one of the first people I contacted after Nicole Ewalt informed me of the trial date in Pennsylvania. She expressed an immediate interest in attending Lane's upcoming hearing. Todd Ewalt had been there to support them by attending their daughter's hearing, and she was determined to honor his wife, Darlene, in the same way. The two of us agreed that it would be best to arrange for our overnight accommodations in downtown Harrisburg. We planned to stay over two nights and wanted to make sure that we were in the same hotel, or at least in close proximity to one another. We would drive down separately on Sunday and be there to support one another the night before the sentencing as well as the night afterward.

Kevin and I had become very fond of Fay and Frank Massaro throughout what had become a lengthy three-year legal process. For them, this hearing would be every bit as traumatic as it would be for the Ewalts. Sitting in court facing their daughter Monica's murderer a second time would inevitably trigger the same feelings of loss and devastation that they had experienced when the trucker responsible for her death was sentenced in a New Jersey courtroom almost two years earlier. Kevin and I wanted to be there for them as well as the Ewalts. Perhaps with us sitting beside them, all of us holding hands, the experience would be less harrowing and the pronouncement of the judge's sentence on Lane equally as gratifying, or even more gratifying, than the time before. I was hopeful that our presence would alleviate some of their despair and help them focus on the finality of the situation: Lane's demise within the prison system for what was left of his pitiful and cowardly life.

Pulling out of our driveway early Sunday morning on June 27, 2010, it was what we New Englanders refer to as a "scorcha." The temperature may have only been in the high eighties, but it was exceptionally muggy, and it felt like a hundred degrees. Not the most ideal weather conditions to be driving with the car top down, but we decided to live it up and make the most out of the driving experience. The commute, however, proved to be more punishing than pleasurable most of the way, with the sun beating down mercilessly and heavy traffic congestion producing choking exhaust fumes. The road noise made conversation a chore, and the drone of eighteen-wheelers barreling by us at a steady pace made us feel vulnerable and exposed. In retrospect, we were not exactly taking a family vacation, so we were in no position to expect too much from this trip. The GPS took us along the most direct route, over the George Washington Bridge. In the past, we had always taken the Tappan Zee and the more scenic route in

our travels to and from Virginia. Going through New York
City was exactly what you would expect, but once we got
out of New Jersey and crossed into Pennsylvania, we were
able to relax and actually began to enjoy the surroundings.
The temperature had changed as well, remaining warm
and sunny but without the oppressive humidity. I was overwhelmed by the natural beauty of the landscape all around
us. We were greeted by a continuous series of picturesque
hills dotted with farmhouses and livestock as far as the eye
could see. The route was clearly traveled by a countless
numbers of long-haulers, and it made me shudder to think
how the serenity and simplicity of quaint communities like
these had been desecrated on those summer nights not so
long ago by a psychopathic truck driver.

   Winding our way through the streets of Harrisburg at
the end of the day, we were relieved to have this part of
our journey complete. Our final destination also proved
to be somewhat of a surprise; we had not known what to
expect of Harrisburg, unaware of its distinction as Pennsylvania's capital or of its magnificence until that moment.
The downtown area was absolutely beautiful, poised on
the east bank of the gleaming Susquehanna River. Our
accommodations were centrally located, only a few city
blocks from the county courthouse in one direction and
the impressive Italian Renaissance–style architecture of
the capitol building even closer in the other. We were awe-
struck by the caliber of restorative work that had obviously been completed or was still in progress on many of
the municipal buildings. I'll never forget the sight of the
magnificent water fountain directly in front of the capitol
building, with its undulating sprays of water released in
varying sequences, directions and heights. We were both
mesmerized by how breathtaking our surroundings were,

and despite the regrettable nature of our visit, it turned out to be an uplifting experience that my husband and I would recall for many years to come.

That same evening, after settling into our hotel room, we met Fay and Frank Massaro for dinner at a popular upscale Mediterranean Italian restaurant that was within walking distance. We were all in good spirits, intoxicated by everything we had experienced in Harrisburg so far, though fueled by an energy that we knew would be short-lived. Once we were face-to-face with Adam Leroy Lane in open court the following day, everything would change. But this night, we hoped to remain untroubled by anything that lay further ahead than dessert. The atmosphere was warm, and we enjoyed a lovely meal together, all of which afforded us the opportunity to chat comfortably. Frank was full of stories, many of which reflected upon his world travels while serving in the U.S. Navy when he was a young man. We shared some laughs, but somehow the conversation steered in the direction of the following day's proceedings. The mood turned darker still when it became clear to Kevin and me that the Massaros were wholly unaware that the death penalty had been taken off the table and that Lane was only going to receive a life sentence. I thought that I had articulated this piece of information to Fay myself, though perhaps not as clearly as I thought. I could sense the disappointment in Frank's demeanor upon learning of the plea-bargain agreement.

At the end of the night, we all headed back to the hotel in virtual silence. It had been a long day, and we all wanted to be well rested and refreshed for the hearing in the morning and the emotional toll that it would surely bring.

It was not to be a restful night, however; first, we were required to change hotel rooms because of the air-conditioning not functioning properly. So we packed up our things and headed down to a new room, where I fell asleep thinking about how a broken air-conditioning system had helped save our daughter's life three years before and wondering if Adam Lane was sleeping next door in the courthouse jail. And then, in the middle of the night, we were awoken by the sound of a shrieking alarm and a recorded message telling us to vacate the building immediately. Kevin and I looked at each other as if to say, "Now what?" We soon found ourselves outside in our pajamas at a quarter to five in the morning alongside hundreds of other sleepy and confused hotel guests. We did not see Fay and Frank in the throng, and we were quickly allowed back inside, never fully knowing what had prompted the sudden evacuation. A couple hours later, when we got up via our personal alarm clock, we bumped into the Massaros after breakfast. None of us spoke much that morning, and when we headed to the courthouse, it felt more like a funeral procession than a hearing.

# Chapter 28

LIFE

Monday, June 28, 2010, was the day we had all been waiting for. With closure to this endless nightmare clearly in sight now, my anxiety level was as high as ever. After almost three years of delays and false alarms, I was half expecting something else would go wrong to let us down again.

We were outside the courthouse with the Massaros, about to go inside, when I spotted Nicole Ewalt approaching the building from the opposite direction. We stopped and waited for her, and I gave her a big hug. She introduced us to Jess and Kevin Johnston, her parents' best friends, who had accompanied the family to the hearing. We had only a short time to chat before the proceedings began when it suddenly dawned on me that these were the Johnstons who had sent us a personalized Christmas card after Lane had been identified as Darlene's murderer. I clearly remembered the card and the handwritten message, which expressed their gratitude to us for catching her killer and asserted that if it had not been for us, they may never have known who murdered their best friend. I recalled their sentiment touching me deeply at the time, and I was pleased to meet them in person.

The Johnstons' presence instantly made Kevin and me feel more at ease. I could see why the Ewalts liked to have them around. They had such naturally warm dispositions that were very reassuring, something I desperately needed at the time. Swirling around in my head throughout the entire trip had been concerns that my husband and I might have overstepped our bounds, that perhaps we should not have intruded upon a very personal family matter that did not necessarily involve us. Never did I feel that more than when we walked into the conference room, where the Ewalt family was gathered prior to the hearing, and I saw the look of complete and total anguish on Darlene's son Nick Ewalt's face. It was almost more than I could bear. I wondered if our presence served merely as a harsh reminder to Nick and the rest of his family that, while we were standing there beside them in the courtroom, Darlene was merely a memory.

Then it was time for the hearing to begin. We were escorted to the courtroom by the victim advocates, Jennifer Storm and Tanya Bartlebaugh, and the district attorney, Edward Marsico, and we filled in special gallery seats that were reserved for the families of the victims. Promptly, Dauphin County Judge Todd A. Hoover entered and announced that the court was in session.

Adam Leroy Lane was then led into the courtroom by two uniformed police officers. Five others were positioned around the room. I noticed that none of them were carrying firearms, and I realized that this was for the safety of everyone, including Lane himself.

Lane strode inside as if he were a grand marshal leading a parade. You could hear the low groans of disgust from the gallery the moment he entered. He had a repugnant, self-satisfied smirk plastered on his face that he seemed to intentionally exaggerate as he made his way past the family members seated in the front rows. He did not seem to possess an ounce of remorse for what he had done, and no compassion whatsoever for the survivors.

He did not look anyone directly in the eye, including the judge, who asked the defendant if he had anything to say before the charges against him were read.

"I ain't got nothing to say," he responded, with a southern accent so thick his words were all but unintelligible. However, there was a very clear absence of emotion in his voice.

Judge Hoover recited a host of charges against Lane that included murder in the first degree, possession of a weapon, loitering and prowling at night. The aggravating-circumstances requirement that would have automatically called for the death penalty had been dropped.

"How do you plead?" the judge asked Lane when he finished.

"Guilty," Lane answered, without hesitation.

The judge informed Lane that by pleading guilty to the charges and accepting the sentence of life in prison, he was waiving his right to a jury trial and everything that this fundamental civil liberty allowed, such as the right to file motions for the cross-examination of witnesses, present witnesses on his behalf, subpoena records and testify on his own behalf. Judge Hoover further advised the defendant that by copping a plea, his appeal rights were also limited, although he did have ten days to file an appeal to modify the sentence and thirty days to file an appeal with the state. He was ordered to pay restitution in the amount of $6,800 to cover the costs of Darlene Ewalt's funeral expenses. He owed the Crime Victims Compensation Fund $5,000, which was the maximum compensation that the fund paid out to families at the time, and $1,800 was to be paid directly to Todd's mother, Margaret Moran, who had paid for Darlene's funeral arrangements.

It was so sad that such details had to be discussed. It made it seem as if Darlene Ewalt's entire life amounted to nothing more than $6,800. Of course, that was not the case at all. To everyone except Adam Lane, she was precious and priceless, and that is something that must never be forgotten. That was why we were all there that day.

At one point, District Attorney Marsico unexpectedly acknowledged to the court that Kevin and I were seated in the gallery among the victims' families and friends. I instantly flushed with embarrassment; I had been feeling self-conscious to begin with. If this had been an actual trial, we would have been called to testify. Along with Patricia Brooks, I knew that prosecutors were highly anticipating what we would reveal to the jury. In fact, prior to entering the courtroom, Ed Marsico had pulled Kevin aside to speak with him. The district attorney told Kevin that he had been looking forward to his witness examination of both of us, which he believed would have provided the jury with compelling testimony that would have perfectly tied up their case against Lane. But this was not a trial, and although our presence was not required, I hoped everyone understood that we were there that day simply to support the families of the victims, and not to draw attention to ourselves.

As uncomfortable as it may have been for us to be specifically named in open court, however, it also seemed to provide an element of surprise for Lane. He raised his head slightly, though he did not look around. He now knew, at least, that the family who had stopped him was there to bear witness to his punishment in the end.

When it came time for the victims' statements, I braced myself. I had been holding back a lot of emotions of my own, and although I had been successful up to that point, I was not sure I would be able to make it through this. I fully understood by then just how important an element these statements were to those involved in any criminal trial that stems from a violent act. In giving the victim's family members the opportunity to express their personal emotions to the court and the perpetrator, it helped them work through the grief process and facilitate closure, which is so vital.

The first to speak was Nicole Ewalt. She identified herself as Darlene's only daughter. She had been nineteen years old, just out of high school, at the time of her mother's murder. Nicole tried to put into words the disarray that her life had been in since Adam Lane took her mother away from her. She choked back tears, the anger evident in her trembling voice as she went on to tell the court that her mother would not be there to see her get married and that it would be just one of many milestones in her life that she would never be able to share with her mother. One day, Nicole said, she would have children of her own who would never know their grandmother Darlene, never embrace her or feel the warmth of her love.

Her sentiments were heart-wrenching, and as tears stung my eyes, I looked at those around me, many reaching for tissues, too. One young female reporter was even crying openly. Toward the end of Nicole's statement, her demeanor began to change. As the pitch of her voice rose, so did the pace of her speech. In talking about some of the circumstances of how the trucker happened to wander onto her parent's property from the highway, and then questioning the reasons Lane had for killing her mother, she could no longer fully contain her fury.

In closing, Nicole said, "I would like to know *why*, but there isn't a why. . . . He'll rot in hell, where he deserves to be."

Todd Ewalt took the stand next. He needed a moment to collect himself, the depth of his grief plainly visible on his face. When he spoke, it was of the living hell that he and his family had been through. A description that I thought best summarized the tragedy was when he called his wife's murder "an unnecessary, senseless act committed by a coward who took the life of the happiest person I knew." My immediate response was to turn to my husband, reach for his hand, and thank God for all that we were incredibly blessed to still hold dear.

As Nick Ewalt approached the stand, everyone seemed to be collectively holding their breath. I know I was. As he sat listening to the statements his sister and father made before him, he appeared to be seething with rage. I was not sure what he might say or do, but I anticipated some kind of dramatic scene playing out. Maybe a verbal barrage of hate and condemnation. Or something more physical, perhaps. I was completely surprised by Nick's even tone as he petitioned the court to reconsider the death penalty in this case. It had never occurred to me that not everyone was in agreement with the plea deal. Certainly, I had been aware that Nicole and Nick's relationship was not a necessarily close one, but I never suspected that they might have been in opposition regarding the punishment of their mother's killer.

In expressing his further sentiments, it became obvious that what Nick Ewalt wanted most was vengeance on Lane. "I just want him dead," he told the judge. "That's all that matters to me. He's going to get killed in jail, I'm sure of that. He's scared. He's going to be with men. He only attacks women, so he's going to be in a lot of trouble down there."

The last person to take the stand was Darlene's mother, Thelma. She told everyone what a beautiful woman her daughter was, inside and out, how happy and vivacious she was, how much she loved music and dancing and how much her family meant to her. As much as she would miss Darlene herself, Thelma said, *everyone* whom her daughter had come in contact with during her life would miss her.

Thelma left the stand close to tears, and I knew there would be a hole in her heart that would never be filled. In Fay Massaro, Thelma certainly had a kindred soul, and I recall Darlene's mother sometime later asking Fay what their lives were like since their daughter was murdered. Fay's response was, "It's awful. Just awful."

It was impossible not to think how easily those same words could have been my own. But this day was not about me.

At the same time that Adam Leroy Lane was sentenced to life imprisonment for the murder of Darlene Ewalt, he was also ordered to serve a consecutive ten- to twenty-year term for the attempted murder of Patricia Brooks. She had been attacked by Lane in her York County home only four days after Darlene was killed. After entering Patricia's home through an unlocked door in the middle of the night, Lane had used a knife to repeatedly slash the sleeping woman's neck and upper body. When the sounds of her struggles woke her family, Lane retreated from the residence and left Patricia for dead. Luckily, she was promptly taken to a nearby hospital where she was treated and, despite the vicious wounds, managed to fully recover although she still carried the horrendous scars on her body, not to mention the psychological toll of his violent assault.

Beyond her own survival, I am of the belief that Patricia Brooks should come away feeling positive about at least one other aspect of that terrifying experience: namely, that she was able to corroborate the existence of this random stalker who preyed on innocent women in the dead of the night, which in turn helped law enforcement come to the realization that Todd Ewalt had nothing whatsoever to do with his wife's murder. Her strength certainly saved Todd and his family further torment.

Unfortunately, like Shea, Patricia could not attend the hearing that day; they both had obligations that took precedence. Patricia's life had been altered enough by Adam Lane, as had our daughter's. Although I was disappointed that I did not have a chance to meet her, I was very happy that she seemed to have managed to move on. There was so much that I would have liked to say to her, and ask her. I hoped to perhaps someday have that opportunity.

Exiting the courtroom at the conclusion of the hearing, Adam Leroy Lane was once again led directly past the gallery and the family members seated in the front row. Unable to contain herself, Fay Massaro yelled out, "You're a piece of garbage. You belong in the dump!"

Lane, who had had a smug, almost contented look on his face, turned slightly toward the gallery and scanned the crowd. Like Fay and everyone else, Kevin and I were watching him closely with the same burning hatred. He seemed to be feeding off all of the negativity directed at him. Then, he focused on us. It was very brief, but I was sure he recognized us. In that same instant, when his eyes locked on mine, I felt a touch of evil, sensing that he wished me dead along with his other victims. The intensity of his glare was chilling, but I refused to look away. It may not have been much, but this small measure of power I had over him at that moment would last me a lifetime. He would not harm me, he did not harm my daughter, and he would never harm another woman again. Unfortunately, he would not be put to death.

Like Lane, we all got a life sentence that day.

Monica Massaro and Darlene Ewalt were the only ones who received a death sentence.

---

The Ewalts gathered for a family luncheon at a restaurant just across the river immediately following the sentencing hearing. It was the kind of thing you have after a funeral, and what they were essentially doing was officially putting Darlene to final rest while at the same time paying tribute to her life. Hopefully, today's final outcome would also give them the closure they had been seeking for three years. They were kind enough to ask Kevin and me to join them, which of course we did, feeling extremely honored to be a part of the commemorative gathering. An invitation was extended to Fay and Frank Massaro as well, but they regretfully declined. It had been an emotionally draining day for both of them, and they did not think they could hold up. Todd certainly understood, and he even offered to drive them back to their hotel. We said our good-byes to them before they left because we knew they had already decided to pass on another night's stay in Harrisburg and head directly home while it was still light.

The lunch itself was lovely, but more important, it gave

us a chance to spend time with some very nice people. It was good to see Nicole Ewalt laughing and smiling with her family. With everyone sharing stories about Darlene, it made me think she was sitting right there in the room with us, just like I believe she was with my family the night Lane entered our home and attacked my daughter, Shea. Like Monica Massaro, Darlene had been our guardian angel, watching out for us and protecting us against Adam Leroy Lane.

A bit later, as we were all speculating about Lane's bleak future in prison and considering all the horrible things that might happen to him there, Todd mentioned something that I found intriguing. He told us that the prison where he thought Lane might actually end up being incarcerated was the same one where many years earlier he had once visited when he was an amateur boxer and he had a bout with one of the inmates. He described it as very cold, dark and damp even in the hottest summer months. It was an image of utter desolation and loneliness, he recalled, with no freedom, no privacy, and no comfort. It was not death, but the thought of Lane languishing in some of the most miserable conditions imaginable was a consoling thought.

As we were leaving, Todd offered to shuttle us back across the Susquehanna River into town, just as he had done for the Massaros. It had gotten hot and very humid, and he must have thought we were crazy when we thanked him but declined, telling him that we preferred to walk. We just felt like the exercise would do us more good, giving us a chance to take in the full beauty of Harrisburg and its ancient river, and some extra time to reflect on the road behind us and to start to think about the journey that still lay ahead.

After making our way back into the city, we decided

to stop at an upscale restaurant and martini bar, where we stayed for a time, enjoying the nightlife of Harrisburg. There were many young professionals who made the evening very entertaining for this middle-aged couple from up north.

As we were crossing the street to our hotel, I happened to look up and see a bus pass by with an advertisement that caught my eye. In large letters along the side of the bus were the words, "Justice isn't served until crime victims are."

How apropos, I thought. It took almost three years, but the state of Pennsylvania observed the tenet emblazoned on the side of the bus.

---

At the crack of dawn the next morning, we were up and headed home. We ended up taking Interstate 78 east into New Jersey. Just a little over an hour into the drive, we spotted the exit for Bloomsbury, the town where Monica Massaro had lived and, sadly, died.

Kevin immediately looked at me. "What do you think?" he asked. "Should we stop?"

I was thinking the same thing, and wanting to honor the memory of Lane's other murder victim and our guardian angel, I nodded.

We took a long, winding road down into the quiet, tree-lined community. It was an eerie feeling to be looking around at the same sites and landmarks that Lane would have seen as he searched for an opportunity to kill under the cover of darkness on July 29, 2007. We were hoping to locate Monica's house and ideally the beautiful park bench that had been dedicated to her memory. But nothing caught our attention as we drove through what appeared to be the center of town. Then we were approaching a hill crest, leaving the small residential area and about to give up, when we suddenly spotted the railroad tracks that Lane had walked along after killing Monica, discarding the contents of her pocketbook as he went. We knew we were very close, and then Kevin saw the sign for Main Street. From the photos and news pieces I had seen, I knew I would recognize the house as we crept slowly down the road. I noticed the Realtor sign first, driven into the small front yard. It was very sad to think that someone else would be residing in the home that Monica had made for herself.

As Kevin started to brake, I said, "No. Just keep going."

I did not think we should stop. It may not have been a memorial site, but it was not a sideshow attraction either. We drove past her house in silence, and less than a half mile away, we came across the truck stop and travel center where Lane had parked his rig before taking his fatal walk down Main Street to Monica's door. I was surprised at just how close the truck stop was to her house. I recalled one newspaper account that said there was no barrier between the Bloomsbury residents and the lurking predators who frequented the travel center at the edge of town, but I now fully understood just how invasive this truck stop was to the community, especially compared to the one off the interstate near our own home.

We turned around and headed back in the direction we had come, and as we passed Monica's house again, I heard myself calling out to Kevin to stop the car. All of a sudden I felt the need to tell Monica that finally this terribly tragic story had come to an end, that her killer was permanently behind bars and would be for the rest of his miserable life. I wanted her to know that what had happened to her and Darlene would never be forgotten.

We pulled over, and I said a prayer for her as we sat in

the car contemplating the very spot where she had taken her last breath and left this earthly existence behind. I only hoped that somehow I was able to convey to her that I had felt her energy the night we were able to overpower Lane and save our daughter. I am certain that her spirit was joined by that of Darlene and my mother-in-law, Mary Lou, in helping us defeat an evil that would otherwise have destroyed our family. There will never be another explanation for me as to why Kevin and I awakened when we did, which was just in time to prevent Lane from murdering Shea.

By the time we got back home to Chelmsford, our family had come full circle in this bitter saga. We were lucky that our family made it though intact, but never would we forget the events that altered so many lives forever during those hot July weeks in 2007. The experiences I had strengthened me, and I can say without exaggeration that I more fully appreciate the diverse beauty of life that surrounds me.

Although it may take a lifetime to heal the emotional scars suffered by my daughter and Patricia Brooks, nothing will ever bring Darlene Ewalt and Monica Massaro back to their family and friends. All we can hope for is that somehow we will all find peace in the knowledge that Adam Leroy Lane has finally been brought to justice.

# Afterword

Sadly, it seems unlikely that the cases described in this book were in fact the only crimes perpetrated by Adam Leroy Lane. Maybe someday we will find out the darkest of truths about this deranged individual. Law enforcement task forces reached out to every department and municipality they could to try to determine if any unsolved crimes similar in mode and method to those Lane had been convicted of in July 2007 had been committed elsewhere, and in confidence, we were told that there is at least one other possible murder victim whom they believe they may yet be able to tie to Lane. However, thus far, there has not been enough significant evidence to warrant further investigation.

Adam Lane has never admitted to any other crimes, though the implication is that he might well have been a burgeoning serial killer when he was apprehended in our home. I hope there are no additional victims or families who have suffered at the hands of Adam Leroy Lane. If there are, I hope this coward will do the only humane thing he has probably ever done in his despicable life and release all these families from purgatory and tell them what happened to their loved ones. I will forever feel blessed that our family is not among those that continue to suffer, and I can't help but feel the plight of all these families must be acknowledged and never be forgotten.

Throughout this process, I have constantly questioned how someone like Lane could become a cold and calculating killer. Did he ever have the capacity to value life in the first place? Assuming he did, what was the turning point where he no longer valued human life and became consumed with the desire to cause pain and suffering in the most inhumane way? Would Lane have struck out on the road in search of the most sadistic means by which to quell his anger and satisfy his desires if someone had cared enough to notice the signs so many years ago? Could this whole tragedy have been averted if circumstances in Lane's life had been different?

It has now been several years since what has come to be known within our circle of family and friends as "the incident." To this day, I still lie in bed at night and think about the events that occurred in the room next to ours, while at the same time I'm grateful that we were spared the tragedy that could so easily have happened. Why were we so fortunate when others were not? In recent news there has been coverage of an eerily similar case involving a violent and random home invasion. The occupants weren't nearly as lucky as we were. The terror I imagine that mother and daughter must have experienced brings back the horror of our own encounter and the certainty that if my husband hadn't been home, as hers was not, our fates would have been the same. I will always be haunted by the "what ifs." Certainly that husband, whose wife was murdered in his absence, must agonize over the same sort of questions. What if he had been home that night? What if my husband had not? What if things had been different?

The simple truth is we are a family that has been fortunate enough to live to tell about our ordeal with a seasoned killer. There are several miraculous circumstances surrounding our survival that have profoundly affected our perspective towards life and the gift that it truly is. We came too close to losing a child in the most horrific and devastating means imaginable, and the recognition of our good fortune brings with it the burden of knowing that while we were spared, others suffered the ultimate loss. We cannot bring back those lives, but we can do our best to honor them; we can work towards preventing the same sort of tragedy from ever occurring again.

On Mother's Day, in a gesture that touched me infinitely, my beautiful daughter gave me a bracelet inscribed with the words "life is a journey . . . not a destination . . . enjoy the moments." By the grace of God, our family will continue to do just that.

## Penguin Group (USA) Online

*What will you be reading tomorrow?*

Patricia Cornwell, Nora Roberts, Catherine Coulter,
Ken Follett, John Sandford, Clive Cussler,
Tom Clancy, Laurell K. Hamilton, Charlaine Harris,
J. R. Ward, W.E.B. Griffin, William Gibson,
Robin Cook, Brian Jacques, Stephen King,
Dean Koontz, Eric Jerome Dickey, Terry McMillan,
Sue Monk Kidd, Amy Tan, Jayne Ann Krentz,
Daniel Silva, Kate Jacobs...

You'll find them all at
**penguin.com**

*Read excerpts and newsletters,
find tour schedules and reading group guides,
and enter contests.*

Subscribe to Penguin Group (USA) newsletters
and get an exclusive inside look
at exciting new titles and the authors you love
long before everyone else does.

PENGUIN GROUP (USA)
penguin.com